Skills for Living

Group Counseling Activities for Elementary Students

Rosemarie Smead Morganett

Research Press
2612 North Mattis Avenue
Champaign, Illinois 61822
www.researchpress.com

Composition by Tradewinds Imaging
Printed by Malloy Lithographing

ISBN 0–87822–347–9
Library of Congress Catalog Number 94–65700

CONTENTS

Handouts

ACKNOWLEDGMENTS

It is with love and gratitude that I express appreciation to the children, counselors, colleagues, and therapists who have encouraged me over the years and given me the opportunity to share the skills and knowledge I have gained from them. Teaching group-work skills and being a support person through my writing and workshops has given me indescribable satisfaction, and I am grateful for the opportunity to continue this work in the future.

I want to thank the leadership and members of the Association for Specialists in Group Work for the opportunity to share our goals, ethics, standards, and skills in workshops throughout the country. I also wish to convey my gratitude to my dear friends at Research Press—Ann Wendel, Russ Pence, Karen Steiner, and crew—for their expert advice and editing, as well as for their unflagging support.

PART 1

GETTING STARTED

Children come into this world facing complex challenges. Given loving, supportive, and affirming adults whose basic needs have been met and who are making progress on their own life's journey, children can quickly learn positive coping and social skills. It is clear, however, that a large percentage of our youth do not have the adults in their lives to help them move in positive directions. Although many adults believe that values and life skills should come from the home, this is not the reality of the 1990s. And even children who have experienced positive parenting are exposed to situations the best of parents never had to deal with in their own childhoods. Thus, in many cases it is the school and the counselor who must teach and remediate where children's behaviors have already become problems.

This book can help counselors in the school or mental health setting create meaningful group experiences for children who for whatever reason are behind in social and life skill development. The group agendas have been developed with children from second through fifth grade in mind. Although each topic stands alone, children can benefit from more than one topical group experience. The sessions are presented sequentially within each agenda so that basic information and skills are presented before more advanced ideas. Children need not have had previous counseling experience to benefit.

In small groups, children master important affective and behavioral competencies associated with the following topic areas:

Peace Begins With Me:
Peacemaking Skills

I'm Somebody Special:
Building Self-Esteem

Friends: Getting Along With Others

KIDS: Kids in Divorce Stress

Grieving and Growing:
Learning From Losses

I CAN Kids: Control Anger Now!

I'm Responsible

Good Citizen's Club

These topics represent personal and social issues that frequently become problematic for elementary-age children, as identified by school and mental health counselors.

Why Group Counseling?

Not every child is a good candidate for group counseling, and not every problem is amenable to change through it. However, some things cannot be learned through self-study or with the help of one other person, even if that person is a very capable counselor. Some particular qualities of the group counseling experience make it especially effective:

1. Groups are children's natural medium for playing and learning.

2. Groups provide a safe and accepting environment to practice new behaviors and to receive the support of others for doing so.

3. Groups offer role models for positive attitudes, social values, and behaviors.

4. Groups show how working together is important and provide models for giving and receiving help.

5. Groups are a place in which children can learn to tolerate and respect others' differences, as well as to empathize with others.

6. Groups teach children how to trust and how to share ideas, attitudes, and feelings honestly.

Getting Organized

Group counseling is not just what happens during a 30- to 40-minute session with children; rather, it involves your knowledge, preparation, state of mind and skills, and ability to use your skills on a moment's notice. Having spent some time in preparation before the group begins will save you a great deal of frustration later on because as the group gets going you won't have time to take care of these details. The following suggestions will help you make the group go smoothly.

Make Basic Preparations

Most counselors have so many clients, projects, and responsibilities that it is difficult to see the timeline of the group, to picture when it will be occurring during the coming weeks. Take a few minutes to plan when the process will occur, leaving sufficient time before and after the sessions to do necessary paperwork and follow-up. If there is too much going on at a particular time for you to give the group your full attention, wait until you do have time to provide this important service for children.

You will also want to make a number of contacts before the group begins. For example, you might need to invite a guest to visit for a certain session or consult with a specialist in a particular area of counseling. You will need to contact potential referral sources, such as other counselors, teachers, administrators, parent groups, and so forth, to let them know the topic of the group and ask for referrals. And you will need to contact the children who express interest in participating in order to screen them.

Physical preparations are also important. You will need to arrange an appropriate space for the group to meet—one that allows confidentiality to be preserved. Don't use an area that is incompletely closed off, or other children, staff, counselors, teachers, or parents might overhear what is being said. Be sure the room is available at the times you need it. It can be disruptive to a group to be displaced after sessions have started. Many children who have been selected for a group experience are already insecure about their problems or issues; they don't need more insecurity by being moved during group or having someone who needs something from the room interrupt the session.

It is essential to have paperwork completed before group begins, so start organizing it in advance. Paperwork refers to publicizing the group, getting parent/guardian consent forms signed, making copies of any handouts the children will need for certain sessions, making charts you might need, and so forth. (Sample forms are provided in Appendix A).

Other materials and resources also need to be assembled before the group begins. For example, several of the sessions suggest that you locate a book on a particular topic. In order to avoid last-minute frustrations, you will need to obtain and read the resource(s) named or ones similar to them. You will also need a few simple supplies, such as a roll of newsprint, drawing paper, crayons or markers, hand puppets, tape, glue, and the like. A supply of some kind of small rewards to encourage and reinforce children for working on issues or skills between sessions is also helpful. Healthy snacks of some sort are optional but recommended at the end of each session. The group needs to be a rewarding experience different from the classroom—one way to make it a fun time as well as a learning time is to offer snacks.

Review Group-Work Process and Practice

Even if you are a seasoned mental health professional, unless you are very familiar with time-limited, topic-driven group work with children you will need to review a few basic ideas about group work. Many excellent texts cover the topic in breadth and depth—for example, Gerald Corey and Marianne Corey's (1992) *Groups: Process and Practice*, George Gazda's (1989) *Group Counseling: A Developmental Approach*, and Samuel Gladding's (1991) *Group Work: A Counseling Specialty*. It is not the purpose of this book to provide extensive discussion of theory or philosophy, but you will be best prepared if you review well.

One area that you need to be particularly aware of concerns the four stages a group experiences. These are the initial, transition, working, and termination stages, and every group moves through them, although at different rates (see Corey & Corey, 1992). You will benefit by understanding that these stages are an essential aspect of every group, that each stage the group goes through is characterized by specific behaviors that you can see and experience, and that by your skill you can facilitate movement from one stage to the next. If you are unaware of the behaviors associated with each stage, you will be less able to do your part to help the group move on.

Another area to review is group dynamics, the magical glue that pushes and pulls groups, the human interaction that underlies the motivation for growth and change. Major dynamics and "curative factors" to be aware of are trust, cohesion, universality, hope, altruism, imitative behavior, interpersonal learning, and catharsis (Yalom, 1975). The more you know about the dynamics of human behavior in groups, the more effectively you will be able to use your skills to bring about growth and change in your young clients.

Know Your Ethics

Ethical guidelines for group counselors have been developed by the Association for Specialists in Group Work (ASGW), a division of the American Counseling Association; these are reproduced in Appendix B. In our litigious society, it is unconscionable for the counselor involved in group work to be unaware of ethical practice as spelled out by our professional organization. Especially review sections on confidentiality, the screening and selection of members, imposing counselor's values, and dual relationships.

ASGW (1991) has also developed professional standards for the training and practice of group workers in four areas of specialization: task/work groups, guidance/psychoeducational groups, counseling/interpersonal problem-solving groups, and psychotherapy/personality reconstruction groups. These standards can give you a basis for evaluating your own training and the need for further training. They also clearly demonstrate that group work is indeed a specialty—an advanced form of the therapeutic endeavor—and that persons conducting groups need to have specialized training and supervision.

Learn and Practice Skills and Techniques

In conducting workshops in group counseling techniques, I find over and over that even persons who have been doing group work for years have gaps in basic skills and techniques. Yes, it is important to know theories and process, but it is also essential to have a firm grasp of nuts-and-bolts techniques, specific things to say and do and avoid doing. For example, it is important to know when, why, and how to use activities and exercises in groups. It is essential to know how to draw out the silent child, cut off the monopolizer or arguer, change focus from topic to person to activity, deal with problem members (fighter, refuser, resister), and cope with crises in groups.

One important skill is the use of open-ended questions. Closed questions (those answered yes or no, or in just a few words) shut down communication, whereas open-ended questions like the following keep group members talking:

> What is it like for you?
>
> What could you do about_____.

Who else in the group feels like that?

Whom do you connect with?

Where in your body do you feel that feeling?

Would you be willing to_____.

How else could you do that?

Would you share that with us?

What would you do differently?

What were you aware of?

What makes it difficult?

How do you feel about_____.

Another skill important in group work is linking, or connecting. The leader uses this skill to help group members recognize mutual thoughts, feelings, or behaviors. The leader needs to initiate this process early on, in the first session, to teach members to think about and express their connections. Children especially have not learned to empathize (that is, to think about how other children are thinking or feeling) or to appreciate how their experiences might be mutual. By asking linking questions, the leader can help stimulate this awareness, deepen the focus of discussion, and draw in members who might not be participating. Some examples of linking questions are as follows:

> Who else feels this way?
>
> I wonder if anyone shares Jill's feelings?
>
> Does anyone think the same way as Shawn on this topic?
>
> Darrin, would you ask if anyone else connects with you about this?

Avoid Counselor Burnout

Group work is one of the most exciting forms of counseling. Being a part of a process that generates growth and behavior change is rewarding, challenging, and ever new. It is also draining, exhausting, and the cause of big-time burnout. When I hear a counselor saying, "Oh, yes, I'm doing four groups right now," I wonder how long this counselor will be doing four groups—or how well. Although group work generates energy, it also takes a great deal of emotional and physical strength to keep in tune with all of the complex verbal and nonverbal human interactions going on simultaneously.

No one else in your life is going to take responsibility for managing your stress. You must manage your stress for yourself, or you may temporarily lose the capacity to care. Pace yourself! Do one or two groups well rather than getting yourself "grouped out." Make a special effort to be rested, alert, and emotionally available to your young clients. Perhaps some extra sleep the night before? Or perhaps a few minutes with your office door shut, closing your eyes and centering yourself before going to group?

Counselors new to group work frequently want to tackle the worst problems, the children with the most severe needs and deficits—right away! This is not an approach in your best interests or the best interests of the children involved. There will always be more children than you can possibly serve. If you are new to this type of group work, I recommend that you stack the deck in your favor. Don't try to take on the children with the worst problems all at once. Start off by selecting a topic you are familiar with and a group of kids who will work well together, who will cooperate and be successful. You have to learn sometime, and now may be your time to learn. As you practice on the "easier" topics and children, you will gain confidence and skills and eventually be able to tackle the harder topics, issues, and behaviors. Don't let others (administrators, directors, teachers, parents) pressure you into taking a group full of youngsters with severe problems—it is your ethical responsibility to decide what the composition of the group should be, not someone else's. If you are constantly busy dealing with acting-out and otherwise disruptive behavior, you have not mastered the selection process, and both you and the children will feel angry and frustrated.

Group-Work Timeline

Group counseling is a process that begins long before the first session and extends long beyond the last session. In general, the following steps are the foundation of the group counseling experience:

1. Conduct needs assessment
2. Develop written proposal
3. Advertise the group
4. Obtain parent/guardian consent
5. Conduct pregroup interview
6. Select group members
7. Administer pretest
8. Conduct sessions
9. Administer posttest
10. Conduct postgroup follow-up and evaluation

Some of these tasks will overlap others—for example, you may be doing two or even three of the preparation tasks at the same time. The process will vary according to your setting and circumstances, so adjust, add to, and omit as needed.

Step 1: Conduct Needs Assessment

A needs assessment is the first step in a systematic attempt to serve the young clients in your setting. Not only does a needs assessment tell you what topics are important, it provides you with data useful in persuading administrators and teachers to permit children to leave the classroom for the group experience. Finally, after the intervention has been conducted, the needs assessment can be used along with information from the postgroup evaluation to demonstrate accountability to school administrators, colleagues, parents, and group members.

Both formal and informal needs assessments exist. An informal assessment might consist of asking parents, teachers, administrators, and children what topics and skills they believe are needed, then keeping a tally of the topics mentioned. More formally, surveys like those included in Appendix C may be conducted.

In addition to specific topical groups, you may want to consider offering some more general, non-topic-driven group experiences. That way some growth areas not covered by the specific topics will also receive attention.

Step 2: Develop Written Proposal

A proposal is a document with a purpose. First, it helps you organize what you are going to focus on in the group, describing the goals, objectives, and content of the group. Second, it serves as an aid to answer questions about the nature of the group to administrators, parents, teachers, colleagues, and referral agencies. If you are in an elementary school setting where group counseling has never been a part of counseling services and no one is familiar with group counseling, there will be many questions from both colleagues and parents about what will happen.

You will need to have done your homework in advance by having a solid, clear proposal.

The written proposal should include the following types of information. These guidelines are based generally on recommendations provided by Corey and Corey (1992).

1. Description and Rationale

Describe the group as a time-limited group experience to learn new skills, practice more adaptive behaviors, and share ideas, thoughts, feelings, and interests on specific topics.

What is your purpose in conducting the group?

Whose needs does it meet?

What topics will be explored?

2. Objectives

What objectives do you have in mind for the group?

Are the objectives reasonable for the age and abilities of the participants?

Are the objectives clear? Measurable? Reasonable for length of group?

3. Logistics

Who will lead the group?

What are the leader's qualifications?

Who will be responsible for making sure ethical guidelines are followed?

How will group members be selected?

When will the group meet? If during class time, do all parties (teachers, parents, students) agree?

How many members will be selected, and what are the criteria for inclusion?

Is there a plan to provide services for those who are not selected?

Where will the group meet, and for how long?

Will the group be closed or open to new members as it progresses?

How will the situation be handled if a member wants to drop out?

4. Procedures

What kinds of techniques will you be using? (Possibilities include relaxation exercises, role-playing, behavioral modeling, self-improvement homework, self-reinforcement, and so on.)

How and when will you explain the risks involved in being in a group? (These might involve the chance of hostile confrontations by other group members, the risk that others might not keep disclosures confidential, the chance of experiencing or reexperiencing psychological pain, and so forth.)

How will you protect members from being hurt physically or psychologically?

Will you take special precautions because participants are legal minors?

How will you explain confidentiality and its limits?

How will you handle requests from parents or others who might want you to divulge a child's confidences?

How will you obtain informed consent from the parent or guardian and informed assent from the child?

Will you require both parents to sign an informed consent if there is a noncustodial parent?

Are you using any recording devices or conducting any research?

How will you ensure safety and confidentiality of counseling records?

5. Evaluation

How do you plan to determine whether a member has changed due to exposure to the group experience?

How are you going to determine whether your goals and objectives have been met?

What follow-up procedures do you anticipate?

Who will receive evaluation data about the group?

How will evaluation data be stored? Who will have access?

How do you plan to evaluate leader performance?

You can also include specific outlines of the sessions for some of the group topics you plan to cover. This book offers many such outlines; you can also develop other outlines on your own.

Step 3: Advertise the Group

After you have received approval for the group counseling experience, you will want to let all of the school administrators know what is happening. In many schools, the assistant principal sees students who are having academic or behavioral difficulties and will be in a position to refer potential group members.

You are in the best position to determine how to advertise group counseling experiences in your setting. Use whatever media are available, including newsletters to teachers and parents, bulletin board announcements, notices at information centers, and so on. Let all of the teachers know by making announcements at faculty meetings, posting notices in the teachers' lounge/dining area, and just generally passing the word. Written flyers can also be circulated to announce the group.

If you have included the teachers and administrators in the needs assessment, they will already know what is happening and will be able to keep an eye out for referrals. The children will refer themselves when they hear what is happening, and usually you will have many more children who want and need to be in the group than space will allow.

Step 4: Obtain Parent/Guardian Consent

In many schools, parents or legal guardians must provide a written informed consent in order for minor children to participate in group counseling. Specific information needs to be provided about the group so that the child and the parent/guardian can make an intelligent decision about whether or not to participate. Cormier and Cormier (1991) have developed a general checklist for informed consent that incorporates the following points:

1. Description of each strategy, including activities involved

2. Rationale for or purpose of the strategy

3. Description of the therapist's role

4. Description of the client's role

5. Description of possible risks or discomforts

6. Description of expected benefits

7. Offer made to answer client's questions about strategy

8. Client advisement of the right to discontinue strategy at any time

9. Explanations in clear and nontechnical language

10. Summary and/or clarifications to explore and understand client reactions

The importance of obtaining informed consent from the parent/guardian, as well as from the student, cannot be overstated. One good way to provide the necessary information is to use a letter and form similar to those provided in Appendix A. Check your school policy on the requirement for a consent from both custodial and noncustodial parents, and be sure to look into this matter before making any final selection of members. It might not be advisable to select a child whose noncustodial parent refuses to give permission. The noncustodial parent's objection may influence the child and the custodial parent and become a source of confusion for the child, resulting in an inability to participate fully.

Step 5: Conduct Pregroup Interview

The ethical guidelines of our counseling specialty require us to screen potential members for a group so that we may obtain informed consent (or, in the case of minors, assent). We also need to ascertain the child's level of commitment to the group and obtain other information that will help in deciding to admit the child to the group. Even though it is a lengthy process, interviewing each prospective group member is important because group counseling has the potential to be harmful under certain conditions. It is our responsibility to check out potential problems and screen out children who are not appropriate candidates.

Sometimes counselors have difficulty explaining to teachers, administrators, or parents why a child who seems to have a great need for counseling services might not be a good group member. One way to explain this is to use the following analogy: Suppose you decide you would like to have cosmetic surgery. You choose a reputable surgeon, make an appointment, and discuss what you would like to have done. Before putting you on the list for the next available operating time, the surgeon will send you for a series of tests to obtain information on your suitability as a candidate for surgery. If you are a suitable candidate, then you may find yourself getting ready to go under the knife. If results indicate that for some reason you are not a good candidate, you will be informed that it would not be in your best interests to proceed. It is the same way with group counseling: Some children are simply not suitable candidates for group counseling. They may need more intense, individual work, or they may be in a personal crisis and would not work well in the group.

Screening helps you ask the right questions to determine whether the group setting is appropriate for a particular child. The TAP-In Student Selection Checklist, included in Appendix A, is designed to help you objectify and standardize the interview process. The acronym TAP stands for Tell, Ask, and Pick. It will help remind you of the information you need to inform the child about, the questions you need to ask the child, and the guidelines you need to follow to help you make the selection, thus helping you "tap-in" to the student's world.

In using the checklist, it is important to talk with the child for a while to develop rapport and to tell the child that he or she is being interviewed for a place in the group. Tell the child that being in the group is very special, that only a few students will be selected, and that parent permission is required. Tell the child that you will need to share a number of things, ask some questions, and write the information down so you can remember it.

Step 6: Select Group Members

One of the most important issues concerns selection of the individuals who will make up the group. Just as you must stop and think about whether each child is a good candidate, you must also look at the group composition as a whole. The group is like a team: Players must be chosen so that they complement one another. It is a good idea to avoid selecting too many of any one type of player to the exclusion of other types.

General Selection Guidelines

Specific guidelines are given in the introduction to each group agenda to help you select children who might be appropriate candidates for that topic. Although research is inconsistent on the selection of group members, the following general guidelines will help you decide. Use your good judgment in selecting members and develop your own feelings on what will work in your setting and for your topic.

Select

1. A range of skill levels and levels of problem severity so each child will have at least one positive behavioral model

2. Children no more than 2 years apart chronologically

3. Children with approximately the same social, emotional, intellectual, and physical maturity

4. Children with high "social hunger" (those who respond well to social influence)

5. Children who work well with other children in group situations such as classroom or team work

6. Children with different racial, cultural, ethnic, and socioeconomic backgrounds

7. Children of both genders

Do not select

1. Siblings or relatives who might feel they have to adhere to familial roles or expectations within the group or who may not self-disclose, fearing information will be shared with another family member

2. Children who are suicidal or who have a psychiatric diagnosis that would indicate they are receiving therapy elsewhere

3. Children who habitually lie or steal for attention

4. Children who are involved in an ongoing crisis, such as a death/loss of a loved one, unless the group is specifically geared toward this issue

5. Children whom you strongly suspect are being abused

6. Children whose parents are divided against having the child participate

7. Children who are so different from the rest of the group that they might be scapegoated (for example, a single child from an ethnic minority or with a disability)

8. Children who are extremely aggressive, either verbally or physically

Homogeneity and Heterogeneity

The factors of homogeneity and heterogeneity are paramount in selecting group members who will be likely to work together for everyone's benefit. *Homogeneity* refers to likenesses (for example, children who have experienced a death in the family). The more alike the group members are, the sooner they will relate to one another and develop a sense of cohesion or "we-ness." This is important for short-term group counseling experiences such as the ones in this book; if the group were to go on for 20 or more sessions, you could choose a more heterogeneous group and allow other factors to pull the group together and enhance growth over time. In the elementary school, such extended group counseling is usually neither possible nor advisable.

Heterogeneity is usually the critical factor in the success of your group counseling effort in this setting and with this age group. Why? Because heterogeneity provides the differences that are needed for each child to have a role model from which to learn. After all, learning from models is what group counseling is all about. Rule number one in selection, then, is that *each member needs other members from whom he or she can learn appropriate behaviors.*

A lack of heterogeneity is why short-term groups that are overloaded with children having a particular problem are usually unsuccessful. If you have a group in which all the children have failed the last two grading periods, how are you going to model enjoying studying, being successful at taking exams, wanting to learn, and the like? There will be no one in the group who has had these experiences, and therefore they won't be modeled. What if the group is overloaded with children who have problems acting out anger? Again, these children will have no models for other, more appropriate ways to behave.

A general rule is to have the group be homogeneous for the problem but heterogeneous for aspects of dealing with the problem, such as coping skills, personality resources, values, and attitudes. In composing a group on the topic of divorce, then, you would choose only children whose families have experienced a divorce (homogeneous), choosing one or two with remarried parents and stepbrothers and sisters, one or two with one remarried parent and the other dating, one or two with neither parent remarried, and perhaps one or two with an absent parent (heterogeneous). In this way, the children relate to one another because of the divorce, but they bring different experiences in dealing with the results of the divorce.

Other Selection Issues

Children who are not appropriate candidates for one particular group might be appropriate for another group in the future or for one in a different setting. It is important to see that children who are not selected receive services if they need them.

Another issue concerns the fact that some children are quite upset when they are not selected, even though you tell them frequently during the selection process that not everyone will be chosen. They experience not being selected as a rejection from a valued adult, and some feel angry or depressed. This is hard on the counselor as well as the child, but it is important to abide by your decisions for the good of the whole group. You might refer such a child to individual counseling or to a group in another setting.

Step 7: Administer Pretest

Accountability is an important issue in group work. A pretest and posttest can give the counselor valuable information about whether the group counseling experience has been effective in changing the skills, attitudes, and/or behaviors of the individual group member and the group as a whole.

Simple Likert-type pretests/posttests for each group agenda are provided in Appendix C. They are intended to be administered individually, thus giving the group leader a good deal of control in explaining the questions and response choices. These comparatively unsophisticated measures will not give you "proof" of anything. If you need more accurate information for research purposes, you might want to use standardized test instruments to obtain your data. However, if your purpose is to obtain general information about the effectiveness of the topics and activities—and your skill in delivering group services—these pretests/posttests will likely be sufficient.

The pretest/posttests included here may also help you to select group members. You may decide to use the pretest as part of the criteria for selection, administering it to all of the children you interview. For example, if you are looking for children with relatively low self-esteem and a child does not indicate on the pretest that this is a problem area, you might want to pass him or her up in favor of a child whose pretest indicates a potential difficulty. Alternatively, you could administer the pretest to children after the selection and before the first session. Because the number of sessions and time are limited, do not use a session to administer a pretest or posttest.

Step 8: Conduct Sessions

The next step is to conduct the sessions. Some of the agendas provided have more than enough stimulus material for one session and can be used for two sessions, especially if your time is limited to 20 to 30 minutes. In other words, you can extend the eight sessions to ten, twelve, or more. Eight sessions with eight children seem to work very well in many elementary school settings. Having fewer than eight sessions does not allow the group process to evolve, nor does it allow for the topic to be covered in enough depth to result in attitudinal changes.

Step 9: Administer Posttest

After the group has ended, use the same instrument you used as a pretest as the posttest. It is important not to wait more than a week or two to give the posttest; if you do, you increase the chance that you are really measuring maturation and/or learning from other sources, and your results thus may be contaminated. You could have the group members stop by your office for a few minutes to take the posttest and give you any other feedback you need to make changes in the group format or content. You might also develop some type of feedback form on leader skills, if you are willing to accept the feedback. Such a form would allow for responses to questions like "What did you like about the way the leader led the group?" and "What do you think needs to be changed?"

Step 10: Conduct Postgroup Follow-up and Evaluation

Approximately 4 to 6 weeks after the end of the group, it is appropriate to reconvene the group members for a brief session to allow them to share their accomplishments and perceptions of what happened in the group and to convey any new ideas you might have to help them work on their issues in the future. They will also need encouragement and support to continue with any behavioral changes they have made. Group members are usually happy to get together again and support one another's progress.

The postgroup evaluation is essential from an accountability standpoint. The information obtained can be used for the following purposes:

1. For reporting to administrators, teachers, or parents the direction of change that may have occurred in the group as a whole as a result of participation

2. To compare pretest and posttest responses for each member to help that member achieve behavior change goals

3. To obtain an idea of the group leader's effectiveness

4. To assist the group leader in improving the group in the future

You might want to write a brief report describing your experience and giving general data results from the pretest/posttest comparison. Remember that the data from these tests belong to the students taking the test and must be kept confidential. Except in extreme circumstances, individual scores may not be shared unless the child gives permission. Be sure to omit all identifying information on reports of general data.

Conducting the Sessions

As you prepare for the group, you will need to consider the following logistical issues.

Group Size

For children at the elementary level, the recommended number of students for a group counseling experience is six to eight. This number is, of course, the ideal, and it is possible to have a successful group experience with fewer or more participants. However, six to eight seems to be a good number because it allows for a variety of ideas and behaviors and permits the leader to let students form dyads for specific activities. If there are more than eight, the students less inclined to self-disclose tend not to be heard. Fewer than about six children means that the time will be concentrated on only those children. Some children cannot tolerate the pressure of constantly sharing and disclosing. There will also be fewer ideas and viewpoints to be shared.

Scheduling

The group counseling experiences outlined in this book have a minimum of eight sessions or meeting times. In terms of group counseling, eight is a very small number of sessions to have expectations for permanent behavioral change—the best that can be hoped for is some attitudinal change. Some children will change behavior, but you should not expect long-term change in ingrained maladaptive behaviors.

You can schedule the sessions to occur once per week, if that suits your school's schedule, or you can schedule them twice weekly for 4 weeks. The latter option works just as well for many of the groups. Some topical areas that include practice on skills for behavior change may require a week between sessions for practice to occur. Having the sessions more than twice weekly is not recommended. Be sure to check the school calendar before you schedule the group so that there are no weeks the group cannot meet. For trust and cohesion to develop, continuity is essential.

The length of the sessions may vary according to your daily schedule. Younger children (approximately second-grade level) can sustain a 30-minute session fairly easily. Fourth- or fifth-grade children can work successfully and accomplish more in a 40-minute session, if this is possible.

Another consideration is the concern of parents, teachers, and children about missing a particular subject in school. This issue is especially important when a child is already having academic difficulty and then has to miss a class periodically to attend group. You might want to vary the time the group is held so children do not miss the same subject each time they attend. One way to deal with this is to have group first period/hour in the morning one week, second period/hour the next week, and so on. If you have an activity period when all of the children are available, this would be ideal. Whatever you do, try to avoid putting the child at further risk for academic problems and distress.

Setting

Confidentiality is a major issue in all group counseling, and ensuring that children have a place where they will feel comfortable disclosing without someone overhearing will help them develop a feeling of security. Choose a room that closes completely and be sure you hang a sign on the door reminding people not to enter during the session. You may need to let some of your colleagues and/or secretaries know that group is not to be disturbed unless there is an emergency. It is up to you to set the tone and let others know how important the issue of privacy is to group counseling.

You will need enough chairs, cushions, pillows, or bean-bag chairs for the leader and all group members to be able to sit in a circle. Do not sit around a table because the table will distract the children and serve as a barrier. Be sure that each child in the group can see every other child and the leader clearly. You will need to have a table or some other flat surface available for drawing, a chalkboard or some kind of easel chart to write on occasionally, a box for your puppets and drawing materials, and, of course, a box of tissues! It is not recommended that you take the group outside or to other places where there will be many distractions unless doing so serves a specific purpose in the session.

Session Organization and Agenda

Each group session in this book is divided into three sections: an Ice Breaker or Review, Working Time, and Process Time. The first session in each agenda begins with the Ice Breaker, an activity designed to introduce children to one another, establish norms for the session, and help children begin to become comfortable with the group format. For this activity, spend as much time as you need to help children relax and get comfortable. You will also need to work on the ground rules and discuss confidentiality in the way specified in the sessions.

The longest part of the session is the Working Time, when you conduct the major business of the day. At this time there is usually some activity or exercise directly related to bringing about the content goals of the group. Young children cannot sustain continued "talk therapy." Their natural modality is play, so the working time of the group involves action-oriented psychological work. Some activities are less action oriented than others—for example, the leader might read a story on the topic. In other groups the children will be making something, drawing, or engaging in role-plays to learn more acceptable behavior.

Managing the time during each activity is critical because the third section of each session, the Process Time, is the most important of all. This time is devoted to maximizing the learning experiences of the session. Open-ended questions are used to stimulate the children to think through what they have learned, make connections with other group members, clarify the concept taught, and decide how they are going to work on their behavior. If Process Time is eroded, the children may leave the session without a clear idea of what they have experienced.

Leadership Style

Leadership style can be thought of as a continuum of control over the group. At one end of the continuum is *leading*, or complete control over the content and expectations of the session. This is similar to a classroom situation in which the teacher presents the subject in lecture style and each child interacts independently with the teacher and the books or materials in front of that child. Questions are also unilateral, between teacher and student, and little if any interaction takes place among the class members. The leader is prepared to assess the degree to which the children have assimilated the material presented.

On the other end of the continuum is the leadership style of *facilitation*. Facilitation involves shared responsibility for what happens in the session; the leader provides stimulus material, but the focus is on interpersonal actions, not on learning specific content. Group classroom guidance and skills training are content oriented, whereas group counseling is process oriented. The intent and outcome of the two approaches are different. In group counseling, the purpose is to provide a safe environment for children to explore their feelings, values, attitudes, and ideas about themselves and their behavior, with behavior and attitudinal changes as a result. The group members are encouraged to participate fully by making connections or "linking" with one another and being supportive and encouraging of one another's situations and attempts to change behavior. In other words, the focus is not on content but on the process of becoming a better human being.

This concept may be new for someone accustomed to the content-oriented approach of the educational setting. But letting go of some control needs to happen for group counseling to succeed. Although content and skills are presented in the agendas in this book, they are meant only as stimuli—they are not cast in concrete. The leader needs to be willing to give up the rigidity of an agenda for the needs of the moment. Many times in group work with children a member of the group will arrive with a fresh issue related to the topic and be obviously hurting over the incident or situation. If the agenda is rigidly followed, the child with the issue will not be psychologically present in the group and the other children will likely wonder what is going on. Perhaps the child will behave in an uncharacteristically aggressive way or be very withdrawn. If it is appropriate in the specific situation, it is the leader's responsibility to forego the planned agenda and help the child deal with the issue in the context of the group.

Young children are used to being in a more structured classroom setting than older children. Depending on their classroom experiences, their level of self-esteem, and other factors associated with personality and experience, they may be confused by the idea of sharing responsibility for what goes on in the group. They may have difficulty addressing their statements to another group member rather than to the leader, for example. Their hesitation can be overcome rather easily by the leader's establishing and reinforcing interaction among members. Children

become accustomed to the new pattern of communication quickly and appear to enjoy the freedom to interact with one another and the leader on a different level.

Group Norms

One of the group leader's most important tasks is to establish norms for conduct and interaction in the group. *Norms* are expected ways of behaving that are reinforced by the leader and other group members. Two types of norms are important in the group. *Ground rules* are explicit (usually written) statements about behavior that is allowed, not allowed, and expected in the group. It is the leader's responsibility to establish basic ground rules for the group and then ask group members to add to them, usually at the first session. Children thus have "ownership" of the rules for the group and are more likely to comply. Some basic ground rules with which to begin might be "Everyone gets a chance to talk," "No hitting or fighting in group," and "Take turns."

Although unwritten, other group norms are also extremely important. As a behavioral model for the group, the leader takes responsibility for demonstrating and reinforcing these norms. The children will pick up the normed behaviors very soon if the leader is consistent in setting and reinforcing them. Some important unwritten norms are as follows:

1. Talk directly to other group members when referring to something about them, not to the leader. (Say, for example, "Tell Jill what you think about that.")

2. Praise for effort, not just for results. (Say, for example, "Sherelle, you worked really hard on_____. I appreciate your efforts. Who else can encourage Sherelle?")

3. Come to group on time. (Each session, say, "Thank you for coming to group on time." If necessary, this could be a ground rule.)

4. Share feelings. (Most children can't distinguish between feelings and thoughts. Sharing your own feelings will help children understand that it is safe to do so and will be appreciated. Say, for example, "I felt sad this morning when I heard your cat died. How do you feel about it?")

5. Take responsibility for your own actions. (Say, for example, "I didn't close my car window, and the rain came in and ruined your papers. I take responsibility for that.")

If as the leader you model appropriate behavioral norms, the children will begin to feel comfortable doing the same. Be aware of the emerging norms in your group so you can support positive norms and eliminate negative ones.

The "Magical Glue" of Groups

The interpersonal forces that cause the tug and push among members of any group or any relationship are called *dynamics*. The most important group dynamic in this context is that of trust, which must develop and grow among the group membership. Without trust there is no involvement, movement, or growth because members will not feel comfortable enough to self-disclose and work on their problems. The children in your group will have different trust levels depending on their previous experiences in relationships. Because the population for a group experience is one in which the members already have issues that have become problematic, it is likely that some will lack trust in this new situation. Be patient when you encounter resistance—or as Virginia Satir called it at one family therapy conference, "justified caution"—in your young members. Use your modeling skills to develop trust. Trust yourself and the group process and bring issues out in the open as they occur to prevent hidden agendas from developing. Be aware that trust develops slowly and must be nurtured and encouraged.

Another important dynamic that works to bond the group is a sense of cohesion, or "we-ness." Cohesion also develops slowly, as the group members take risks to share themselves and their hurt, anger, painful experiences, and efforts at healing. In the beginning of the group there exist only individuals; the sense of being a group with a purpose is not yet present. Group cohesion can be nurtured by the leader but grows only after members share activities, reveal feelings, undergo and work out problems, and discover that they have painful experiences in common. When cohesion develops, you will be able to sense a spirit of cooperation in the group, shared pleasure in one another's accomplishments, and a willingness to continue sharing and undertaking self-improvement activities.

Your direct and indirect connections can foster the group's sense of cohesion. Take time to point out group members' connections with one another and help them make mental and emotional connections by using open-ended linking statements. For example, say, "That must have been very painful for you, Shawn. Who else in the group can connect with what Shawn is feeling? Tell him." A less direct way of accomplishing this is to make a note of something—for example, "It sounds as though all of you have been hurt and angry over a divorce."

Things That Go Bump in the Group

Group work is challenging. However, certain facets of this specialty are difficult to deal with, requiring growth to meet the personal and professional demands. The following are issues that have a particular impact on groups.

My Middle Name Is "Flexible"

Counseling children demands that you have a certain amount of flexibility because their problems and issues cycle so rapidly. With regard to group work, it is important to be flexible in terms of dealing with the immediate feelings children bring to group, giving up some of your control by encouraging members' ownership of group interactions, and encouraging members to be independent thinkers and questioners, in touch with their own feelings as a valuable part of themselves. Many times counselors have come from an authoritarian background in their families of origin, have been educators for many years, and feel the need to be in charge in their environment. In order for group counseling to be group counseling, not classroom guidance or education, the leader must have the personal security and flexibility to encourage children to be independent and to own their feelings, thoughts, and behaviors. It may take a great deal of courage to give up needing to be the teacher in order to be the counselor, but if you are able to do so the result in the long run will be more socially and emotionally responsible youth.

Play as Therapy

Play, not talk therapy, is the natural medium of interaction among children. Children's verbal skills are insufficient to express complex experiences, and their cognitive level of development does not allow for the reasoning necessary for more formal therapy. The group experience for children needs to be built around play—drawing, being read to, making things, acting out a scene in dress-up clothes, and the like. The younger the children, the quicker they will become restless and inattentive to the message, so vary your approach. Talk for a short time, then have the group do something, then get back together and share.

Be sure that the attitude of learning as fun is present. Some of the session topics are pretty serious—for example, the importance of funerals. Try to attach something enjoyable to each session so the element of pleasure is always involved. Snacks at the end of sessions serve this purpose, as do small rewards for behavioral change. Sometimes teachers or parents do not understand why children participating in the group are receiving rewards or snacks for learning something they should know in the first place. The children are in the group because they are experiencing emotional pain beyond what is normal and because they need to learn new skills. In many cases they have not learned to be reinforced by the things that adults in the learning environment think they should be reinforced by, such as good grades on tests or report cards. These children often need immediate and tangible rewards to increase their motivation to work on problem behaviors.

Behavioral Homework

Although the primary goal of the group is not skills training, in which the development and transfer of training to everyday situations is the goal, the group sessions do provide the opportunity to practice new skills. The children watch peers perform appropriately, practice the behavior together, and are then encouraged to practice the behavior outside the session.

A caution is in order regarding behavioral homework: You must decide whether the suggested homework is appropriate for one member, several members, or the whole group. It is best to invite group members to do the behavioral homework rather than assign it as would be done in the classroom. Many children are already overwhelmed by what is going on in their lives—they don't need you to give them more pressures or anxieties. If you make sure they have a choice in the matter, you will find that some children will become involved in between-session practice and that these children will provide good models for the others. Later on in the group, it is likely that more children will become involved.

Be sure that you explain the purpose of practicing a certain behavior outside the group. If students do not understand what you are suggesting, few will comply. One way you can tell whether or not students understand is to ask them to repeat what you have asked them to do and

why. If they cannot tell you right there during the group what you are asking them to do between sessions, then you can be sure they aren't going to remember after the group session is over.

Finally, if some students do undertake behavioral homework between sessions, you must remember to discuss and reward their efforts at the beginning of the next session. Each session in this book includes prompts for you to bring up issues from the previous session, including homework.

Challenging Behaviors in the Group

In every group there will be some children whose behavior challenges the leader and the other group members. The monopolizer, the hostile, acting-out child, and the silent refuser are among those who present the leader with a unique opportunity to grow personally and to model appropriate responses for the other group members. It will be important for you as leader to see these situations as opportunities and to approach them in a positive manner, not allowing yourself to become angry or punitive yourself.

Children who monopolize can be distinguished by their frequent interactions in the group without their sharing very much personally. Usually, they comment about other children or other situations outside of the group but refrain from actually disclosing or working on their own issues. It is important to stop monopolizers from rambling or taking too much "air time" before the other children get aggravated by these interruptions. You must be careful not to cut off a legitimate addition to the conversation, however, or such children will feel that you don't like them or don't want to hear what they have to say. You can cut them off gently, explaining why you are doing so by saying, for example, "Marcus, I need to stop you here so that we can let the other kids have a turn today. You have had a lot of air time, and it's their turn. You can have a turn again another time" or "Paula, you need to talk about your feelings and behavior, not other people's feelings and behavior who are not here. You are the one here in the group. You can have another chance to talk about how this relates to you in a little bit."

Hostile, acting-out children present a special problem in a group. Part of the issue revolves around whether they should have been selected for the group in the first place. Each child must bring some positive behaviors to the group for the others to learn from. If a child is so hostile that he or she cannot contain the behavior and will present the leader with continual challenges, then that child is robbing the rest of the group of the opportunity to work on their problems and should probably not participate. The child may benefit from individual therapy to deal with the source of the anger and frustration. However, if hostile, acting-out behavior erupts in group on an occasional basis, it can be used as grist for the group mill—exploring what these feelings are, where they come from, and how to deal with them. You could say, "Tim, it seems you're very angry about what Jamal said about you. How do you feel right now? Could you tell us? I'll help you with your angry feelings and will help Jamal and you talk about it if the two of you would like to work this out." In this way, the child and everyone else involved has an opportunity to learn how to express and resolve explosive feelings.

Threats to Confidentiality

The issue of confidentiality arises again and again in group work with children. It is the leader's responsibility to uphold ethical guidelines, which indicate that the child is the client and that the confidences of the client are to be respected, not shared purposely or inadvertently with others, no matter how interested in the child's welfare they are. Trust is at the heart of counseling, and if a child believes the counselor cannot be trusted to keep secrets safe, he or she will not self-disclose. It is therefore essential that you continually clarify what confidentiality means to all the parties concerned.

Although children have the right to have their confidences kept, certain limits do exist. These limits may be discussed under the categories *harm, abuse,* and *courts.* Appendix A includes a sign you may reproduce to hang in your office and/or group room to help remind you and the children to discuss confidentiality on a regular basis.

Harm

Harm means anything that would indicate that the child has, is, or will do harm to self or others. This includes overt behaviors—for example, a child who makes comments about suicide or "getting even" with someone. It also includes covert behaviors, as in the case of an adolescent who believes she is pregnant but has not confirmed this fact nor received any medical care.

Abuse

The second major limit to confidentiality, abuse, refers to knowledge of child abuse. All states have laws requiring that child abuse be reported; thus, a counselor must limit confidentiality and report the situation to the appropriate authorities if a group member reports being abused or knowing that another child is being abused.

Courts

The third limit to confidentiality, courts, means that if the court subpoenas records, the counselor may have to reveal information that would otherwise be held confidential.

How To Stop Needing This Book

In the final analysis, leading a group counseling experience is a little like conducting a symphony orchestra. Like leading, conducting is determined by the culture that you are in, the sophistication of the participants, the temperament and skills of the conductor/leader, and many other variables. When learning to conduct, a person needs to consider who he or she is and how best to express that sense of individuality, as well as the various technical aspects of the art. The person needs to apply a great deal of sensitivity to understand and provide for the input each member of the orchestra needs. Some orchestra members will be watching the conductor carefully for every nuance of instruction. Others might need very little in the way of input to play their instrument and the particular piece in a masterful fashion. So it is with the group.

As you develop your group counseling leadership skills, it is essential that you tune in to both your needs and way of being and the needs of the children in your group. By keeping both sets of needs in harmony, you will begin to develop a balance in your professional life that will allow group work to meet the needs of many more of your young clients.

Because of the complexities of multiple human interaction, group work is one of the most delicate mental health services we can provide. Most counselors need assistance to get started in group work. In addition, children present us with special challenges due to their rapid developmental changes in the cognitive, physiological, emotional, and academic areas. Becoming more aware of who you are as a counselor and what your own needs and abilities are is important in terms of discovering and practicing group leadership skills. On the other hand, it is important to be constantly aware of the needs and abilities of your youthful group members.

So, how do you stop needing this book? There is an apocryphal story that when one famous concert violinist was asked by a passerby how to get to Carnegie Hall, the violinist said, "Practice, practice, practice!" It seems that there are so many skills, tasks, and issues related to the practice of group counseling that one wonders if providing services for a number of children at once saves any time at all. What you need, then, is practice. And practice comes only after you have the courage to get started.

References and Suggested Resources for Professionals

Association for Specialists in Group Work. (1991). *Professional standards for training of group counselors* (2nd ed.). Alexandria, VA: Author.

Bowman, R.P. (1987). Small group guidance and counseling in the schools: A national survey of school counselors. *The School Counselor, 34*, 256–262.

Carroll, M., & Wiggins, J. (1990). *Elements of group counseling: Back to the basics.* Denver: Love.

Corey, G. (1990). *Theory and practice of group counseling* (3rd ed.). Pacific Grove, CA: Brooks/Cole.

Corey, G., & Corey, M.S. (1992). *Groups: Process and practice* (4th ed.). Pacific Grove, CA: Brooks/Cole.

Cormier, W.H., & Cormier, L.S. (1991). *Interviewing strategies for helpers* (3rd ed.). Pacific Grove, CA: Brooks/Cole.

Duncan, J.A., & Gumaer, J. (Eds.). (1980). *Developmental groups for children.* Springfield, IL: Charles C Thomas.

Gazda, G.M. (1989). *Group counseling: A developmental approach* (4th ed.). New York: Allyn & Bacon

Gibson, R.L., Mitchell, M.H., & Basile, S.K. (1993). *Counseling in the elementary school.* New York: Allyn & Bacon.

Gladding, S.T. (1991). *Group work: A counseling specialty.* New York: Macmillan.

Morganett, R.S. (1990). *Skills for living: Group counseling activities for young adolescents.* Champaign, IL: Research Press.

Rose, S., & Edelson, J. (1987). *Working with children and adolescents in groups: A multimethod approach.* San Francisco: Jossey-Bass.

Scheidlinger, S. (1984). Short-term group psychotherapy for children: An overview. *International Journal of Group Psychotherapy, 34*, 573–585.

Thompson, C., & Rudolph, L. (1988). *Counseling children* (2nd ed.). Pacific Grove, CA: Brooks/Cole.

Trotzer, J.P. (1989). *The counselor and the group.* Muncie, IN: Accelerated Development.

Yalom, I.D. (1975). *The theory and practice of group psychotherapy* (2nd ed.). New York: Basic.

PART 2

GROUP AGENDAS

Peace Begins With Me: Peacemaking Skills

In suggesting ways to improve social relations among children, Vivian Paley (1992) stresses the need to start early. And in fact, in the hope of breaking the cycle of violence and preventing hate crimes, racial conflict, and disregard for human rights, schools, school districts, and cities all over the country are conducting projects to teach children to build bonds of peace, friendship, racial and ethnic cooperation, negotiation skills, and understanding.

Teaching peace and peacemaking is a rather new concept, prompted by changes in elementary school social studies programs and movements to address equality issues and rights among minority groups, promote global understanding, and emphasize acceptance of cultural diversity. The skills of peacemaking are not clearly defined, nor do many texts or curricula exist to foster and encourage children's growth in this area. The bibliography for this group agenda reflects this recent interest in the topic, listing fewer resources than for other topical areas such as divorce or loss.

One related area of endeavor, social skills training, has blossomed in the last two decades, primarily as a result of efforts by professionals involved in the disciplines of special education, school counseling and psychology, and mental health. These disciplines have developed various approaches for teaching more peaceful ways of getting along—for example, anger management, conflict resolution and negotiation, and appropriate assertion. Peacemaking certainly incorporates the values of understanding and accepting others' individual differences, but it also includes the dimension of developing the social ethic of global harmony. As such it is a more encompassing, future-oriented, and preventive approach than social skills training.

Peacemaking as an educational concept is on the cutting edge and will not appeal to everyone as a topic for group counseling. However, the ability to cooperate and solve conflicts in a peaceful way will serve children throughout their lives. It is my own belief that if there is to be peace in the world, it will come through group work of some kind.

Group Goals

1. To teach appreciation of the beauty of individual differences

2. To teach empathy skills so that children may better understand one other

3. To help children learn to appreciate cultural, racial, and religious diversity

4. To raise awareness of our responsibility to become citizens of the world, and care for animals, the environment, and other people

5. To give children the opportunity to work collaboratively and cooperatively on a project they can share with others in the school

Selection and Other Guidelines

To determine group composition, follow the general selection guidelines presented in Part 1, especially allowing for a variety of differences in skill level and needs. Differences in the group will provide a built-in opportunity for the study of diversity. If you have children from different cultures in your setting, choose several to be in the group. Do keep participants relatively close in age—no more than 2 years age difference.

This group topic is specifically recommended for the child who has the following needs:

1. To appreciate individual differences

2. To acquire empathy skills and become more sensitive to others' feelings

3. To build self-esteem and expand areas of competence

4. To learn respect for diversity

5. To learn empathy for peers with physical or emotional differences

6. To acquire a broader range of positive social experiences

In addition to the specific information conveyed in the sessions, this agenda gives children a real experience in working cooperatively. Specifically, throughout the sessions group members have the opportunity to create quilt blocks related to the topic of each session. Session by session, the topics are expressed in the children's blocks and added to the quilt, which when finished can be hung on a dowel for display wherever the group chooses. The quilt thus becomes the embodiment of the group experience and individual beliefs. The quilt-making experience results in group cohesiveness in short order, and the children love it!

The quilt can be made of various materials, according to the skill level of the children, available resources, and the permanence desired. In addition to materials specific to each session, you will want to have the following on hand:

> Fabric that can easily be cut with a pinking shears into 12 × 12–inch squares (a light canvas or heavy cotton/polyester works best)
>
> Permanent fabric markers or fabric paint (found in the wearable-art section of craft shops or fabric stores)
>
> Glitter or other embellishments
>
> Various colored yarns
>
> Large needles
>
> A large manila envelope for each child to store squares, needle, and yarn
>
> A dowel rod about 8 feet long

You will need to purchase 2 to 3 yards of material in eight different colors. Precut eight squares in each color, one for each of the eight children in the group. You will also need a length of fabric about 8 feet long to make a sleeve at the top from which to hang the quilt.

One way of arranging the quilt is to devote a single color to each session topic. For example, suppose you choose light blue material for Session 1. Children would draw their different images of peace on the light blue blocks. These eight blocks, sewn together, would then become the first row across the top of the quilt. The next session topic would use blocks of a different color—for example, yellow—which would make up the second row of the quilt. A more multi-colored, "crazy quilt" effect will result if you let each child choose his or her own color for a given session topic. If a child is missing for a session, you might ask that child to come in before the next session to complete a square so there will be no missing blocks.

Be sure to allot at least 45 minutes for each session. If you have shorter sessions, you might want to increase the number of sessions and do the stimulus work during one session and the quilt-making work during the next session.

Each session closes with an optional snack from a different culture or country. Children enjoy sampling the different foods, and for many the snack provides a good incentive for group participation. Some ideas include Chinese rice crackers, stone ground corn chips, egg rolls, tortillas, bagels, and so forth.

References and Suggested Resources for Professionals

Print Resources

African-American experience: An HBJ resource guide for the multicultural classroom. (n.d.). Orlando, FL: Harcourt Brace Jovanovich.

A-gay-yah: A gender equity curriculum for grades 6+. (n.d.). (Available from Educational Development Center/WEEA, 55 Chapel Street, Newton, MA 02160)

Berck, J. (1992). *No place to be: Voices of homeless children.* Boston: Houghton Mifflin.

Black images in contemporary children's books. (n.d.). (Available from Edit Cetera, 528 Belair Way, Nashville, TN 37215)

Can't we all just get along? A manual for discussion programs on racism and race relations. (n.d.). (Available from Study Circles Resource Center, P. O. Box 203, Pomfret, CT 06258)

Carlsson-Paige, N., & Levin, D. E. (1985). *Helping young children understand peace, war, and the nuclear threat.* Washington, DC: National Association for the Education of Young Children.

Common bonds: Anti-bias teaching in a diverse society. (n.d.). (Available from Association for Childhood Education International, 11501 Georgia Avenue, Suite 312, Wheaton, MD 20902)

Contemporary concerns. (n.d.). (Eight-book series available from Carolrhoda Books, 241 First Avenue North, Minneapolis, MN 55401–9907)

Democracy's next generation II: A study of American youth on race. (1992). (Available from People for the American Way, 2000 M Street, N. W., Washington, DC 20036)

Larch, D. (1985). *Father Gander's nursery rhymes: The Equal Rhymes Amendment.* Santa Barbara, CA: Advocacy Press.

Martz, L. (1992). *Making schools better: How parents and teachers across the country are taking action—And you can too.* New York: Times.

Matiella, A. C. (1991). *Positively different: Creating a bias-free environment for young children.* Santa Cruz, CA: Network.

Miller-Lachmann, L. (1991). *Our family, our friends, our world: An annotated guide to significant multicultural books for children and teenagers.* New Providence, NJ: R. R. Bowker.

Milne, T. (1992). *Kids who have made a difference.* Northampton, MA: Pittenbruach.

Multicultural books for children. (n.d.). (Free 4-page bibliography available from *The Boston Globe*, P. O. Box 2378, Boston, MA 02107–2378)

Paley, V. G. (1992). *You can't say you can't play.* Cambridge, MA: Harvard University Press.

Teacher's resource guide: North American Indians. (n.d.). (Free resource available from Anthropology Outreach and Public Information, NHB MRC 112, National Museum of Natural History, Smithsonian Institution, Washington, DC 20560)

Teaching Tolerance. (Free periodical available from Southern Poverty Law Center, 400 Washington Avenue, Montgomery, AL 36104)

Willhoite, M. (1991). *Families.* Boston, MA: Alyson.

Organizations and Awards

Fellowship of Reconciliation (P. O. Box 271, Nyack, NY 10960)

> *Begun in 1914, this international peace organization develops projects and materials for adults and children concerned with domestic and international peace.*

Grinnell Peace Project Award (c/o Iowa Peace Institute, P. O. Box 480, Grinnell, IA 50112)

> *An award for student proposals that promote peace or nonviolent solutions to conflict.*

1000 Crane Club (Contact Walter Enloe, Institute of International Studies, 278 Social Sciences Building, University of Minnesota, Twin Cities, MN 55455)

> *For elementary and middle school children who wish to be involved in peacemaking projects worldwide. Begun by children in Hiroshima International School, Japan.*

Bibliography for Children

Adoff, A. (1982). *All the colors of the race.* New York: Beech Tree. (Grades 4–8)

Blackwood, M. (1987). *Derek the knitting dinosaur.* Minneapolis: Carolrhoda. (Preschool–Grade 4)

Booth, Z. (1987). *Finding a friend.* Mount Desert, ME: Windswept. (Preschool–Grade 3)

Brown, I. (1992). *Before the lark.* Hillsboro, OR: Blue Heron. (Grade 4 and up)

Brown, T. (1987). *Someone special just like you.* New York: Henry Holt. (Kindergarten–Grade 3)

Carlson, N. (1990). *Arnie and the new kid.* New York: Penguin. (Kindergarten–Grade 3)

Carrick, C. (1985). *Stay away from Simon!* New York: Clarion. (Grades 2–5)

Cohen, B. (1983). *Molly's Pilgrim.* New York: Bantam Skylark. (Grades 2–5)

Golant, M. (1987). *It's O.K. to be different!* New York: Tor. (Preschool–Grade 2)

Hoffman, M. (1991). *Amazing Grace.* New York: Dial. (Preschool–Grade 6)

Hudson, W. (1991). *Jamal's busy day.* Orange, NJ: Just Us. (Preschool–Grade 2)

Kates, B. (1992). *We're different, we're the same.* Racine, WI: Golden Books. (Preschool–Grade 3)

Levine, E. (1989). *I hate English.* New York: Scholastic. (Kindergarten–Grade 3)

Litchfield, A. (1977). *A cane in her hand.* Racine, WI: Whitman. (Grades 3–6)

Martin, B., Jr. (1987). *Knots on a counting rope.* New York: Henry Holt. (Grades 4–7)

Peterson, J. (1977). *I have a sister, my sister is deaf.* New York: HarperCollins. (Kindergarten–Grade 3)

Rabe, B. (1981). *The balancing girl.* New York: Unicorn. (Kindergarten–Grade 3)

Roy, R. (1985). *Move over, wheelchairs coming through! Seven young people in wheelchairs talk about their lives.* New York: Clarion. (Grades 4–7)

Simon, N. (1976). *Why am I different?* Chicago: Whitman. (Grades 1–3)

Stanek, M. (1989). *I speak English for my mom.* Niles, IL: Whitman. (Grades 2–5)

Stein, S. (1974). *About handicaps: An open family book for parents and children together.* New York: Walker. (Preschool–Grade 4)

Vigna, J. (1992). *Black like Kyra, white like me.* Morton Grove, IL: Whitman. (Grades 2–6)

Whitney, D. (1989). *Creatures of an exceptional kind.* Atlanta, GA: Humanics. (Preschool–Grade 3)

Wright, B. (1991). *My sister is different.* Milwaukee, WI: Raintree. (Kindergarten–Grade 6)

Getting Started

Goals

1. To introduce children to the group experience and help them begin to get acquainted
2. To establish ground rules and discuss the issue of confidentiality
3. To discuss the purpose of the group and prepare children for the sessions ahead
4. To help children become aware that the group is a safe environment for sharing ideas, feelings, and behaviors
5. To introduce the idea of the quilt project as an expression of children's peacemaking knowledge and skills

Materials

Easel pad and marker

Examples of different peace signs (the sign from the 1960s, American Sign Language symbol, or the same from other cultures)

Quilt materials for each child

A snack from a different culture or country *(optional)*

Group Session

Ice Breaker

1. Welcome the children to group. Go over the purpose of the group and explain some of the topics you will be discussing. Tell children about the quilt project and enlist their ideas as well as answer questions about why they will be making the quilt and what they will do with it when it is finished. Explain that they will share what they have learned with other children and display the quilt in a prominent place in the school.

2. Discuss basic ground rules for the group, giving a few examples:

   Everyone gets a chance to talk.

   No hitting or fighting in group.

   Take turns.

   Ask group members for input to encourage "ownership" of rules. List these on an easel pad so everyone can see, then post the ground rules in the room where group is held during every session. (It is especially important to have compliance on rules during this agenda because the sessions require a good bit of moving around—group members need to be careful for safety's sake.)

3. Next go over the confidentiality rule and its limits. For example, you might say:

   When we talked about your being in the group, I told you that whatever we say in our group is *confidential*. That means what we say is private. You may talk about your own thoughts, feelings, and actions, but you may not share anything others in the group talk about. There are some special times when I would have to share what you say—if you say something about harming yourself or others, if you share something about child abuse, or if the court (a judge) asks me about what goes on.

4. Go around the circle and have the children share their names, their favorite food from another culture or country, and what they think *peace* is.

Working Time

1. Begin a discussion of what peace is and what peacemaking skills might involve. Have group members contribute their ideas, then share the idea that peacemaking has to start inside each person's heart before it can spread all over the world. Talk about the effects of people's not knowing peacemaking skills (for example, conflicts, wars, starvation, homeless and mentally ill persons sleeping on the streets, fighting and shooting in the cities).

2. Show group members the various peace signs and tell them that the first project for the quilt will be for them to create a square showing themselves doing something peaceful, such as sharing something with someone who has less than they do, displaying a peace sign, shaking hands with someone after an argument that has been worked out, meeting someone from another country, and so forth. Ask group members for their own ideas.

3. After you have brainstormed various ideas of peace, distribute the quilt materials. (If you hand out all of the various colored quilt squares at once, children can choose from among them, then store the ones not used in individual manila envelopes.)

4. Have children begin their first drawing. Encourage discussion among children as they work. You might want to have an extra piece of fabric for each child to do a practice drawing—working on cloth is different, and there is no way to erase mistakes.

5. After the children have finished their blocks, have them work together to stitch the blocks into one long row. (One way of accomplishing this is to have the children work first in pairs, then groups of four, then all together. Either you or the group members can decide who will do the actual stitching.)

6. After the blocks have been stitched together, spread them out on a large table or the floor so everyone can see. Encourage the children to explain what their quilt blocks are about to the entire group.

7. If time permits, have the children sew on a fabric sleeve wide enough to accomodate a dowel to hang the quilt. (You could also do this yourself later.)

8. Have children put away their quilt materials for the next session.

Process Time

1. Discuss the following questions:

> What did you learn about what peacemaking skills are?
>
> What does *peacemaking* mean to you?
>
> Why is it important to know how to get along with one another?
>
> Does anyone else in the group have ideas like yours? If so, tell that person how you feel the same.
>
> What did you like about starting our peacemaking quilt?
>
> What do you think we should do with our quilt to share what we are doing with the rest of the school?

2. Share snacks, if desired. Before saying good-bye, thank group members for attending and remind them of the meeting time for the next session.

Different Races, Smiling Faces

NOTE: If your group does not include much cultural or ethnic diversity, for this session you may wish to invite other children or adults from inside or outside your setting as guests. These guests' involvement in the discussion will help bring home the session's message. Be sure the guests know what the topic of discussion will be and are prepared to share their ideas and feelings on the topic without getting upset if and when prejudices are discussed. If guests of different races or backgrounds are not available, you can use pictures, books, poems, or any other materials you think would work to stimulate discussion.

Goals

1. To establish the norm of reviewing what happened during the previous session and give children an opportunity to discuss anything they still have questions about

2. To clarify where different races started and why people's appearance is different

3. To share the information that although there are differences in skin color, eye color or shape, and so forth, beneath these differences we are all the same, with the same feelings, needs, joys, and pains

4. To allow children to talk freely about their reasons for liking or disliking different races in order to dispel myths of prejudice

5. To expose children to cultural diversity

Materials

A globe or world map

Quilt materials for each child

A snack from a different culture or country (*optional*)

Group Session

Review

1. Welcome the children to group. If you have guests, introduce them.

2. Briefly go over the ground rules and review the confidentiality rule.

3. Ask whether there is any "unfinished business" from the last session, on what peace is and why it is important. Ask whether anyone noticed a situation or heard anything on television about a situation in which peacemaking skills would be useful.

Working Time

1. Discuss with children (or have guests lead discussion of) different races and skin colors. Explain that our skin color is different because of our genes and because we have different amounts of *melanin* (the pigment that causes coloring in each person). Explain that people who come from a certain part of the world develop certain likenesses that become "built in." These likenesses stay with them when they move from that part of the world.

2. Share the idea that some people believe that certain colors of skin are better than others and that they believe this so strongly that they have fought terrible wars over it. Explain that some people in our country felt that it was all right to keep African Americans in slavery because they had dark skin and were therefore not as good as people with white skin. Tell group members that during World War II many Japanese Americans who were loyal to the Allies were made to stay in internment camps just because of their skin color and cultural background. Show on a globe or map where Africa and Asia are.

3. Discuss the idea that even though we have some differences on the outside, we all share the same feelings, such as happiness, sadness, anger, fear, and jealousy. We all want to be treated with respect. We all want to grow up and get a good education and be good citizens in whatever culture we belong. We all have hopes and dreams of doing something good in our lifetimes. We now know that we are all human beings and we all have the right to the same freedoms.

4. After you have talked about the different races and how we are alike and different, brainstorm some ideas for quilt blocks on this topic. Have the children get started making the blocks.

5. After children have finished their quilt blocks, have them stitch them together, then share with the group.

6. Have children put away their quilt materials for the next session.

Process Time

1. Discuss the following questions:

   What did you learn about why people have skin of different color?

   What has happened to people because their skin was this color or that color?

   Are people really different?

   In what ways are we more alike than different?

   What can we learn from being friends with people of all races?

   What is good about learning to be at peace with all people?

2. Share snacks, if desired. Before saying good-bye, thank group members for coming and remind them of the meeting time for the next session.

We All Love to Eat

> NOTE: If you know that any of the group members are from another culture or country and that parents might provide a special snack, contact them ahead of time and ask. If this isn't possible, you can bring something yourself.

Goals

1. To share the idea that although different countries have different customs, religions, ways of being governed, and so forth, the love of cooking and eating together is a bond we share

2. To help children recognize that a lot of the food we eat has its origin in another country and a different ethnic group

3. To give children the opportunity to share a special dish or treat from their own culture

Materials

A cookbook with recipes from different countries

A piece of newsprint, approximately 8 feet long, taped or affixed to the wall

Markers

A globe or world map

Quilt materials for each child

A snack from a different culture or country

Group Session

Review

1. Welcome the children to group. Briefly go over the ground rules and the confidentiality rule.

2. Ask whether anyone has anything left over from the last session, on being a different race or having different skin color but having the same feelings inside. Did anyone notice on the news or at home ways the peacemaking skills of understanding and working things out could be of help?

Working Time

1. Show the children the cookbook with recipes from different countries. Share some of the food ideas, such as goulash from Hungary, sauerbraten from Germany, fried rice from China, kimchi from Korea, and so on.

2. Ask group members to name some of their favorite foods, and, if they know, in what country those foods originated. As they share, have them find the country on the globe or map then write the names of the countries and foods on the sheet of newsprint. For example:

> Italy: Pizza, lasagna, spaghetti, pepperoni
>
> Mexico: Tacos, tortillas, burritos
>
> France: French bread, croissants, beignets

3. Ask group members if they have some special family dishes that might be from their grandparents or from the country their family originally came from. If you have Native American children in the group, ask them to tell about some foods that are native to this country (for example, corn and squash).

4. Have children make their quilt blocks, illustrating such things as people making bread, putting pizza in an oven, or making tea.

5. Tell children to stitch their quilt blocks together, then share with the group.

6. Have children put away their quilt materials for the next session.

Process Time

1. Discuss the following questions:

> You have worked on your quilt three times. What do you think of it now?
>
> What does the quilt say to you?
>
> What do you want to do with it when you are finished?
>
> What did you learn today about people from different places and their food?
>
> How does food bring us closer together?
>
> What meals are special to you?
>
> What is it about good food that links us closer to one another?
>
> What did you learn about yourself today?

2. Share the special snack. (Be sure to thank anyone who brought food!) Before saying good-bye, thank group members for their hard work and remind them of the meeting time for the next session.

All Kinds of Worship

Goals

1. To explore the idea that there are many different religious beliefs and ways to worship
2. To explore the different names the deity is called and the different kinds of buildings in which worship takes place around the world
3. To allow children to question one another and share their religious beliefs in a supportive environment
4. To reinforce acceptance of others' religious beliefs

Materials

Pictures of various religious figures in ceremonial garb, such as shamans, bishops, rabbis, mullahs, preachers, and priests

Pictures of different places of worship, such as temples, cathedrals, churches, and mosques

Quilt materials for each child

A snack from a different culture or country *(optional)*

Group Session

Review

1. Welcome the children to group. Briefly review the ground rules and the confidentiality rule.
2. Ask whether anyone has anything they want to share from the last session, on the idea that many of the foods we eat come from other countries and that food is a special way we can bond together.

Working Time

1. Ask the children to share what they know about different ways of worshipping. Invite them to describe what their own religious leader wears when talking to them on their special day of worship. Show them pictures of other forms of religious dress.
2. Ask the children to describe some of the churches or other places of worship that they have seen or visited—for example, mosques, temples, cathedrals, chapels. Show children the pictures, then ask the following questions:

    What do these places look like?

    Why are they built the way they are?

    What is the purpose of these places?

3. Discuss the fact that different people have different beliefs and that some people choose not to believe in a higher being. Point out that it is not our place to judge whether someone's beliefs are right or not—everyone has the right to believe what he or she wants in our country.
4. Discuss the idea that different religions and cultures have different names for a higher power—for example, God, Yawheh, Allah, Krishna.
5. Have children get their quilt materials and depict what they would like. They might draw a religious symbol, person, or place.
6. Encourage children to stitch their quilt squares together and then share them with one another.
7. Have children put away their quilt materials for the next session.

Process Time

1. Discuss the following questions:

    What are some of the places called where people go to worship?

    Who else in the group goes to the same kind of place you do?

    Why do people believe in a higher power?

    Does everyone believe in a higher power?

    What are some of the names of religious leaders?

    What do you like about your own place of worship?

    What do your religious beliefs help you to do?

2. Share snacks, if desired. Before saying good-bye, thank group members for attending and remind them of the meeting time for the next session.

Xenophilia

NOTE: This session is based on a project developed by the Burnaby, British Columbia, Multicultural Society to help the children of Burnaby experience and express multicultural awareness. For more information about this project, contact Dr. Eugene Kaellis, Co-Executive Director, Burnaby Multicultural Society, 250 Willingdon Avenue, Burnaby, British Columbia, Canada V5C 5E9.

Goals

1. To help children learn about bias and prejudice against people who are different
2. To encourage appreciation and respect for people's individual differences
3. To promote the understanding that personal qualities and character are more important than external appearances

Materials

Dictionary

Quilt materials for each child

Snacks from a different culture or country (*optional*)

Group Session

Review

1. Welcome the children to group. Briefly go over the ground rules and the confidentiality rule.
2. Ask group members if they have anything left over from the previous session, on how people worship in many ways.

Working Time

1. Get out the dictionary and encourage group members to look up the word *xenophobia* (fear of foreign things or people). Explain that this fear is based on misunderstanding people because you don't know anything about them or because they may wear strange-looking clothes, talk differently, or go to a different place of worship. (Be careful to differentiate between this idea and justifiable caution of strangers and other issues related to children's personal safety.)
2. Then have children look up the word *xenophilia* (attraction for foreign things or people). Explain that it is the opposite of xenophobia.
3. Ask children to close their eyes and imagine a town named Xenophilia, with men, women, and children of every color, size, shape, language, hairstyle, dress, religion, diet, belief, custom, educational background, and financial status. Encourage children to tell you what they see when they imagine the town:

    What do the people in the town look like?

    What kinds of clothes are they wearing?

    What kinds of cars are they driving?

    What customs and holidays are they celebrating?

Talk about the word *prejudice*, explaining that the people in Xenophilia have no prejudice about one another's differences because they are all so very different!

4. Let children open their eyes. Ask if they think people in their school are prejudiced against others in the school who are different. Discuss the following questions:

>How do you know?
>
>Why does prejudice hurt everyone?
>
>Can you tell what someone is like inside just by looking at the person?
>
>What can we do to help people understand that there are better ways to get along than hate and prejudice?
>
>What can you do if a person is prejudiced against you?

5. Distribute the quilt materials and have group members make quilt blocks illustrating what they think Xenophilia is like, with all its different kinds of people.

6. Have the children stitch their quilt blocks together and share them with the group.

7. Have children put away their quilt materials for the next session.

Process Time

1. Discuss the following questions:

>What did you like best about the story of Xenophilia?
>
>What do you think it would be like to live where there were people from all over the world? Would that make it harder or easier to accept everyone?
>
>What is the difference between xenophobia and xenophilia?
>
>What did you learn about prejudice today?
>
>Why do you think some people are prejudiced against others?
>
>What can you do when someone says something about another person that shows prejudice?
>
>Why should you stand up for your beliefs?

2. Share snacks, if desired. Before saying good-bye, thank group members for coming and remind them of the meeting time for the next session.

Peace to All Creatures

Goals

1. To introduce the idea that we are responsible for taking care of the earth and the creatures on it

2. To help children become aware of the need to take care of their own yards, neighborhoods, communities, and country

3. To give children information about organizations that help preserve land, mountains, forests, oceans, and animals

Materials

Pictures of endangered species

Publications from several wildlife and environmental organizations, such as the National Wildlife Federation, World Wildlife Fund, Nature Conservancy, National Parks, Audubon Society, or Humane Society (*Ranger Rick*, for children ages 6 through 12, is especially good. Write the National Wildlife Federation, 1400 Sixteenth Street, Washington, DC 20078–6420 for subscription information.)

Quilt materials for each child

A snack from a different culture or country *(optional)*

Group Session

Review

1. Welcome the children to group. Briefly go over the ground rules and the confidentiality rule.

2. Ask group members whether they have any "unfinished business" relating to the last session, on understanding and appreciating people's differences. Did they notice any examples of prejudice or hear about anything going on in the news that is the result of prejudice? Remind group members that it is important to get to know people and not judge them by how they look or speak.

Working Time

1. Ask children if they know what the word *extinct* means and clarify that some animals are already extinct and that others are endangered species, meaning that they are in danger of becoming extinct. Show the pictures of endangered species.

2. Discuss the fact that some animals become extinct because people kill them to make ornaments, wearing apparel, and remedies. Others become extinct because people destroy the places where they live (for example, by cutting down forests or draining marshlands).

3. Show group members the wildlife and environmental publications and share the idea that many people support and help our environment. Explain how these magazines give us ideas about how to be good citizens of the earth, how to recycle and reuse, and how to keep animals from becoming extinct.

4. Discuss the idea that all the meat we eat comes from living animals and that there is an ancient Native American tradition that we should show special respect for the animals that give their lives for us to eat. Tell group members that some vegetarians believe it is wrong to eat animals and that they eat only non-animal foods. Other people are vegetarians for health or religious reasons. More and more restaurants are having meatless choices. Some people give up eating meat for a day a week for both health reasons and because they care about animals and the environment.

5. Ask children how they think they can help animals. Talk to them about taking good care of their pets, not leaving them outside to fend for themselves all of the time. Pets need love and attention every day, as well as the right food and water. It is important to spay and neuter animals, too. Otherwise, puppies and kittens will have to be put to sleep because no one wants them. Mention that another way to help animals is to put up bird feeders. Some people feed squirrels and raccoons, too. Tell group members that birds are fun to feed and watch, but that once people start putting out seed they must keep it up because the birds depend on this food to make it through the cold weather.

6. Give children time to work on quilt blocks relating to the session topic, then have them stitch their blocks together. Encourage them to share and discuss their quilt blocks with the group.

7. Have children put away their quilt materials for the next session.

Process Time

1. Discuss the following questions:

> What did you learn about taking care of the world we live in?
>
> Why is it important to recycle and reuse things and not just throw them away?
>
> What is an endangered species?
>
> How can we help save endangered species—and why is it important to try?
>
> What did you learn about how you can help animals?

2. Share snacks, if desired. Before saying good-bye, thank group members for their participation and tell them that the group will meet only two more times after this session. Remind them of the meeting time for the next session.

Understanding Homelessness

NOTE: This session includes two options: Option A involves a prearranged field trip to a homeless shelter to help serve a meal. This option requires two blocks of time: the first to prepare children for the trip and give them an opportunity to create quilt blocks related to the topic and the second to conduct the field trip and process that experience. Option B, requiring only one session, involves discussion of a book about homelessness as a starting point; children complete their quilt blocks within this same session time.

Goals

1. To help children understand the concept of homelessness

2. To encourage awareness that there are people in our own communities who need help and love from us

3. To suggest that sharing and caring for others is necessary and can be a fulfilling experience

Materials

A book about homelessness, such as *No Place to Be: Voices of Homeless Children,* by Judith Berck (Houghton Mifflin, 1992)

Quilt materials for each child

A snack from a different culture or country *(optional)*

Group Session: Option A

Review

1. Welcome the children to group. Remind them of the ground rules and the confidentiality rule.

2. Ask whether anyone has anything to add from the last session's topic, on helping animals and caring for the earth and our environment.

Working Time

1. Prepare the children for their visit to the homeless shelter by reading from a book about homelessness. Some ideas to stress are as follows:

   There are people right here in our own communities who need our help. We don't have to go to another country to find people who need help.

   A homeless shelter is one place in our community that helps people who are poor.

   Anyone can become homeless. Not just adults are homeless—kids can lose their homes, too.

   Homeless people are not just in cities but are in smaller towns, too.

   Many churches have soup kitchens or meals for people who are hungry. The people who come there may not be homeless but are still very needy.

2. Have children create quilt blocks depicting their feelings about homelessness. Ask them to stitch their blocks together, then share them with the group.

Process Time: Before the Field Trip

1. Discuss the following questions:

    > What did you learn about homeless people today?
    >
    > Why is it important to help people in our community?
    >
    > How can helping make a more peaceful world?
    >
    > What else can you do to be a caring member of our community?
    >
    > What would it be like if you had to pack up one suitcase and leave home? What is so important to you that you would want to have it with you?
    >
    > What do you think homeless people want most in all the world?
    >
    > What do you think it feels like to be hungry and not know where your next meal is going to come from?
    >
    > Have you ever felt "homeless" because of a divorce, death, or some other event?
    >
    > What hope is there for homeless children? How can we help?

2. Share snacks, if desired. Before saying good-bye, thank group members for coming and go over any details about the field trip arrangements.

Process Time: After the Field Trip

1. Help children express their feelings about the visit. The following discussion questions may help:

    > What did you learn from the visit about people who are homeless?
    >
    > How did you feel about the people you saw?
    >
    > What places or organizations are there in our community to help people, and what do they do? (Group members might research this topic.)
    >
    > What does *volunteer* mean? Where could you or your parents volunteer?
    >
    > What good does it do for you to give your time and help to others in our community?
    >
    > How do you feel when you help others?

2. Share snacks, if desired. Before saying good-bye, thank group members for coming. Tell them the next session will be the last one and remind them of the meeting time.

Group Session: Option B

Review

1. Welcome the children to group. Remind them of the ground rules and the confidentiality rule.
2. Ask whether anyone has anything to add from the last session's topic, on helping animals and caring for the earth and our environment.

Working Time

1. Read from and discuss a book about homelessness. Some ideas to stress are as follows:

    > There are people right here in our own communities who need our help. We don't have to go to another country to find people who need help.
    >
    > A homeless shelter is one place in our community that helps people who are poor.
    >
    > Anyone can become homeless. Not just adults are homeless—kids can lose their homes, too.

Homeless people are not just in cities but are in smaller towns, too.

Many churches have soup kitchens or meals for people who are hungry. The people who come there may not be homeless but are still very needy.

2. Discuss the following questions:

What would it be like if you had to pack up one suitcase and leave home? What is so important to you that you would want to have it with you?

What do you think homeless people want most in all the world?

What do you think it feels like to be hungry and not know where your next meal is going to come from?

Have you ever felt "homeless" because of a divorce, death, or some other event?

3. Have children create quilt blocks depicting their feelings about homelessness. Ask them to stitch their blocks together, then share them with the group.

Process Time

1. Discuss the following questions:

What did you learn about homeless people today?

Why is it important to help people in our community?

How can helping make a more peaceful world?

What else can you do to be a caring member of our community?

What hope is there for homeless children? How can we help?

What places or organizations are there in our community to help people, and what do they do? (Group members might research this topic.)

What does *volunteer* mean? Where could you or your parents volunteer?

What good does it do for you to give your time and help to others in our community?

How do you feel when you help others?

2. Share snacks, if desired. Before saying good-bye, thank group members for coming. Tell them that the next session will be the last one and remind them of the meeting time.

Saying Good-bye

Goals

1. To give children the opportunity to review and process what they learned during the group experience

2. To help children decide how to display their quilt and share their ideas about peace with other children in the school

3. To model saying good-bye to one another in a healthy way and help group members learn that saying good-bye marks the beginning of a new phase of their relationship

Materials

Quilt materials for each child

A snack from a different culture or country *(optional)*

Group Session

Review

1. Welcome the children to group. Remind them of the ground rules and explain that the confidentiality rule holds even after the group is over.

2. Give group members the opportunity to discuss anything left over from the last session, on the topic of homelessness.

3. Talk about how group members have shared their personal ideas, feelings, and behaviors during the group. Tell them you appreciate their willingness to grow and learn new things.

Working Time

1. Process what happened and what children learned during the group sessions by asking the following questions:

   What did you learn that peacemaking means?

   How can you be a peacemaker in your own life?

   How can you let other kids know about peacemaking skills and that you think they are important?

   What did you learn about different races of people?

   What are some of the things that are the same about all human beings?

   What did you learn about foods from other countries and cultures?

   What was it like to learn about the different ways people worship?

   How can you help animals? What are you willing to do?

   What did you learn about homeless people?

   What did working on the quilt during each session mean to you?

2. Ask children what they would like to do to display their quilt when they finish. Let them brainstorm their own plan. (You may need to schedule a follow-up session or two to carry out the plan.)

3. Ask group members to decide what to draw for the quilt today. Some possibilities are children of different races and cultures showing the "peace" sign, children waving good-bye to one another, and a circle of children from all cultures holding hands and singing.

4. Let group members work on their quilt blocks, sew them together, and share them with the group.

Process Time

1. If appropriate, tell group members that you will be available to help them with their problems individually.

2. Spend the remaining time singing songs together and sharing snacks, if desired. End with a group hug.

I'm Somebody Special: Building Self-Esteem _____

Disagreement exists about how positive self-esteem is related to mental health. Nonetheless, virtually every system of psychology recognizes self-esteem as an important human need. Research is scanty on the exact nature of self-esteem, the mechanism of its achievement, and its impact on our values, goals, and motivation. However, studies do indicate that negative behaviors such as delinquency, substance abuse, acting out, poor social skills, and anger management difficulties are associated with low self-esteem (Battle, 1980; Brookover, Thomas, & Patterson, 1964; Bynner, O'Malley, & Bachman, 1981; Kahle, Kulka, & Klingel, 1980; Norem-Hebeison, 1975; Purkey, 1970). Under the assumption that these links are important, substantial study has been conducted to develop techniques and methods to enhance self-esteem in children.

Group counseling has been used with growing frequency to help children identify problematic issues and behaviors and to teach new skills and behaviors to improve children's thoughts and feelings about themselves (Amerikaner & Summerlin, 1982; Burke & Van de Streek, 1989; Campbell & Myrick, 1990; Gerler, Kinney, & Anderson, 1985; Gwynn & Brantley, 1987; Omizo & Omizo, 1987). Branden (1987) and others who have conducted long-term studies in the area of self-esteem believe that the feelings of being lovable and capable are central. Some of the ways suggested to help children gain more positive self-esteem include developing self-awareness (of feelings, thoughts, abilities, desires, needs), self-acceptance (not disowning the self), and self-expression (using assertion appropriately). The noted Harvard psychologist and researcher Carol Gilligan (1982) has made us aware that we cannot necessarily apply the research conducted on the development of self-esteem in boys to girls, that different psychological and sociological factors may be at work for each gender, and that "lovable" and "capable" are only part of the self-esteem picture.

The sessions in this group agenda attempt to incorporate Branden's and Gilligan's views that caring relationships are centrally important to self-concept. In addition, they attempt to

encourage Stanley Coopersmith's (1967) four criteria for self-esteem: (a) a feeling of significance, (b) a feeling of competence, (c) a feeling of virtue (the development of moral and ethical standards), and (d) a feeling of power (the ability to influence one's own and others' lives).

The activities here are also based on an expanded definition of self-esteem, one that encompasses more than the psychological component of individual functioning. We are involved not only in our own growth and development but in the development of our society as a whole. Thus, our children can enhance their self-esteem not only by individual achievements but also by working to address the major social issues of our time: poverty, racism, ageism, sexism, and other debilitating conditions. This group agenda is therefore based on a conceptualization of self-esteem that seeks an environment in which human dignity is respected and in which individual, cultural, social, and cooperative learning activities are emphasized.

Group Goals

1. To help children identify feelings about self

2. To promote recognition that we are all part of a larger world

3. To help children learn to name feelings (in other words, increase their affective vocabulary)

4. To encourage children to communicate their strengths to others, including other children

5. To help children begin to understand that good choices/decisions and positive behaviors result in positive thoughts and feelings of self-esteem

6. To engage children in cooperative learning activities in order to increase their sense of self-worth and confidence

Selection Guidelines

The general selection guidelines presented in Part 1 apply to this group agenda. School personnel can determine with some accuracy which children need help to improve self-esteem. Body language, interpersonal behaviors, academic status, motivational status, stress management ability, and coping skills all give clues as to where the child stands in this regard.

The following specific behaviors indicate that a child may be a good candidate for this topical group:

1. Lack of self-confidence, reflected in the reluctance to take risks (for example, avoiding competition in academics or sports, choosing easy tasks or classes to avoid failure, avoiding activities that might involve conflict)

2. Low motivation to continue tasks or to socialize

3. Lack of positive friendship behaviors

4. Insecurity, low frustration tolerance, or anxious behaviors

5. Few friends or playmates at school and home, reflected in not being selected for games and activities

References and Suggested Resources for Professionals

Amerikaner, M., & Summerlin, M. (1982). Group counseling with learning disabled children: Effects of social skills and relaxation training on self-concept and classroom behavior. *Journal of Learning Disabilities, 15*, 340–343.

Battle, J. (1980). The relationship between self-esteem and depression among high school students. *Perceptual Motor Skills, 51*, 157–158.

Branden, N. (1967). *The psychology of self-esteem*. New York: Bantam.

Branden, N. (1987). *How to raise your self-esteem*. New York: Bantam.

Brookover, W., Thomas, S., & Patterson, A. (1964). Self-concept of ability and school achievement. *Sociology of Education, 37*, 271–278.

Burke, D., & Van de Streek, L. (1989). Children of divorce: An application of Hammond's group counseling for children. *Elementary School Guidance and Counseling, 24*, 112–118.

Bynner, J. M., O'Malley, P. M., & Bachman, J. G. (1981). Self-esteem and delinquency revisited. *Journal of Youth and Adolescence, 10*, 407–441.

Campbell, C., & Myrick, R. (1990). Motivational group counseling for low-performing students. *Journal for Specialists in Group Work, 15*, 43–50.

Coopersmith, S. (1967). *The antecedents of self-esteem*. San Francisco: Freeman.

Gerler, E., Kinney, J., & Anderson, R. (1985). The effects of counseling on classroom performance. *Journal of Humanistic Education and Development, 23*, 155–165.

Gilligan, C. (1982). *In a different voice*. Cambridge, MA: Harvard University Press.

Gladding, S. (1991). *Group work: A counseling specialty*. New York: Macmillan.

Gwynn, C., & Brantley, H. (1987). Effects of a divorce group intervention for elementary school children. *Psychology in the Schools, 24*, 161–164.

Kahle, L. R., Kulka, R. A., & Klingel, D. M. (1980). Low adolescent self-esteem leads to multiple interpersonal problems: A test of social adaptation theory. *Journal of Personality and Social Psychology, 39*, 496–502.

Norem-Hebeison, A. A. (1975). Self-esteem as a predictor of adolescent drug abuse. In National Institute on Drug Abuse, *Predicting adolescent drug abuse*. Washington, DC: Author.

Omizo, M., & Omizo, S. (1987). The effects of group counseling on classroom behavior and self-concept among elementary school learning disabled children. *Exceptional Child, 34*, 47–64.

Purkey, W. (1970). *Self-concept and school achievement*. New York: Prentice Hall.

Bibliography for Children

Brown, M. (1949). *The important book.* New York: HarperCollins. (Preschool–Grade 3)

Brown, S. (1992). *Gentle rain and loving sun: Activities for developing a healthy self-concept in young children.* Muncie, IN: Accelerated Development. (Preschool–Grade 2)

Carlson, N. (1988). *I like me!* New York: Puffin. (Preschool–Grade 2)

Carr, J. (1990). *I am curious about me.* New York: Scholastic. (Preschool–Grade 2)

Caseley, J. (1990). *The cousins.* New York: Greenwillow. (Grades 1–4)

Cooper, I. (1991). *Frances four-eyes.* New York: Knopf. (Grades 3–6)

Crowdy, D. (1990). *Pride.* Chicago: Children's Press/The Child's World. (Preschool–Grade 3)

Dini, G. (1983). *The heart that followed me home.* Mahwah, NJ: Paulist. (Kindergarten–Grade 4)

Fleming, B. (1992). *Scott the dot: A self-esteem tale for children.* San Luis Obispo, CA: Impact. (Preschool–Grade 4)

Hallinan, P. (1991). *I know who I am.* Center City, MN: Hazelden. (Kindergarten–Grade 4)

Johnson, J. (1991). *Celebrate you: Building your self-esteem.* Minneapolis: Lerner. (Grade 5 and up)

Krauss, R., & Johnson, C. (1955). *Is this you?* New York: Scholastic. (Kindergarten–Grade 3)

Kroll, S. (1987). *I'd like to be.* New York: Putnam Berkeley Group. (Preschool–Grade 2)

Loomans, D. (1991). *The Lovables in the kingdom of self-esteem.* Tiburon, CA: H. J. Kramer. (Preschool–Grade 3)

Lopshire, R. (1986). *I want to be somebody new.* New York: Random House/Beginner Books. (Kindergarten–Grade 3)

Moser, A. (1991). *Don't feed the monster on Tuesdays! The children's self-esteem book.* Kansas City, MO: Landmark Editions. (Kindergarten–Grade 6)

Palmer, P. (1977). *Liking myself.* San Luis Obispo, CA: Impact. (Kindergarten–Grade 4)

Plattner, S. (1992). *Connecting with myself.* Belmont, CA: Fearon. (Kindergarten–Grade 3)

Rayner, C. (1989). *The don't spoil your body book.* Hauppauge, NY: Barron's. (Grade 3 and up)

Schwartz, L. (1978). *I am special.* Santa Barbara, CA: Learning Works. (Grades 1–4)

Schwartz, L. (1991). *Hannah the hippo: Understanding self-esteem.* Santa Barbara, CA: Learning Works. (Kindergarten–Grade 3)

Seuss, Dr. (1969). *My book about me: (By me, myself).* New York: Random House. (Kindergarten–Grade 8)

Sinykin, S. (1990). *Come out, come out, wherever you are!* Center City, MN: Hazelden. (Grades 1–5)

Getting Started

Goals

1. To introduce children to the group experience and help them begin to get acquainted
2. To establish ground rules and discuss the issue of confidentiality
3. To discuss the purpose of the group and prepare children for the sessions ahead
4. To help children become aware that the group is a safe environment for sharing ideas, feelings, and behaviors
5. To identify feelings as a special part of us and give children practice expressing them

Materials

Easel pad and marker

Construction paper (cut into name-tag-size pieces)

Crayons/markers

Safety pins

Puppets, toy animals, or masks (enough so each child has a choice)

Feeling Faces Chart (Handout 1)

A healthy snack, such as raisins in individual boxes, fruit, crackers, or juice *(optional)*

Group Session

Ice Breaker

1. Welcome everyone to group. Go over the purpose of the group and explain some of the topics you will be discussing.
2. Pass out the crayons or markers and pieces of construction paper, instructing group members to write their names, then pin the tags on. (You could use premade name tags with adhesive on the back for younger children, if desired.)
3. Tell the children that to help them get acquainted you would like them to choose a puppet, mask, or toy animal who will introduce them to the group.
4. Model what you want children to do by choosing something to "speak" for you. Share your name, favorite food, and what you want to learn about in group.
5. After each child has had a turn sharing this information, discuss basic ground rules for the group, giving group members some examples:

    Everyone gets a chance to talk.

    No hitting or fighting in group.

    Take turns.

    Ask for group members' input to help them develop "ownership." List all the ground rules on the easel pad so everyone can see. Post the ground rules during every session.

6. Next go over the confidentiality rule and its limits. For example, you might say:

> When we talked about your being in the group, I told you that whatever we say in our group is *confidential*. That means what we say is private. You may talk about your own thoughts, feelings, and actions, but you may not share anything others in the group talk about. There are some special times when I would have to share what you say—if you say something about harming yourself or others, if you share something about child abuse, or if the court (a judge) asks me about what goes on.

Working Time

1. Distribute a copy of the Feeling Faces Chart (Handout 1) to everyone. Explain that feelings are a special part of us that help us understand ourselves and other people: Some feelings make us feel warm and fuzzy, like love, affection, joy, and happiness. Other feelings make us feel cold and prickly, like fear, sadness, or anger. Feelings are not good or bad, and it is important to recognize and be able to share our feelings as part of who we are.

2. Go around the circle, letting children pick out a few feelings from the chart. After each child has shared a feeling, ask the others if they have ever felt that way. Encourage those who feel the same way to address one another directly and say, "I connect with you, _____ . I felt that way when _____ happened." This will help children be better able to identify their feelings and the situations when they are likely to arise.

Process Time

1. Discuss the following questions:

> What did you learn about in group today?
>
> What did you learn about yourself in group today?
>
> How do you feel now about coming to group?
>
> Do you have anything you want to say to anyone else before we end the group?
>
> What feelings do you think you might have before we meet again that you could come back and tell us about?

2. Thank the children for coming to group and share snacks, if desired. Before saying good-bye, remind them of the meeting time for the next session.

Feeling Faces Chart

HAPPY

LOW

Cheerful
Glad
Pleased
Amused
Relieved

MEDIUM

Delighted
Excited
Bubbly
Tickled
Glowing

HIGH

Elated
Ecstatic
Jubilant
Overjoyed
Radiant

SAD

Resigned
Blue
Glum
Gloomy
Ignored

Forlorn
Dejected
Slighted
Defeated
Burdened

Miserable
Crushed
Helpless
Worthless
Depressed

ANGRY

Peeved
Bugged
Annoyed
Ruffled
Cross

Disgusted
Irritated
Hostile
Riled
Biting

Fuming
Furious
Outraged
Hateful
Burned up

AFRAID

Uneasy
Tense
Anxious
Nervous
Puzzled

Alarmed
Fearful
Strained
Shaky
Jittery

Panicked
Horrified
Terrified
Petrified
Desperate

Feely Feelings

Goals

1. To develop the norm of reviewing what happened during the previous session and give children an opportunity to discuss anything they still have questions about

2. To help children learn that sharing feelings is an important part of healthy, lasting relationships and of feeling good about ourselves

Materials

Feeling Faces Chart (Handout 1, p. 46)

A healthy snack, such as raisins in individual boxes, fruit, crackers, or juice *(optional)*

Group Session

Review

1. Welcome the children to group. Briefly go over the ground rules, asking if there are any the children would like to change or add. Review the confidentiality rule.

2. Make sure children know one another's names; continue to use name tags if they still do not know each other by name yet.

3. Review the Feeling Faces Chart (Handout 1), asking group members if they had any special feelings since the last session that they can remember and would be willing to share. Let them each have a turn—reinforce their sharing.

Working Time

1. Tell the children that you have a story to read to them about knowing who we really are, then read the following.

Houndie and Mutsy

In the home of Rosi and Phillip Jefferson lived two dogs named Houndie and Mutsy. Houndie was a beautiful Afghan hound, with flowing, silky hair and ears and a curled up tail like a monkey's. She was so beautiful that people would stop Rosi and Phillip when they were out walking the dogs and ask what kind of dog she was. They would say things like "Oh, that dog is so regal, she looks like a queen."

Now Mutsy, who was no special kind of dog at all, just kind of hung back and followed on the walks, looking very dejected and sad indeed when this happened. In fact, Mutsy was joked about and called an "arf" dog, for "arf terrier" and "arf everything else"! This was a joke because it sounded like "half and half." Poor Mutsy—nobody said he was beautiful or regal or even cute. In fact, Mutsy had an unusual way of walking because his leg had been broken when he was just a tiny puppy, and it had grown together crooked. So Mutsy walked with a sway and a hitch and dragged his leg a little, making him look even more discombobulated!

One day after their walk, Mutsy and Houndie were talking to each other, the way dog friends do. Mutsy said, "Houndie, I think the world of you as my best friend, and I know you like me very much, too. But when we are on walks with Rosi and Phillip and people say nice things to you and mean things to me, I feel like crying, like getting angry at them and chewing their shoes, like saying 'Hey, notice how pretty my markings are, and that I have an excellent nose,' but I don't—I just stand there and cry to myself. Would you be willing to stick up for me and not take all of the attention, and pay attention to how I feel? I like myself just how I am, and I need to know my friends accept me for who I am, too, not how pretty or ugly I am."

Houndie didn't realize that her friend Mutsy felt so terrible, awful, and horrible about being teased and discounted by the kids and grown-ups in the neighborhood. She said, "Oh, Mutsy! I'm sorry! I haven't been a very good friend to you. I haven't been loyal to your friendship because I forgot you when you needed me. I like for people to say how pretty I am, and I didn't realize that you need people to see that you have many special things about you, too, even though they aren't on the outside. I want everyone to know that being different on the outside does not mean that you are not beautiful on the inside. You are the most loving, loyal, honest, and special friend I have ever had. I will try hard to be more aware of your feelings and to appreciate you."

The next day, Phillip and Rosi took the dogs for their walk. Houndie pranced in her high-stepping style, and Mutsy came along behind, dragging his leg a little, but with a friendly attitude in his heart. The neighbors were working in their yard and said to Phillip and Rosi, "Oh, my, Houndie is such a gorgeous creature!" Houndie knew they were saying lovely things about her beauty. She tossed her head and stepped highly, her long hair flowing. She looked like the queen of the desert. Houndie looked back at Mutsy, who was staring down. She knew he must be feeling rejected and ugly. She ran to him and whispered in dog language in his ear, "Mutsy, it looks as though you feel rejected and unappreciated because those people don't know what a beautiful dog you are inside. I do. And I appreciate all of you."

Mutsy realized that he was not going to be able to change the opinion of some people about his looks, but he felt very proud of his friendship with Houndie. He could ask for things he needed, he could tell Houndie his true feelings, and she would listen to his ideas and make him feel special for who he was, not what he looked like on the outside. Mutsy knew that he and Houndie had a very special friendship!

2. Help children respond to the following questions:

> What do you think Mutsy felt like when he was called names and rejected by people in the neighborhood? Have you ever felt this way?

> What did Mutsy do about getting the positive feelings he needed and the recognition for who he was inside? How could you do something like that?

> Can you change other people's feelings and thoughts?

> Can you change your own feelings and thoughts?

> After Mutsy asked Houndie to pay attention to his feelings and his true self, she watched and listened to him to know how he was feeling. Who could you watch and listen to so you could let them know you understand?

> What kind of feelings and recognition are important in friendship?

> How do you feel when you share your feelings with your friends?

Process Time

1. Discuss the following questions:

   What did you learn about in group today?

   What do you think is important about sharing feelings?

   Did you connect with anyone in group today? If so, tell that person how you feel.

   How do you feel about sharing your feelings with others?

   What would you be willing to do before the next session to share your feelings or to have your feelings understood better?

2. Share snacks, if desired. Before saying good-bye, thank the children for coming and remind them of the meeting time for the next session.

Pictures of Me

Goals

1. To give children the chance to share their ideas of who they are—what they are capable of and what they would like to become capable of

2. To help children understand that people have different strengths and weaknesses and that these differences are OK

Materials

Feeling Faces Chart (Handout 1, p. 46)

Assorted magazines (especially those with pictures of children performing various activities: doing school activities, playing outside, being involved in sports, helping with household tasks, going to religious services, doing homework, and so on)

Scissors

Glue

Large sheets of construction paper

Crayons/markers

A healthy snack, such as raisins in individual boxes, fruit, crackers, or juice *(optional)*

Group Session

Review

1. Welcome the children to group. Briefly go over the ground rules and review the confidentiality rule.

2. Ask children what feelings they noticed having since they were together last time. Let them all have a chance to share. Refer to the Feeling Faces Chart (Handout 1) as needed.

3. Discuss the following questions:

> Which of your feelings do you like the best?
>
> Which of your feelings do you dislike and want to end?
>
> What could you do to have more positive feelings?
>
> What could you do to have fewer negative feelings?

Working Time

1. Place the magazines in the middle of the group. Let the children sit on the floor around the magazines and choose a couple to look at. Pass out the scissors, glue, and sheets of construction paper.

2. Thumb through a magazine and find a picture of someone who illustrates some feeling, behavior, or action that represents you. Show it to the children and tell them why it represents you. For example, if you are a woman and you find a picture of a woman carrying a briefcase to work, you could say this is a picture of a professional person like yourself.

3. Encourage children to look through the magazines and find pictures representing themselves, cut them out, and glue them to the construction paper.

4. Help the children find four or five more pictures representing what they can do, what they hope to do better, or what they cannot yet do but would like to do. Have them cut out the pictures in different shapes (hearts, squares, diamonds, triangles, and so forth) and glue them to the paper. Let them decorate their pictures with the crayons or markers.

5. When the children have finished, have them sit down again in their group circle to share the pictures they have chosen to represent themselves.

Process Time

1. Discuss the following questions:

> What did you learn from "picturing" yourself?
>
> What do you like best about yourself?
>
> What do you want to work on to improve or change?
>
> What did you notice about others' pictures?
>
> How are we alike?
>
> How are we different?

2. Thank the children for coming to group and share snacks, if desired. Before saying good-bye, remind them of the meeting time for the next session.

Changing and Growing

NOTE: This session is best held outdoors. Select a place for the group to go and sit together where they can observe nature.

Goals

1. To present the idea that everything in life changes as it grows, matures, and dies within its own life span

2. To establish the idea that we have more control over some of these changes and less control over others

3. To help children identify the things they can and cannot change

Materials

A healthy snack, such as raisins in individual boxes, fruit, crackers, or juice *(optional)*

Group Session

Review

1. Welcome the children to group. Briefly go over the ground rules and the confidentiality rule.

2. Ask group members whether they had any particular feelings since the last session that they would like to share. Reinforce them for sharing, telling them that this is a safe place to talk about their feelings.

Working Time

1. Ask how children feel about being outside instead of inside for this session. Explain that the purpose of being outside is to notice how things in nature grow and change, just as we do.

2. Ask the children what they notice in nature that changes as it grows. Point out whatever in the environment illustrates this idea: trees of different maturity, flowers just opening or fading, growing or dying leaves, new shoots coming out of the ground, and so on. Stress that everything has its own life span and that everything changes.

3. Tell the children that we too grow and change over our lifetimes but that we have more "input," or ways of making things go the way we want them to. For example, we don't have a lot of control about what our bodies look like when we are 15 years old because we are still growing and our genes are telling our bodies what they are supposed to be shaped like. But we do have quite a bit to say about how our bodies look when we are 50 years old because we can choose to eat healthy things during our life, exercise regularly, and not smoke or drink alcohol. Other things about life we have less control over, like other people's behavior, getting a new teacher, having to go to a new school, or parents divorcing.

4. Discuss the following questions:

>What things about yourself are changing and growing?
>
>What can you change? How can you do that?
>
>What things can't you change in your life? How can you deal with that?
>
>What can you do when you get upset over other people's behaviors?
>
>What can you do when you get angry, hurt, or sad about things you can't change?
>
>Do you connect with anyone in group today? If so, tell that person how you feel.

Process Time

1. Discuss the following questions:

>What did you learn in group today?
>
>What was it like for you to hear what other kids think about?
>
>What was it like to feel a part of the group?
>
>How are you feeling about learning things in group so far?
>
>What might happen before the next session that you could change or do something about?
>
>What might happen before the next session that you could not do anything about?
>
>How might you feel about this? (Children may have difficulty naming future feelings, but let them try.)

2. Share snacks, if desired, and thank the children for coming to group. Before saying good-bye, remind them of the meeting time for the next session.

I Can!

Goals

1. To instill the idea that each person has special talents and gifts to use for his or her own good and the good of others
2. To help children recognize feelings of being capable
3. To encourage children to share their talents with others in the group

Materials

Drawing paper

Crayons/markers

A healthy snack, such as raisins in individual boxes, fruit, crackers, or juice *(optional)*

Group Session

Review

1. Welcome the children to group. Briefly go over the ground rules and review the confidentiality rule.
2. Ask the children if they had any more thoughts or feelings since the last session, on how things grow and change and what we can and can't change. Have group members experienced any changes in their own lives since the last session?

Working Time

1. Pass out the art materials and ask the children to draw two things they do that they are proud of. Explain that they will be sharing their drawings with the rest of the group. Let children sit on the floor if they wish so they can draw comfortably.
2. Circulate and give individual praise and encouragement—let the children know you appreciate their drawings and their willingness to share.
3. Call children back to the group circle and ask who would like to share first. Let each child have a turn making an affirming statement—for example, "I like the way I can draw what I feel," "I am good at being friendly," or "I can help others a lot." Be sure to praise children for their efforts and not just their accomplishments.

Process Time

1. Discuss the following questions:

   What did you learn in group today?

   What was it like to share your pictures of your talents?

   What was it like to hear about other kids' talents?

   How do you feel about yourself after talking about your talents?

   What talents would you like to work on and improve?

   What person in your life would you be willing to share these pictures with and tell your good feelings about your talents?

2. Thank the children for coming to group and share snacks, if desired. Before saying good-bye, remind them of the meeting time for the next session.

What Do I Value?

> NOTE: Before beginning this session, tape a large sheet of newsprint to the wall for each group member, including yourself. Make three columns on your own sheet: *A Little Important, Medium Important,* and *Very Important.* List under these three headings some of the things you value (for example, rose garden, children, car, parents, time alone, church, friendships, pet dog, being honest, giving time to help others, and having fun with family/friends).

Goals

1. To help children recognize what they value and to encourage them to articulate their values to others

2. To help children realize that what we value makes us unique and that such differences are not just OK but are what make us really special

3. To encourage children to accept others' differing values

4. To introduce the idea that what we think is important is a special part of ourselves and shouldn't be given up just to be liked by others

Materials

Large sheets of newsprint

Tape

Crayons/markers

A healthy snack, such as raisins in individual boxes, fruit, crackers, or juice *(optional)*

Group Session

Review

1. Welcome the children to group. Briefly go over the ground rules and review the confidentiality rule.

2. Ask whether children shared their drawings from the last session with anyone and, if so, how they felt about talking about their talents and successes. Ask whether children noticed the talents of family members or friends: How did it feel to know that other people have things they can do well and need to have recognized?

Working Time

1. Introduce the idea that we all have *values,* or things we believe. Some of these things are a little important, some are medium important, and some are very important.

2. Show group members your previously completed values chart, then encourage them to make a values chart for themselves, telling them that they will have the chance to share with everyone when they finish.

3. Give group members time to write—help them express their ideas if they need it. Try to encourage the children as their developmental age permits to think of abstract values as well as material goods. Even little ones value friends, hugs, honesty, and the like.

4. Have group members bring their completed values charts back to the circle and share what they think is a little important, medium important, and very important.

5. Point out that we all value different things. Some of the things are going to be like what our friends value, and some of the things are going to be different. Stress that it is OK to be different, even if our friends don't like what we value.

6. Ask children what they can do if one of their friends says something negative about what they value:

   What can you say or do to defend your values?

   When should you look at your values and make some changes?

Process Time

1. Discuss the following questions:

   What did you learn in group today?

   How can you show your friends that you respect what they value?

   What can you do if other people don't like what you value?

   What kind of situations can you think of where people may try to get you to do things that are against your values? (For example: taking drugs, smoking, drinking alcohol, or running with the wrong crowd.)

   How do you know if something is not good for you and needs to be changed?

   Would you be willing to notice before the next session what you value and how you feel about it?

2. Share snacks, if desired. Thank the children for coming to group. Before saying good-bye, remind them of the meeting time for the next session. Mention that there will be only two more sessions before the group is over.

Appreciating Friends

Goals

1. To give children the opportunity to explore and clarify what they value about friends
2. To help children understand how to tell their friends what they value about them and about the friendship
3. To encourage awareness that friendship skills are important to us and to getting along in life and that we feel good about ourselves when we can be a good friend to others

Materials

A play telephone

A healthy snack, such as raisins in individual boxes, fruit, crackers, or juice *(optional)*

Group Session

Review

1. Welcome the children to group. Briefly go over the ground rules and review the confidentiality rule.
2. Ask whether group members have anything they want to say about the last session, on what we value in our lives.

Working Time

1. Use the following questions to help children explore what they like about having friends—best friends, boyfriends, girlfriends, and so on. Be sure to use your linking/connecting skills after questions—for example, "Who else likes the same thing as Latisha?" and "Who can connect with what Shawn has said?"

    What would life be like if you had no friends at all?

    How do you feel when your friends go away on vacation or aren't around for you to play with in the summer?

    What do you miss most when a friend moves away?

    How important is it to have at least one good friend?

    What do you think are your best friendship skills?

    Would you rather have a lot of friends you knew just a little or a few friends you knew very well?

    What are you willing to give up to keep a friend?

    When your friends get in an argument, what do you do?

    When you and a friend get in an argument, what do you do?

    Would you like it if your friend called you up and told you just why it is that he or she likes having you for a friend?

2. Tell group members that the play telephone you have will give them the chance to practice saying what they value about their friend. Tell them that they will have a turn to call a friend and tell that person what they value about the friendship. Model the process: "Hello, Margie, this is Susan. I was thinking about our friendship, and I just wanted to tell you that it means a lot to me to have you as a friend because you always care about what I do, even when you don't think it is a good idea. I appreciate that."

3. Let each child who wants to use the phone make a call to a friend. Give plenty of praise and support for their efforts.

Process Time

1. Discuss the following questions:

> What was it like for you to share nice things about your friendship with your friend? How did you feel?
>
> How do you think your friend would feel hearing those things?
>
> What did you like about telling these things to your friend?
>
> What didn't you like?
>
> What do you think will happen if you share positive things about your friends with them?
>
> How important do you think it is to do this?
>
> Would you be willing to really tell your friend how you feel about him or her?

2. Remind the children that the next session will be the last and that they will be saying good-bye to each other then. Discuss any special ideas they might have for the last session to help them remember the group.

3. Share snacks, if desired. Thank the children for coming to group and remind them of the meeting time for the next session.

Saying Good-bye

Goals

1. To give children the opportunity to review and process what they learned during the group experience

2. To reinforce children's good feelings about who they are

3. To model saying good-bye to one another in a healthy way and help group members learn that saying good-bye marks the beginning of a new phase of their relationship

Materials

A full-length or hand-held mirror

Whatever snacks or other materials group members have chosen to celebrate the last session

Group Session

Review

1. Welcome the children to group. Briefly go over the ground rules and explain that the confidentiality rule continues even after the group is over.

2. Ask if children have anything they want to bring up from the last session, on what they value in their friends. Give them a chance to tell what happened if they actually spoke with a friend.

Working Time

1. Review what children learned during the other sessions by asking the following questions:

    What did you learn from the story of Houndie and Mutsy about our need to be positive to one another?

    What did you learn from "picturing" yourself and your achievements?

    What things about you are changing and growing?

    Do you think everyone has special talents or gifts? What are yours?

    What did you learn about having values and standing up for them?

    What is important to you about having friends?

2. Ask the following types of general questions as well:

    What was the best thing that you learned from being a group member?

    What topic did you think helped you the most?

    What do you like about yourself now that you didn't before you came to group?

3. Tell the children that you are very pleased with their efforts to learn about themselves and to share their thoughts and feelings with one another. Stress that it is important to be appreciated by others, but it is more important to appreciate ourselves.

4. Show group members the mirror and tell them that they have the opportunity to make a statement of appreciation to themselves. Model this type of statement: "What I appreciate most about myself is that I am a caring person."

5. Ask who would like to go first and pass that person the mirror. Have the person fill in the same sentence stem: "What I appreciate most about myself is _____."

6. Let everyone have a turn, then thank the children for participating.

Process Time

1. Discuss the following questions:

> What was it like for you to tell yourself in the mirror that you appreciated something about yourself?
>
> What did you learn from doing this activity?
>
> Would you be willing to practice telling yourself one thing you appreciate about yourself each day?
>
> What do you think would happen if you told someone else that you appreciate him or her?

2. Let the children know again how much you value their hard work. If appropriate, tell them that you will be available to help them with their problems individually.

3. Celebrate in the way children have chosen.

Friends: Getting Along With Others_____

Social and interpersonal skills training is a relatively new phenomenon, arising in the 1970s as a convergence of education and psychotherapy. The impetus for such training was in part the educational requirement of mainstreaming and the need to help children with special needs succeed in regular classrooms (Goldstein, 1988). During the 1970s some behavioral theorists and therapists began to explore the role of thinking processes in behavior change. Cognitive-behavior therapy as a major stream of therapeutic practice was put into effect by such theorists as Albert Bandura (1969, 1977, 1986), Donald Meichenbaum (1977), and A. T. Beck (1976).

As skills training methods became more common in therapy, the educational community began to adopt and expand these methods for use with children in the school setting. Today, school psychologists, school counselors, and mental health professionals in the community regularly use skills training methods to address a range of behavioral and emotional problems (Corey, 1991; Goldstein, 1988), including difficulties in meeting, making, and keeping friends. A deficiency in these skills can result from a number of causes and be maintained by continued negative interactions in the classroom and on the playground.

This group experience is designed to help children learn the specific skills that can help them increase positive interactions. This in turn will increase the chances that they will be able to maintain healthy friendships that will have a positive influence on development. Sessions provide the opportunity for children to see friendship skills modeled and practice skills in a safe and supportive environment. Perhaps most important, children will be able to express the feelings and thoughts they have about the stresses they have experienced as a result of their lack of a peer support system.

Group Goals

1. To help children begin to build trust in the process of interacting and disclosing in a group of peers and become comfortable sharing feelings and ideas

2. To clarify the concept of friendship

3. To encourage knowledge of what skills are valued and not valued in friendships

4. To help children learn positive skills by seeing them modeled by other group members

5. To expand children's ideas about friendships with people of all ages and animals, as well as same-age peers

6. To help children learn that all friendships come to an end and that there are positive ways to end friendships

7. To encourage awareness that it is important to cooperate as a member of a team or community

Selection and Other Guidelines

The success of this group experience depends heavily on the general guidelines for selection presented in Part 1. Be sure not to overload the group with children who have the same type of skill deficits. A good mix might result from choosing one or two children who are shy and lack the skills or know-how to meet new friends, one or two who are aggressive and need to learn to be respectful of others, one or two who have friends but can't keep them, and one or two who have good friendship skills but need the opportunity to express their feelings about transition issues such as moving and losing old friends.

It is important to include at least some children who can model appropriate friendship behaviors. Keep in mind also that although skill acquisition is important, it is secondary to the group experience. Focus on sharing ideas, behaviors, thoughts, and feelings about friendships as well as on the acquisition of skills.

The following are some indicators that might be present in children who would be good candidates for this group:

1. Lack of ability to initiate friendships

2. Lack of ability to keep friends over a period of time expected for the age group

3. Inappropriate possessiveness or difficulty sharing

4. Difficulties in adjusting or making friends resulting from a recent move

5. Difficulties that reflect a lack of age-appropriate social responsibility, such as initiating fights, excessive arguing and teasing, or inability to apologize

References and Suggested Resources for Professionals

Agras, W. S. (Ed.). (1978). *Behavior modification: Principles and clinical applications* (2nd ed.). Boston: Little, Brown.

Bandura, A. (1969). *Principles of behavior modification.* New York: Holt, Rinehart & Winston.

Bandura, A. (1977). *Social learning theory.* New York: Prentice Hall.

Bandura, A. (1986). *Social foundations of thought and action: A social cognitive theory.* New York: Prentice Hall.

Beck, A. T. (1976). *Cognitive therapy and emotional disorders.* New York: International Universities Press.

Bellack, A. S., & Hersen, M. (1977). *Behavior modification: An introductory textbook.* Baltimore: Williams & Wilkins.

Corey, G. (1991). *Theory and practice of group counseling* (3rd ed.). Pacific Grove, CA: Brooks/Cole.

Cormier, W. H., & Cormier, L. S. (1991). *Interviewing strategies for helpers: Fundamental skills and cognitive behavioral interventions* (3rd ed.). Pacific Grove, CA: Brooks/Cole.

Goldfried, M. R., & Davison, G. C. (1976). *Clinical behavior therapy.* New York: Holt, Rinehart & Winston.

Goldstein, A. P. (1988). *The Prepare Curriculum: Teaching prosocial competencies.* Champaign, IL: Research Press.

Kazdin, A. E. (1978). *History of behavior modification: Experimental foundations of contemporary research.* Baltimore: University Park.

Lazarus, A. (1971). *Behavior therapy and beyond.* New York: McGraw-Hill.

Lazarus, A. (1981). *The practice of multimodal therapy.* New York: McGraw-Hill.

Lazarus, A. (1982). Multimodal group therapy. In G. M. Gazda (Ed.), *Basic approaches to group psychotherapy and group counseling* (3rd ed.). Springfield, IL: Charles C Thomas.

Meichenbaum, D. (1977). *Cognitive behavior modification: An integrative approach.* New York: Plenum.

Thoresen, C. E., & Coates, T. J. (1980). What does it mean to be a behavior therapist? In C. E. Thoresen (Ed.), *The behavior therapist.* Pacific Grove, CA: Brooks/Cole.

Wilson, G. T. (1978). Cognitive-behavior therapy: Paradigm shift or passing phase? In J. P. Foreyt & D. P. Rathjen (Eds.), *Cognitive behavior therapy: Research and applications.* New York: Plenum.

Wolpe, J. (1969). *The practice of behavior therapy.* New York: Pergamon.

Bibliography for Children

Berenstain, S., & Berenstain, J. (1982). *The Berenstain Bears get in a fight.* New York: Random House. (Preschool–Grade 2)

Berenstain, S., & Berenstain, J. (1983). *The Berenstain Bears and the truth.* New York: Random House. (Preschool–Grade 2)

Berry, J. (1988). *Being destructive.* (Available from Paperbacks for Educators, 426 West Front Street, Washington, MO 63090) (Kindergarten–Grade 3)

Berry, J. (1988). *Being mean.* (Available from Paperbacks for Educators, 426 West Front Street, Washington, MO 63090) (Kindergarten–Grade 3)

Berry, J. (1988). *Breaking promises.* (Available from Paperbacks for Educators, 426 West Front Street, Washington, MO 63090) (Kindergarten–Grade 3)

Berry, J. (1988). *Cheating.* (Available from Paperbacks for Educators, 426 West Front Street, Washington, MO 63090) (Kindergarten–Grade 3)

Berry, J. (1988). *Fighting*. (Available from Paperbacks for Educators, 426 West Front Street, Washington, MO 63090) (Kindergarten–Grade 3)

Berry, J. (1988). *Interrupting*. (Available from Paperbacks for Educators, 426 West Front Street, Washington, MO 63090) (Kindergarten–Grade 3)

Berry, J. (1988). *Lying*. (Available from Paperbacks for Educators, 426 West Front Street, Washington, MO 63090) (Kindergarten–Grade 3)

Berry, J. (1988). *Stealing*. (Available from Paperbacks for Educators, 426 West Front Street, Washington, MO 63090) (Kindergarten–Grade 3)

Berry, J. (1988). *Teasing*. (Available from Paperbacks for Educators, 426 West Front Street, Washington, MO 63090) (Kindergarten–Grade 3)

Birney, B. (1991). *Oh, bother! Someone's fibbing!* Racine, WI: Golden Books. (Grades 1–4)

Bourgeois, P. (1991). *Franklin fibs*. New York: Scholastic. (Preschool–Grade 2)

Buscaglia, L. (1988). *A memory for Tino*. Thorofare, NY: Slack. (Preschool–Grade 12)

Carlson, N. (1983). *Loudmouth George and the sixth-grade bully*. New York: Puffin. (Preschool–Grade 3)

Carlson, N. (1987). *Arnie and the stolen markers*. New York: Puffin. (Preschool–Grade 3)

Cohen, M. (1985). *Liar, liar, pants on fire*. New York: Dell. (Kindergarten–Grade 6)

Deeter, C. (1991). *Finding the green stone*. Orlando, FL: Harcourt Brace Jovanovich. (Grades 3–7)

Duncan, R. (1969). *When Emily woke up angry*. Hauppauge, NY: Barron's. (Preschool–Grade 2)

Elliott, P. (1991). *Fluffy and Sparky: A story about true buddies*. San Bernardino, CA: Borgo/Planetary Publications. (Preschool–Grade 3)

Galvin, M. (1987). *Ignatius finds help: A story about psychotherapy for children*. New York: Magination. (Kindergarten–Grade 6)

Goffe, T. (1991). *Bully for you*. New York: Child's Play. (Grades 2–6)

Grimes, N. (1991). *Oh, bother! Someone's fighting!* Racine, WI: Golden Books. (Grades 1–4)

Mayer, M. (1983). *I was so mad*. Racine, WI: Golden Books. (Preschool–Grade 3)

McGuire, L. (1992). *The terrible truth about third grade*. Mahwah, NJ: Troll. (Grades 2–4)

Millman, D. (1991). *Secret of the peaceful warrior: A story about courage and love*. Tiburon, CA: Starseed. (Kindergarten–Grade 4)

Mitchell, E. (1969). *The temper tantrum book*. New York: Puffin. (Preschool–Grade 2)

Powell, R. (1990). *How to deal with friends*. Mahwah, NJ: Troll. (Preschool–Grade 2)

Sanford, D. (1990). *Once I told a lie: And you'll never guess what happened*. Portland, OR: Multnomah. (Kindergarten–Grade 2)

Sanford, D. (1990). *Once I was a thief: And you'll never guess what happened*. Portland, OR: Multnomah. (Kindergarten–Grade 2)

Sharmat, M. (1984). *My mother never listens to me*. Morton Grove, IL: Whitman. (Preschool–Grade 3)

Simon, N. (1974). *I was so mad*. Niles, IL: Whitman. (Preschool–Grade 3)

Steig, W. (1973). *The real thief*. New York: Farrar, Straus & Giroux. (Kindergarten–Grade 4)

Vigna, J. (1990). *Saying goodbye to Daddy*. Niles, IL: Whitman. (Preschool–Grade 3)

Viorst, J. (1972). *Alexander and the terrible, horrible, no good, very bad day*. New York: Macmillan. (Kindergarten–Grade 4)

Wilde, S. (1988). *Extraordinary Chester*. Santa Barbara, CA: Red Hen Press. (Kindergarten–Grade 3)

Wilhelm, H. (1991). *Tyrone the double dirty rotten cheater*. New York: Scholastic. (Grades 1–3)

Winthrop, E. (1990). *Luke's Bully*. New York: Puffin. (Grades 2–5)

Youngs, B. (1990). *Friendship is forever, isn't it?* Holmes Beach, FL: Learning Tools. (Grades 3–10)

Zolotow, C. (1984). *I know a lady*. New York: Puffin. (Preschool–Grade 3)

Getting Started

Goals

1. To introduce children to the group experience and help them begin to get acquainted
2. To establish ground rules and discuss the issue of confidentiality
3. To discuss the purpose of the group and prepare children for the sessions ahead
4. To help children become aware that the group is a safe environment for sharing ideas, feelings, and behaviors
5. To give children practice in self-disclosing and taking turns
6. To begin to define and clarify the concept of friendship

Materials

Easel pad and marker

Drawing paper

Crayons/markers

Cartoons illustrating how "balloons" show what the characters are saying or thinking

A healthy snack, such as raisins in individual boxes, fruit, crackers, or juice (*optional*)

Group Session

Ice Breaker

1. Welcome the children to group. Go over the purpose of the group, where and when it will be meeting, and some of the topics that will be covered.

2. Discuss basic ground rules for the group, giving a few examples:

    Everyone gets a chance to talk.

    No hitting or fighting in group.

    Take turns.

    Encourage group members to give their input to help them develop "ownership." List all the ground rules on an easel pad, then post them in the room where group is held during every session.

3. Talk about the confidentiality rule and its limits. For example, you might say:

    When we talked about your being in the group, I told you that whatever we say in our group is *confidential*. That means what we say is private. You may talk about your own thoughts, feelings, and actions, but you may not share anything others in the group talk about. There are some special times when I would have to share what you say—if you say something about harming yourself or others, if you share something about child abuse, or if the court (a judge) asks me about what goes on.

4. Have group members find a partner and talk for about 5 minutes. Ask them to share their names, what they like or dislike about their names, and what they like best about having friends. Tell them that after they share this information, you will ask them to present the same information to the group.

5. Have children get back into the group-meeting circle. Ask who would like to go first to introduce his or her partner. Have each child share the information gathered.

Working Time

1. Distribute the drawing materials, then show children the cartoons with the "balloon" sayings. Tell them that the cartoonist draws a balloon above or beside the characters to show what they are saying or to tell something about the characters.

2. Ask group members to draw a picture of their best friend or a person they would like to be their best friend, then draw balloons to the side to show what they like about the person—for example, honest, friendly, plays fair, smiles a lot, sticks up for me, says thanks, good in math, plays soccer with me, shares toys and games. (It will help if you show children a drawing like this that you have made for one of your own friends.)

3. Have the children share their completed pictures with the group.

4. After the last child has shared, ask the group to name things that they would not like a friend to do or say so they can begin to compare positive and negative friendship behaviors and learn what others want in a friend.

5. Discuss what children think are their own best two or three friendship skills or what their best friend would say are their strengths.

Process Time

1. Ask the following questions:

   What did you learn about friendship today in group?

   Does anyone else in the group feel the same way you do? If so, tell that person how you feel the same.

   What do you think you need to improve on to be a better friend?

   What is the most fun about friends?

   What is your biggest worry about having friends?

   Look around the group. Is there anyone you would like to be friends with? Tell that person.

2. Share snacks, if desired. Before saying good-bye, thank group members for coming and remind them of the meeting time for the next session.

All Kinds of Friends

Goals

1. To establish the norm of reviewing what happened during the previous session and give children an opportunity to discuss anything they still have questions about

2. To promote awareness that friendship is a special part of our lives and that we can have friends of different ages, as well as animal and imaginary friends

3. To help children learn the difference between being alone and being lonely

4. To encourage understanding that when we are lonely we can make new friends

5. To help children express their feelings about one another in the group as friendships grow

Materials

A book about friendships between older persons and children, such as *I Know a Lady*, by Charlotte Zolotow (Puffin, 1984), or *A Memory for Tino*, by Leo Buscaglia (Slack, 1988)

A healthy snack, such as raisins in individual boxes, fruit, crackers, or juice *(optional)*

Group Session

Review

1. Welcome the children to group, then briefly go over the ground rules and the confidentiality rule. Encourage group members to ask any questions they may have.

2. Ask group members if they have anything to say about the last session, on what qualities make a person a good friend and what qualities do not.

Working Time

1. Read the story in the book selected.

2. Ask questions pertinent to the story and encourage group members to connect with one another to build group cohesion. For example:

   What older people do you have as friends?

   What kinds of things can you learn from them?

   How can they help you?

   What can you do for them?

   Why is it a treasure to have an older person as a friend?

3. Talk about other kinds of friends, asking questions like the following:

   Do you have any animal friends? Who are those friends?

   How is having a pet as a friend different from having a boy or girl as a friend?

   What is it like when you lose a pet that has been your friend?

   What is the best thing about having a pet friend?

   What about a friend who is "just pretend"? How is that friend different from a friend who is a real boy or girl?

   Who has a pretend friend?

   What is the best thing about having a pretend friend?

4. Encourage group members to talk about times they were alone or felt lonely—for example, when friends were away in the summer, when they stayed at a grandparent's house, or when a sibling went away to college. Ask the following questions:

> What does it mean to be alone?
>
> What does it mean to be lonely?
>
> If you are alone, does it mean that you are lonely?
>
> When is it good for you to have some alone time?
>
> What happens when you don't have any alone time at home and people are bugging you all of the time?

5. Ask the children to pretend to introduce one of their friends, real or imaginary, to the rest of the group. Model the formula for introducing someone. For example:

> Hello, group. I'd like to introduce you to my friend, Amanda. Amanda is an apricot-colored toy poodle. She is 3 years old and knows how to shake hands and roll over. I like her because she always runs to meet me when I come home from school and plays with me when no one else can.
>
> Hello, group. I'd like to introduce you to my friend, Mrs. Flowers. Mrs. Flowers lives next door to me, and I have known her all my life. She makes the best oatmeal raisin cookies in the world and invites me in for some, and we talk a lot.

6. Encourage group members to introduce their own friends. This gives them experience introducing someone, lets the other group members know a little more about them, and encourages sharing and self-disclosure.

Process Time

1. Discuss the following questions:

> What did you learn about different types of friendships today?
>
> What is important about having different kinds of friends?
>
> If you don't have different kinds of friends, how can you meet some?
>
> How do you feel when you don't have enough friends?
>
> Does anyone else in the group feel the same way you do? Tell that person how you feel the same.
>
> Before the next session, would you be willing to try to meet someone who could be your friend? Who would that be?

2. Share snacks, if desired. Before saying good-bye, thank group members for coming and remind them of the meeting time for the next session.

Friendship Zingers

Goals

1. To increase awareness of what kinds of behaviors are damaging to friendships
2. To help children understand how other people perceive their friendship behaviors
3. To encourage children to use brainstorming as a technique to discover alternative ways to deal with friendship situations
4. To help children reinforce one another for modeling and sharing positive behaviors

Materials

A healthy snack, such as raisins in individual boxes, fruit, crackers, or juice *(optional)*

Group Session

Review

1. Welcome the children to group. Briefly go over the ground rules and the confidentiality rule.
2. Ask the children if they have anything they want to share about the last session, on the benefits of having older friends, animal friends, and imaginary friends.
3. Ask whether group members had the opportunity to introduce themselves to a new friend since the last session, and, if so, what this experience was like.

Working Time

1. Discuss the fact that friendships are very precious to us and that they add a great deal to our lives: We have friends all through our lives, and no matter where we live or move, we can keep old friends we love and make new friends. But if we don't treat a friend right or if we behave in a hurtful or embarrassing way, someone might stop being friends with us, just as we might stop being friends with someone if that person treated us badly. Sometimes we make good choices in friendship behavior, and sometimes we make bad choices.

2. Explain that bad friendship choices are "friendship zingers," then ask the children to listen to the following situations as you read them. After you read each situation, ask, "What is the bad choice of behavior (the zinger)? What would be a better choice?"

   #### Situation 1

   Keshia is nosy. She walks up to kids who are talking and listens in on what they are saying. Then she goes and tells other kids what they were saying. No one likes her. Everybody calls her "nibby nose."

   #### Situation 2

   Kareem is a tattletale. Every chance he gets he runs and tells the teacher, his mom, or some other adult about the behavior of one of the other kids. The kids hate this, and no one will ask Kareem to play.

   #### Situation 3

   Paul is rude. He makes cutting remarks about everybody to make a joke. He says nasty things and makes fun of people, and then he can't understand why no one wants to have him for a friend. The more the kids dislike him, the more he is rude and tells them to bug off and get lost.

Situation 4

Karen uses foul language. She thinks it is cute and "grown up," and she puts down other kids who don't want to sound so rough and nasty. She is not aware that it makes her sound foolish and immature or that other kids don't want to be around her.

Situation 5

Lee is always dirty. He does not take a bath for days and days, and he comes to school smelling awful. His fingernails are a mess, and his hair is greasy, smelly, and never combed. His mother is always after him, but he refuses to take care of himself. The other kids don't even like to be around him.

Situation 6

Phil does several unpleasant and annoying things. He picks his nose, spits on the sidewalk, and scratches himself in public. It is embarrassing to be his friend because he does these things, so no one wants to be around him. He thinks he is cool, that the other kids are babies and jerks, and that his behavior is OK.

3. If you have time, encourage children to role-play the situations and change the bad choice of behavior to a good choice. Try at least two or three so they can see the good choice of behavior being modeled.

Process Time

1. Discuss the following questions:

> What did you learn today about things that can turn kids off to you as a friend?
>
> How would you feel if you heard that you were doing some of these things that turn kids off?
>
> What was it like for you to hear about other kids' problems with friendship?
>
> What kind of courage does it take to tell your friend that he or she is doing something that turns you off?
>
> Are you willing to try to change some of the things you might be doing that bother other kids so that you can have friends?
>
> What could you or would you practice before we meet the next time?

2. Share snacks, if desired. Before saying good-bye, thank the children for coming to group and remind them of the meeting time for the next session.

Getting and Giving Help

Goals

1. To encourage awareness that everyone needs both to receive and to give help

2. To help children learn to ask others for the help they need and to tell others they appreciate help when it is given

3. To give children the opportunity to practice being helpful in the school community and to reward them for doing so

Materials

Helpful Behaviors Chart (Handout 2)

Special stickers of some kind

A healthy snack, such as raisins in individual boxes, fruit, crackers, or juice *(optional)*

Group Session

Review

1. Welcome the children to group. Briefly go over the ground rules and the confidentiality rule.

2. Ask whether anyone has anything to share from the previous session, on friendship zingers (behaviors that interfere with friendship):

> Did group members notice anyone with these behaviors? If so, did that person seem to have many friends?

> Did they notice any of these problems in themselves? If so, what did they do to get rid of these behaviors?

Working Time

1. Discuss the fact that we all need a lot of help to make it through life. Discuss the following questions:

> What are some of the things you need help with? (For example: doing homework or chores, making the bed, putting things on high shelves, fixing a bike, going to ball games, going to music lessons, or doing science projects)

> What happens when you need help but are afraid to ask or when you don't have anyone to ask?

> How can you find someone to help you?

2. Tell children that they will each have a turn to practice asking someone else in the group for help. With a volunteer from the group, model the following steps.

> *Step 1:* Turn to the person next to you.

> *Step 2:* Ask the other person to help you do something. (For example: "Marta, will you please help me shut the window?")

> *Step 3:* When the person says yes, be sure to tell the person you appreciate the help.

3. Next have children practice asking for help in pairs.

4. After everyone has had a chance to ask for help, invite group members to try asking someone outside the group for help. Let them know you will be asking them how things went during the next session.

5. Next spend some time brainstorming things children could do to help other people. For example:

> Carrying a package for the principal
>
> Running an errand for the school secretary
>
> Picking up some trash for the custodian
>
> Opening a door for a teacher who has his or her arms full
>
> Asking your teacher if you can help turn all the computers on or off
>
> Straightening up the books and games in the resource room
>
> Helping a friend with math problems he or she doesn't understand
>
> Helping a friend study for a test

6. Distribute the Helpful Behaviors Chart (Handout 2) and explain that children may earn special stickers for performing a certain number of helpful behaviors before the next session. (Determine this number on the basis of the number of stickers you have, how many opportunities you think will present themselves in your setting, and so forth.) Show group members the special stickers, then explain that each time a member helps someone, he or she is to present the chart to the person. The person will initial the chart to show that the child performed the helpful behavior. The group member then brings the chart to the next group session to receive the special stickers.

Process Time

1. Discuss the following questions:

> What did you learn in group today about how to ask for help?
>
> What did it feel like to ask someone to help you?
>
> What did it feel like to be asked by someone for help?
>
> If you help other people, what do you think you will feel like?
>
> What do you think other kids and adults will think of you if they see you being helpful?
>
> What do you think you will get out of being helpful?
>
> What do you think is the hardest thing about being helpful?

2. Share snacks, if desired. Before saying good-bye, thank group members for coming and remind them of the meeting time for the next session.

Helpful Behaviors Chart

Name _____

Week beginning _____

Day	What I did that was helpful	Person's initials	Stickers
Monday			
Tuesday			
Wednesday			
Thursday			
Friday			
Saturday			
Sunday			

Saying "I'm Sorry"

Goals

1. To encourage awareness that apologizing is the right thing to do when you have hurt or inconvenienced someone or when you have behaved badly in some other way

2. To help children decide whether a behavior has hurt someone else and requires an apology

3. To help children learn the specific steps in apologizing

4. To help children understand that they may feel anxious before they apologize but better about having said they were sorry

Materials

A healthy snack, such as raisins in individual boxes, fruit, crackers, or juice *(optional)*

Group Session

Review

1. Welcome the children to group. Briefly go over the ground rules and the confidentiality rule.

2. Ask the children whether they asked anyone for help since the last session:

    If so, how did you feel?

    Did you get the help you needed?

    Did you remember to tell the person you appreciated the help?

3. Next ask group members to talk about their experiences practicing helpful behaviors. Award the special stickers and let each child stand up and take a bow while the others applaud his or her efforts. Be sure to give verbal praise for children's attempts to work on their behavior.

Working Time

1. Point out that there are times when you might do something that causes someone else to be hurt, inconvenienced, or bothered. Ask the following questions:

    How do you think a person might feel toward you when that happens?

    Can you think of a time when someone did something that bothered you?

    What feelings did you have?

2. Explain that an *apology* means saying you are sorry for having done whatever you did because it was not your best behavior. Stress that saying you are sorry isn't easy and that people often have some uncomfortable feelings before they do.

3. Tell the children that you have some situations to read and that after you read them you will ask what happened and what would be a good way to make an apology so both people involved will feel better about the situation.

    #### Situation 1

    You talk to a friend in the hall too long, and the bell rings. Now you have to walk into your classroom late. Your teacher is already talking to the girls and boys about math. She looks at you when you walk in the door.

Situation 2

Your mom asks you to take the garbage cans out to the street so they can be picked up the next morning. You forget to take them out. Now the garbage cans in the garage are overflowing and won't get picked up for another week!

Situation 3

Your little brother got a new toy for his birthday. It is really neat. You ask him if you can play with it, and he says no. You wait until he is gone and then take it and play with it. But you drop it and break it! Now he is going to be double ding-dong mad at you.

Situation 4

Your cousin is always bragging about her new clothes and how rich she is and how much money her dad and mom make. You think it will drive you crazy if you hear that one more time. Sure enough, she starts bragging, so you say in a very cruel tone of voice, "Oh, shut your trap. I don't give a darn." Then you start to feel really bad about being hurtful.

Situation 5

Your stepdad promised to take you to the mall on Saturday to shop for a new gizmo. You have been excited thinking about this all week. Friday night, he comes home from work and says he can't take you this week because he has to work. You are disappointed, and now you'll miss the gizmo game because your old one won't work right. You start yelling and screaming. You run up the stairs into your room and slam the door. Then you realize that he can't help having to work and that you behaved like a 3-year-old having a tantrum.

Process Time

1. Discuss the following questions:

> What kinds of things do you do that you should apologize for?
>
> What kinds of feelings do you have just before you apologize to someone?
>
> Why do you think you feel this way?
>
> How do you feel after you apologize to someone?
>
> Even if you apologize, the other person might still be angry with you. What can you do?
>
> How do you think the other person will feel after you apologize?

2. Share snacks, if desired. Before saying good-bye, thank group members for coming and remind them of the meeting time for the next session.

Ending Friendships

Goals

1. To promote awareness that friendships change, grow, and end
2. To encourage recognition that it is important to say good-bye when we lose a friend to a move, death, or some other event
3. To help children learn that we all get angry with our friends but that being angry does not have to mean that the friendship must end

Materials

A book dealing with having someone die or move away without a good-bye, such as *Saying Goodbye to Daddy*, by J. Vigna (Whitman, 1990)

A healthy snack, such as raisins in individual boxes, fruit, crackers, or juice *(optional)*

Group Session

Review

1. Welcome the children to group. Briefly go over the ground rules and the confidentiality rule.
2. Ask group members whether they had any situations since the last session in which they needed to apologize to someone, then discuss the following questions:

   What feelings did you have before apologizing?

   How did you feel afterwards?

   What did the person say or do?

   Could you tell whether the person felt better toward you?

   Do you think it is best to apologize even if it is a hard thing to do?

Working Time

1. Discuss the fact that when a friendship ends, it is a loss just like the loss of someone who dies. Ask group members what kinds of feelings they might have after a loss—hurt, anger, fear, numbness, and so on.
2. Ask children to brainstorm some of the ways they might lose a friend. For example:

   The friend moves to another town or school.

   Parents divorce and the person has to move.

   There is an argument they can't or don't know how to resolve.

   The friend just won't talk to them anymore.

   The friend gets a disease and has to go to the hospital or even dies.

3. Read the story you have selected, then discuss the following questions:

   Why is it important for us to have a chance to say good-bye before someone goes away or stops having a friendship with us?

   How does saying good-bye help us grieve and heal our hurt feelings?

   How do people say good-bye when someone dies?

What can you do when a friend is leaving or moving away and you feel awful and want to say good-bye?

What if you are angry with the person? Should you still say good-bye?

If you don't get a chance to say good-bye before you can talk to a person face to face, what are some other ways you can say good-bye? (For example: send a video, write a letter, call the person long-distance to tell them)

4. Explain that some grown-ups have a divorce ceremony with all the family members there, just as they had a ceremony when they got married. The purpose for this is to say good-bye to the relationship and to mark its ending, so it is a "good-bye ceremony."

5. Ask the children to think of people in their lives that they wish they could have said good-bye to. Help them think of ways they might do so and encourage them to try.

Process Time

1. Discuss the following questions:

What did you learn today in group about friendships ending?

Why is it important to say good-bye in friendships?

What can you do if you do not have a chance to say good-bye before a friend leaves?

What kinds of feelings could you have if you don't have a chance to say good-bye?

Does getting angry with a friend mean that the friendship is over?

Do your mom and dad get angry sometimes but still love each other?

Because we all get angry from time to time with our friends, what can we do so we don't have to end the friendship?

2. Share snacks, if desired. Before saying good-bye, thank group members for coming and tell them the group will meet only two more times after this session. Remind them of the meeting time for the next session.

I Can Cooperate

Goals

1. To help children learn the importance of cooperating on a task

2. To explore the idea of working for a common purpose to benefit everyone

3. To encourage the realization that many things call for cooperation and that each person has to do his or her part or things will be difficult for everyone else

4. To help children learn that without cooperation some things just don't get accomplished

Materials

Recipe for Orange-Coconut Balls (Handout 3)

Ingredients specified in the recipe

Mixing equipment (bowl and mixing spoon, rolling pin, measuring cup, waxed paper, cookie sheet)

Group Session

Review

1. Welcome the children to group. Briefly go over the ground rules and the confidentiality rule.

2. Ask whether anyone has anything they want to bring up about the previous session, on saying good-bye and ending friendships. Invite children to share their experiences saying good-bye.

3. Remind the children that the next session will be the last one. Discuss any ideas they have for celebrating and saying good-bye.

Working Time

1. Discuss the concept of cooperating, asking children to share their ideas about what cooperating means and why it is important.

2. Ask children to think about what their moms and dads do at work and whether they might need to cooperate with anyone else to get their work done. Let each group member share.

3. Discuss the kind of cooperation that goes on among teachers, the principal, and others who work around the school. Brainstorm what might happen if all of a sudden people stopped cooperating and just did their jobs alone. For example:

> People in the kitchen wouldn't get lunch ready for the kids and teachers.
>
> Secretaries wouldn't get the phone messages to kids when they needed them.
>
> The principal wouldn't meet with parents.
>
> Teachers wouldn't share ideas with other teachers.
>
> Coaches and teams would lose games because team members wouldn't play together.
>
> Kids wouldn't get to use the computers because other kids wouldn't share.

4. Tell the children that they are going to get to do a fun project to learn how everyone has to do a job and do it right or the project won't turn out: They get to help make Orange-Coconut Balls, and everyone can have some to eat.

5. Have children wash their hands thoroughly, then distribute copies of the Recipe for Orange-Coconut Balls (Handout 3). Have the children choose one of the ingredients to prepare or add and circle it on the page. (You may need to revise the steps listed if you have more or fewer than eight children in your group.)

6. Let group members mix the ingredients together and make the cookies. Refrigerate them for the remainder of the session. If a refrigerator is not available, the cookies are edible as is. (The recipe makes about 2 dozen cookies.)

Process Time

1. Discuss the following questions:

> What did you learn about needing to work together and cooperate on projects to get them finished right?
>
> What do you think would happen if when making the cookies just one person did not want to cooperate and do his or her part? How would the recipe change? What would the result be?
>
> How do you think learning to cooperate with others will help you in school now?
>
> What about when you go to high school? How could cooperation help then?
>
> If everyone cooperates and does his or her share, what will happen?
>
> How have we all benefited from working together on the recipe?

2. Share the Orange-Coconut Balls. Before saying good-bye, thank group members for participating. Tell them the meeting time for the next session and remind them that it will be their last.

Recipe for Orange-Coconut Balls

Ingredients

A 10-ounce box of vanilla wafers

A 1-pound box of powdered sugar

1 cup of chopped nuts (walnuts or pecans)

1 stick unsalted margarine

1 average-size can frozen orange juice concentrate

1 small can shredded coconut

Instructions

1. Cream margarine and powdered sugar together. Add just enough orange juice to make mixture creamy.

2. Crush the vanilla wafers with the rolling pin.

3. Add chopped nuts and crushed vanilla wafers.

4. Slowly add more of the orange juice. Stop when the mixture looks as though it will stick together in balls.

5. Take small amounts of dough to roll into balls about an inch around.

6. Roll the balls in the shredded coconut.

7. Put the balls on a cookie sheet, then cover with waxed paper.

8. Put the cookie sheet in the refrigerator.

Saying Good-bye

Goals

1. To give children the opportunity to review and process what they learned during the group experience
2. To encourage and support the personal changes and skills children have learned and practiced
3. To give children the opportunity to say good-bye in a healthy way

Materials

Polaroid camera and film

Construction paper

Glue

Crayons/markers

Whatever snacks or other materials group members have chosen to celebrate the last session

Group Session

Review

1. Welcome the children to group and briefly go over the ground rules. Remind them that the confidentiality rule applies even after the group is over.
2. Ask whether anyone has anything to add about the last session, on the topic of cooperation.

Working Time

1. Help children process what they have learned and experienced by asking the following questions:

    What is a friend?

    What did you learn about having friends of different ages? Friends who are pets or imaginary?

    What kind of "zingers" (things that turn other kids off) did you learn about?

    What is it like for you to ask for help from someone? What is it like to help someone else?

    What did you learn about saying you were sorry?

    Why is it important to say good-bye in friendships and relationships? What happens when you don't get the chance to say good-bye?

    What did you learn about cooperating on a project?

2. Tell the children that they will be saying good-bye to one another today because the group is ending. Thank them for sharing so much of themselves and working so hard on their friendship skills. Show group members the camera and tell them that they are going to make a card with their picture on it. All the group members will autograph the card, just like famous people.

3. Pass out sheets of construction paper and have group members fold the sheets in half from the top down, then turn the paper sideways so that it opens like a greeting card. Take each child's picture.

4. Show children how to glue their pictures on the front of their cards, then have them pass their cards around to the other children in the group. Have each one write something positive about the child whose picture is on the front. Encourage children to write things they learned from that person or what they like or admire about them. (For example: "Jason, you are a good friend. I like you because you are always fair.") Help children spell any words they don't know.

Process Time

1. Discuss the following questions:

> What did you learn from the group that you will remember the most?
>
> Who shared the thing that meant the most to you? Tell that person.
>
> Who helped you the most with your friendship skills? Tell that person.
>
> What did we talk about that was the scariest part of the group to you?
>
> What helped you the most to be a better friend?

2. Thank group members for coming and praise them for sharing their very private thoughts and feelings. Let them know you appreciate how hard they have worked on becoming a better friend and understanding what to expect from friends. If appropriate, tell them that you will be available to help them with their problems individually.

3. Celebrate in the way children have chosen.

KIDS: Kids in Divorce Stress_____

Divorce occurs at a staggering rate in our society, affecting some 40 to 60% of school-age children (Thompson & Rudoph, 1992; Whiteman, 1991). Although divorce has been the topic of a number of short-term studies, only a handful of investigations have attempted to assess the longer term effects of divorce on children. What we do realize at this point is that the process of divorce affects the whole family and that the major variables involved in the child's adjustment appear to be the child's age, coping skills, and gender; the amount of time since the divorce; the amount of preparation received before the divorce; custodial and financial arrangements after the divorce; and parents' post-divorce relationship (Guidabaldi, Perry, & Nastasi, 1987; Hetherington, Cox, & Cox, 1978; Kurdek, Blisk, & Siesky, 1981; Wallerstein & Kelly, 1976).

Although research indicates that some children escape the experience of divorce with relatively few emotional scars, significant percentages show adjustment and personality difficulties in both the home and school settings (Knoff, 1987). In the home, divorce has been related to health problems, decreased coping skills, increased anxiety and aggression, and lowered levels of social interaction. School settings can expect to be the arena for lowered academic functioning, increased emotional adjustment problems, increased retention in grade, and more frequent interactions with school authorities and mental health professionals (Knoff, 1987).

School-age children generally react to divorce with some combination of anger, fear, withdrawal, grieving, reconciliation fantasy, shame, loyalty conflict, sense of loss and confusion, and decreased academic functioning. Although data are conflicting, it appears that divorce affects boys of elementary school age more seriously than girls, with older boys seeming to have more serious adjustment problems (Knoff, 1987). Further research is required to give us more in-depth insight into how the divorce process plays itself out in the social and psychological life span of the individual. In the meantime, it is safe to say that elementary school children experiencing a family divorce are at risk for social, emotional, and academic difficulties.

This group counseling experience could be the single most important factor in the child's ability to cope with divorce trauma. The highly charged emotional content will prove to be a challenge for the counselor as well as the children. Schools would be well advised to develop pre-divorce groups and psychological education activities in the classroom to augment any group counseling effort on this topic.

Group Goals

1. To provide a safe, secure, and reinforcing environment where children can learn new skills to help them cope with the divorce

2. To teach some factual information about divorce that will help children deal with their emotional issues more effectively

3. To give children the opportunity to express their negative feelings about the divorce and what is happening to and around them

4. To encourage children to share their thoughts and feelings with other children who have experienced similar thoughts and feelings (in other words, to promote awareness of universality)

5. To teach the skill of assertively expressing feelings and needs to family members

6. To teach children effective ways of managing their stress

7. To reinforce social support systems that may have been lost due to the divorce

8. To teach children to identify behaviors and situations that increase the chances of ineffective emotional and behavioral responses

Selection and Other Guidelines

In addition to following the general selection guidelines discussed in Part 1, you will want to provide at least one role model for each child in the group. This means having the group homogeneous for the issue of divorce but heterogeneous for other factors, such as length of time since the divorce, coping skills, values and attitudes toward divorce, and adjustment to new family patterns and living arrangements. For example, try to select one or two children whose parents divorced several years ago and have remarried so that the child has adjusted to some aspects of the divorce but is perhaps struggling to get along with stepsiblings. Select another one or two who might have one parent who is remarried and the other one dating. Select one or two whose parents are not remarried, and perhaps one with an absent parent. Choose children who have a range of coping and emotional skills, such as frustration tolerance, ability to express feelings and needs, ability to adjust to classroom demands, and so forth. Overloading the group with children who are severely debilitated by the divorce will result in a lack of mental and emotional energy required for the group's success.

The following specific indicators may suggest that a child is a good candidate for a group intervention on this topic:

1. Currently dealing with a divorce in the family, but not in immediate crisis

2. Expressing feelings of shame, isolation, loneliness, or poor self-esteem

3. Absence of major emotional disturbances

4. Expressing the belief that he or she is in some way responsible for the divorce

5. Exhibiting acting-out behavior to get attention

6. Expressing anger, hostility, and/or defiant attitudes

For this particular group experience it is best to secure permission from both custodial and noncustodial parents. Sensitive family topics frequently surface, and a parent who is strongly opposed to his or her child's involvement can affect how the child participates—possibly even withdraw the child from the group. This is confusing and frustrating to the child and disrupts the group process for the others. Because of the sensitive nature of the topic, you will want to maintain good contact with parents.

References and Suggested Resources for Professionals

NOTE: The Children and Divorce Resource Network provides services and resources for children and families experiencing separation, divorce, and remarriage. For more information, contact the Children and Divorce Resource Network, Beech Acres' Aring Institute, 6881 Beechmont Avenue, Cincinnati, OH 45230. (Telephone: 513–231–6630)

Cautela, J. R., & Groden, J. (1978). *Relaxation: A comprehensive manual for adults, children, and children with special needs*. Champaign, IL: Research Press.

Friedman, J. T. (1984). *The divorce handbook: Your basic guide to divorce*. New York: Random House.

Gardner, R. (1991). *The parents' book about divorce*. New York: Doubleday.

Glass, S. M. (1980). *A divorce dictionary: A book for you and your children*. Boston: Little, Brown.

Guidabaldi, J., Perry, J., & Nastasi, B. (1987). Growing up in a divorced family: Initial and long-term perspectives on children's adjustment. In S. Oskamp (Ed.), *Annual review of applied social psychology*. Newbury Park, CA: Sage.

Hetherington, E., Cox, M., & Cox, R. (1978). Effects of divorce on parents and children. In M. E. Lamb (Ed.), *Nontraditional families: Parenting and child development*. Hillsdale, NJ: Erlbaum.

Jones, M., & Schiller, J. (1992). *Stepmothers: Keeping it together with your husband and his kids*. New York: Carol Publishing Group.

Kelly, J. B., & Wallerstein, J. S. (1977). Brief interventions with children in divorcing families. *American Journal of Orthopsychiatry, 47*, 23–36.

Knoff, H. M. (1987). Children and divorce. In A. Thomas & J. Grimes, *Children's needs: Psychological perspectives*. Silver Springs, MD: National Association of School Psychologists.

Kurdek, L. A., Blisk, D., & Siesky, A. E. (1981). Correlates of children's long-term adjustment to their parents' divorce. *Developmental Psychology, 17*, 565–579.

Margulies, S. (1992). *Getting divorced without ruining your life*. New York: Simon & Schuster.

Stuart, I. R., & Abt, L. E. (Eds.). (1981). *Children of separation and divorce: Management and treatment*. New York: Van Nostrand Reinhold.

Thompson, C. L., & Rudolph, L. B. (1992). *Counseling children* (3rd ed.). Pacific Grove, CA: Brooks/Cole.

Wallerstein, J. S. (1984). Children of divorce: Preliminary report of a ten-year follow-up of young children. *American Journal of Orthopsychiatry, 54,* 444–458.

Wallerstein, J. S., & Kelly, J. B. (1976). The effects of parental divorce experiences on the child in later latency. *American Journal of Orthopsychiatry, 46,* 256–267.

Wallerstein, J. S., & Kelly, J. B. (1980). *Surviving the breakup: How children and parents cope with divorce*. New York: Basic.

Whiteman, T. (1991). *Innocent victims: Helping children through the trauma of divorce*. Wayne, PA: Fresh Start.

Bibliography for Children

Banks, A. (1990). *When your parents get a divorce: A kid's journal*. New York: Puffin. (Grades 3–6)

Berman, C. (1982). *What am I doing in a stepfamily?* New York: Lyle Stuart. (Kindergarten–Grade 6)

Berry, J. (1990). *Good answers to tough questions about divorce*. (Available from Paperbacks for Educators, 426 West Front Street, Washington, MO 63090) (Grades 3–6)

Boulden, J., & Boulden, J. (1991). *My story: Divorce and remarriage activity book*. Weaverville, CA: Boulden Publishing. (Kindergarten–Grade 3)

Brown, L., & Brown, M. (1986). *Dinosaurs' divorce: A guide for changing families*. Boston: Little, Brown. (Kindergarten–Grade 3)

Gardner, R. (1991). *The boys' and girls' book about divorce*. New York: Bantam. (Grades 4–8)

Girard, L. (1987). *A daddy's on Saturday*. Morton Grove, IL: Whitman. (Kindergarten–Grade 3)

Heegaard, M. (1990). *When Mom and Dad separate: Children can learn to cope with grief from divorce*. Minneapolis: Deaconess/Woodland Press. (Grades 1–6)

Jasinek, D., & Ryan, P. (1988). *A family is a circle of people who love you*. Minneapolis: CompCare. (Kindergarten–Grade 6)

Jayanti, A. (1981). *Silas and the mad, sad people*. Berkeley, CA: New Seed Press. (Kindergarten–Grade 3)

Krementz, J. (1984). *How it feels when parents divorce*. New York: Knopf. (Grades 3–9)

Lebowltz, M. (1989). *I think divorce stinks*. Woodbridge, CT: CDC Press. (Kindergarten–Grade 3)

LeShan, E. (1978). *What's going to happen to me? When parents separate or divorce*. New York: Aladdin. (Grades 3–6)

Mayle, P. (1988). *Why are we getting a divorce?* New York: Harmony. (Kindergarten–Grade 3)

Norris, L. (1991). *D is for divorce*. Deerfield Beach, FL: Health Communications. (Preschool–Grade 2)

Osman, T. (1989). *Where has Daddy gone?* Nashville, TN: Ideals. (Kindergarten–Grade 3)

Park, B. (1981). *Don't make me smile*. New York: Knopf. (Grades 4–7)

Perry, P., & Lynch, M. (1978). *Mommy and Daddy are divorced*. New York: Dial. (Kindergarten–Grade 3)

Prokop, M. (1986). *Divorce happens to the nicest kids: A self-help book for kids and adults*. Warren, OH: Allegra House. (Kindergarten–Grade 6)

Prokop, M. (1986). *Kid's divorce workbook*. Warren, OH: Allegra House. (Kindergarten–Grade 6)

Rofes, E. (Ed.). (1981). *The kids' book of divorce: By, for and about kids*. New York: Random House. (Grades 5–8)

Simon, N. (1983). *I wish I had my father*. Morton Grove, IL: Whitman. (Grades 1–4)

Stinson, K. (1984). *Mom and Dad don't live together any more*. San Diego, CA: Firefly. (Kindergarten–Grade 3)

Sullivan, M. (1988). *The parent/child manual on divorce*. New York: Tor. (Grades 4–7)

Watson, J. (1988). *Sometimes a family has to split up*. New York: Crown. (Kindergarten–Grade 2)

Getting Started

Goals

1. To introduce children to the group experience and help them begin to get acquainted
2. To establish ground rules and discuss the issue of confidentiality
3. To discuss the purpose of the group and prepare children for the sessions ahead
4. To help children become aware that the group is a safe environment for sharing ideas, feelings, and behaviors
5. To promote the realization that other children in the school are having the same feelings they are (in other words, that reactions to a family divorce are universal)

Materials

Easel pad and marker

Crayons/markers

A roll of newsprint

Tape

A healthy snack, such as raisins in individual boxes, fruit, crackers, or juice *(optional)*

Group Session

Ice Breaker

1. Welcome the children and go over the purpose of the group and some of the session topics. Stress that the purpose of the group is to focus on the members, to help them get in touch with who they are, and to share with other group members whose families have also gone through a divorce.

2. Discuss basic ground rules for the group, giving group members some examples:

   > Everyone gets a chance to talk.
   >
   > No hitting or fighting in group.
   >
   > Take turns.

   Ask for the children's input to help them develop "ownership." List the ground rules on an easel pad so everyone can see, then post them during every session.

3. Discuss the confidentiality rule and its limits. For example, you might say:

   > When we talked about your being in the group, I told you that whatever we say in our group is *confidential*. That means what we say is private. You may talk about your own thoughts, feelings, and actions, but you may not share anything others in the group talk about. There are some special times when I would have to share what you say—if you say something about harming yourself or others, if you share something about child abuse, or if the court (a judge) asks me about what goes on.

4. Have group members form pairs and share their names, who their family members are, and what they would like to learn in this group and/or something else about themselves (for example, the name of a pet or a favorite food). Let members know that they will be sharing their partner's information with the rest of the group.

5. Reassemble in the group circle and let each pair make their introductions.

Working Time

1. Discuss what the children have just shared with one another, pointing out that each one of them has experienced a divorce in the family and that many have family members that do not live in the home or new family members to learn to live with.

2. Give each child a piece of newsprint long enough to lie down on. Have the children take turns tracing one another's outlines on the newsprint.

3. Next have group members write their names on the chest part of their drawings. Have them write positive things about themselves all over the drawing—for example, good swimmer, likes computers, good baby-sitter, rides horses, soccer goalie, and so forth.

4. Tape the figures up to the wall so group members can walk around and talk about who they are—a sort of "show-and-tell about me."

Process Time

1. Discuss the following questions:

   What did you learn about yourself by writing out your likes/good points?

   What was it like for you to think about your good points?

   What about the feelings and behaviors you don't like about yourself—are they part of you, too?

   What did you learn about other people in the group?

   What did you learn about families going through a divorce?

2. Explain that the next session will be about the people who make up group members' new family. Invite the children to think about just who makes up their family now, including any new people that were not part of the family before the divorce.

3. Share snacks, if desired. Before saying good-bye, thank group members for coming and remind them of the meeting time for the next session.

My Family Then and Now

NOTE: This session could be very emotional for some children. Do not try to suppress children's emotional reactions, but be sure to allow enough time to process the feelings that arise.

Goals

1. To establish the norm of reviewing what happened during the previous session and give children an opportunity to discuss anything they still have questions about

2. To help children clarify the meaning of relationship words associated with divorce and remarriage so they can talk about their situation with others

3. To suggest the idea that other children have new families, too, and that it is OK to discuss one's feelings about these new people

Materials

Dolls, paper dolls, or small statues of adults and children (enough so that several different family configurations are possible)

"Dress-up" clothes (some adult and some children's clothing, such as high heels, purses, briefcases, hats)

A healthy snack, such as raisins in individual boxes, fruit, crackers, or juice *(optional)*

Group Session

Review

1. Welcome the children to group, then briefly review the ground rules and the confidentiality rule.

2. Ask whether any group members have unfinished business from the last session—anything they forgot to say or want to share about their family.

Working Time

1. Discuss the names for members of families who have gone through a divorce. For example:

    Stepmom: Person your dad marries

    Stepdad: Person your mom marries

    Stepbrother: Stepparent's son

    Stepsister: Stepparent's daughter

    Biological mom: Mother who gave birth to you/your genetic mom

    Biological dad: Your genetic dad

2. Encourage group members to share who their family members are now. Tell them that they can put on the dress-up clothes to role-play one family member and select enough dolls to represent the rest of the family. Have them introduce family members to the rest of the group.

3. Let all of the children have a turn, monitoring the time so that everyone gets a chance to share.

Process Time

1. Discuss the following questions:

   What was it like for you to dress like a family member and tell the group about your family as it is today?

   What kinds of feelings did you have about your family?

   How do you express your anger toward your family?

   What is different about where you live now?

   What do you like or not like about your new living arrangements? (Help children connect with others who have similar situations.)

   What did you learn about other group members' families?

   How do you feel now that you know other kids also do things like visit their other parent and stepfamily on weekends?

2. Share snacks, if desired. Before saying good-bye, thank group members for coming and remind them of the meeting time for the next session.

Why People Divorce

Goals

1. To clarify reasons parents divorce

2. To help children understand that they are not to blame for the divorce and that they cannot expect that anything they do or change about themselves will bring about a reconciliation

3. To continue to encourage children to get in touch with their feelings about the loss

Materials

Drawing paper

Crayons/markers

A healthy snack, such as raisins in individual boxes, fruit, crackers, or juice *(optional)*

Group Session

Review

1. Welcome the children to group and remind them of the ground rules and the confidentiality rule.

2. Ask whether group members have anything they want to say about what they learned during the last session, on the names and relationships of new family members.

Working Time

1. Share the idea that sometimes we want things to be a certain way, but they are not that way. For example, you may want your mom and dad to get back together again, but this is probably not going to happen. You might want your mom or dad to stop dating a new person, but that probably won't happen either. Even if it did happen, your parent would probably date someone else again in the future.

2. Ask group members to draw a picture of the perfect situation for them, including all the people they want in the picture. Then have them turn their papers over and draw how it is, with the people, places, or situations that really exist.

3. Have the children share their "ideal" and "real" pictures.

4. Next talk about why parents get divorced. Have group members brainstorm some reasons. For example:

> Parents fight all the time and can't get along.
>
> One or both parents' jobs keep them away.
>
> Parents don't love each other any more.
>
> Parents don't want to be married to each other.
>
> One or both parents want to be married to someone else.

5. Point out that if children are not the cause of the divorce, there is nothing they can really do to change things. Discuss the following questions:

> Have you ever wished, hoped, or dreamed about getting your parents back together? Have you ever tried anything to do this?
>
> Is it a good idea to spend time hoping and wishing this will happen? Why or why not?
>
> How much control do you have over this situation?

What do you think you could do to make things happen?

What would it be better to do than to worry and wish?

Process Time

1. Discuss the following questions:

    What did you learn about your own family situation today?

    How did you feel when you shared your pictures with everyone else?

    Who in your pictures loves you the same today as before the divorce?

    What can you say to your parents to let them know that you understand a little bit better about why they got a divorce?

    If you behaved any differently, would your parents still be living in separate places?

2. Share snacks, if desired. Before saying good-bye, thank group members for coming and remind them of the meeting time for the next session.

Feelings About Divorce

Goals

1. To help children learn to identify the feelings people have because of a divorce

2. To encourage children to express their negative feelings in the supportive group environment

3. To promote the realization that our feelings are a special part of us, neither good nor bad in themselves

4. To help children learn more adjectives to express feelings of all kinds

Materials

Feeling Faces Chart (Handout 1, p. 46)

Magazine pictures of situations that could be interpreted to be about divorce/separation (for example, a man and woman arguing, a child who is visibly upset, a family dinner with only one parent)

A healthy snack, such as raisins in individual boxes, fruit, crackers, or juice *(optional)*

Group Session

Review

1. Welcome the children to group, then briefly go over the ground rules and the confidentiality rule.

2. Ask whether anyone has anything to add about the last session, on why people get divorced.

Working Time

1. Distribute copies of the Feeling Faces Chart (Handout 1). Explain that words to describe feelings, like people, come in "families." In each word family there are words to describe low level feelings (you feel just a little that way), medium level feelings (you feel more strongly), and high level feelings (you feel even more strongly). Illustrate this idea by discussing a "word family" from the chart.

2. Encourage group members to share some of their feelings and comment on their intensity. Using the children's own examples, stress that feelings are not good or bad—they are just feelings and a special part of us. Discuss the idea that we can choose to express our feelings in either positive or negative ways.

3. Pass out one picture of a divorce/separation situation at a time. Ask group members to tell what they think the people in the picture are doing and feeling. For example, if the picture shows a man and a woman facing away from each other, group members might say she is angry and he is sad after an argument.

4. Have the children use the Feeling Faces Chart and look up other words that mean angry and sad (or whatever feeling words are appropriate). Help them understand that divorce is a very intense situation that calls for intense feeling words.

5. Process the rest of the pictures in this way.

Process Time

1. Discuss the following questions:

   What did you learn about levels of feelings today?

   What did you learn about your own feelings today?

   Do any other group members have feelings like yours? Tell them how you feel the same.

   What did you learn about how everyone here has had some of the same things happen to them?

Speak Up

Goals

1. To strengthen children's understanding that feelings have different levels of intensity
2. To help children share a range of feelings with one another
3. To encourage awareness that it is important to share negative feelings in an appropriate way
4. To help children practice expressing their feelings in the group

Materials

Paper cups in small, medium, large, and extra-large sizes (such as those from fast-food restaurants)

Feeling Faces Chart (Handout 1, p. 46)

A pitcher of water

Paper towels

A healthy snack, such as raisins in individual boxes, fruit, crackers, or juice *(optional)*

Group Session

Review

1. Welcome the children to group and briefly review the ground rules and the confidentiality rule.
2. Ask group members whether they noticed any low, medium, or high level feelings in themselves or a family member since the last session. Discuss what happened in the situation.

Working Time

1. Pour some water into each of the four cups. Ask, "What is different about each cup, and what is the same?" Point out that each of the cups contains water, but each has a different amount. Discuss the idea that feelings can be the same in different situations, but they may come in different amounts. Refer back to the Feeling Faces Chart (Handout 1) if necessary.

2. Take one of the smallest cups and fill it until it overflows. Keep pouring until everyone sees you spill quite a bit of water. (Use the paper towels to keep from spilling on the floor.) Stop and ask:

   What happens when you have too much water for the cup to hold? (It spills over and makes a mess.)

   What do you think happens when your feelings get too much for you to hold? (You get angry and they spill over—you either "blow up" or stuff your feelings inside.)

3. Present the idea that it isn't good for us to keep our feelings inside until they spill out without our control. When this happens we usually hurt someone or get hurt ourselves because other people get angry or upset with us. To keep hurtful behavior from happening, we can talk about our feelings before they get out of control.

4. Ask for volunteers to role-play the following situations. After each role-play, help group members identify the feeling and its intensity, then say how they feel and what they need by using the format suggested.

Situation 1

You play on a school team and have missed two games because your dad picked you up on the weekend to take you out of town to spend time with him and his new wife. You don't want to miss another game, and the coach is also irritated with you for missing. You are getting more and more upset as Saturday approaches. You would like to tell your mom and dad how you feel, but you don't know what to say. (Roles: You, your mom, your dad)

How do you feel about this situation?

Is it a small, medium, large, or extra-large feeling?

Do you think you need to share it?

Why?

Say how you feel and what you need: "I feel _____ when _____ happens and I want/need _____."

Situation 2

You are living with your dad. Your mom's new boyfriend has come to pick you up for the weekend instead of your mom. Your dad is furious and won't let you go. You are eager to go because you want to be with your mom for the weekend and play with your friends who live near her. You are upset at your dad and don't know what to do. (Roles: You, your dad)

How do you feel about this situation?

Is it a small, medium, large, or extra-large feeling?

Do you think you need to share it?

Why?

Say how you feel and what you need: "I feel _____ when _____ happens and I want/need _____."

Situation 3

Your stepbrother is a bully and takes things from you whenever no one is around. This makes you furious, but you are afraid to say anything because he has threatened to beat you up if you tell. Also, you don't want to upset your mom because she is upset enough already about things. (Roles: You, your stepbrother, your mom)

How do you feel about this situation?

Is it a small, medium, large, or extra-large feeling?

Do you think you need to share it?

Why?

Say how you feel and what you need: "I feel _____ when _____ happens and I want/need _____."

Situation 4

Your mom and her boyfriend just split up. It took you a long time to get used to the idea of her going out on dates and being around this new man, and now he is gone, too. She just told you that she is going to have a new date come over tonight to watch television. You are sad and also fuming. (Roles: You, your mom)

How do you feel about this situation?

Is it a small, medium, large, or extra-large feeling?

Do you think you need to share it?

Why?

Say how you feel and what you need: "I feel _____ when _____ happens and I want/need _____."

5. If there is time left, ask children to role-play some real situations in which they need help expressing their feelings.

Process Time

1. Discuss the following questions:

   What did you learn about feelings coming in different sizes?

   What can you do to prevent feelings from getting to the point where they spill over and hurt both you and others?

   What did you learn about role-playing?

   Do any other group members have feelings like yours? If so, tell them how you feel the same.

   Do you think you could use your new skills for sharing feelings sometime before the next session? Who would be willing to try and then come back and tell us how that worked?

2. Share snacks, if desired. Before saying good-bye, thank group members for coming and remind them of the meeting time for the next session.

The Myth of the Wicked Stepmother

Goals

1. To help children understand that stepparents are human, too

2. To give children who are living with stepparents and stepsiblings the opportunity to share some of the positive and negative things about living together

3. To give children whose parents have not yet remarried a model for coping with stepparents and stepsiblings

4. To provide the opportunity for children to air their worries and concerns about remarriage

5. To help children understand that the myths surrounding stepfamilies are untrue—that everyone is really just trying to adjust to the situation with the skills he or she has at the time

Materials

The story of Cinderella (any version)

A healthy snack, such as raisins in individual boxes, fruit, crackers, or juice *(optional)*

Group Session

Review

1. Welcome the children to group and briefly go over the ground rules and the confidentiality rule.

2. Ask whether anyone had the opportunity to practice speaking up about feelings before they "spilled over." Discuss what happened.

Working Time

1. Read the story of Cinderella, emphasizing the parts about the wicked stepmother and stepsisters.

2. Point out that the story of Cinderella tells a myth about stepfamilies. Ask the following questions to separate fact from fiction:

   > Have you ever heard of a myth? What is it? (A story that people believe is true.)
   >
   > Do any of you have stepmothers or stepsisters?
   >
   > Do any of the rest of you think you might have them someday?
   >
   > What idea about stepmothers do you get from this story?
   >
   > What are your experiences with stepmothers?
   >
   > Do you think this story is fair to stepmothers?
   >
   > What are the good things about stepmothers?
   >
   > What does the story say about stepsisters?
   >
   > Does anyone have stepsisters this bad?
   >
   > What kind of stepbrothers and stepsisters do you have?
   >
   > What are some bad things about stepfamilies that you have experienced? Some good things?

Process Time

1. Discuss the following questions:

> What did you learn about myths?
>
> How do you know that it is only a myth that stepmothers and stepsisters are wicked and mean?
>
> Do you think that you could be a stepmother or stepfather someday? Would you be wicked and mean?
>
> What did you learn about stepfamilies today?
>
> Are you feeling any different now about stepfamilies than before we talked today?

2. Share snacks, if desired. Before saying good-bye, thank group members for coming, tell them that the group will meet only two more times, and remind them of the meeting time for the next session.

Chill Out

Goals

1. To help children understand what stress is and how our bodies show stress
2. To promote the idea that sufficient sleep, good nutrition, and exercise are important in managing stress
3. To teach progressive muscle relaxation as a skill to help children learn to cope with stress

Materials

A chair for each child

A healthy snack, such as raisins in individual boxes, fruit, crackers, or juice *(optional)*

Group Session

Review

1. Welcome the children to group and remind them of the ground rules and the confidentiality rule.
2. Ask whether anyone has anything left from the last session, on the topic of stepfamilies.
3. Remind children that the next session will be their last one. Discuss any ideas they might have to celebrate the end of the group experience.

Working Time

1. Ask the children whether they know what *stress* means and whether anyone has ever felt "stressed out." Ask them to share some times that were very stressful for them.
2. Explain that our bodies tell us that we have too much to handle with signs like a very fast heartbeat or pulse, sweating, tightness or "butterflies" in the stomach, being unable to fall asleep at night, or just feeling "uptight." Ask group members whether they have ever noticed any of these signs.
3. Discuss the idea that eating right and getting enough sleep and exercise are ways to deal with stress. Discuss the following questions:

    What kinds of things are best for you to eat?

    What are things you can snack on that are good for you?

    What about getting to bed on time? Do some of you stay up too late to get enough rest?

    How many hours of sleep do you need?

    How can you tell if you are not getting enough rest?

    How do you feel if you sit around and watch television for hours and fill up on junk food?

    Why is it good to get out and play or get some other exercise?

4. Tell children that you are going to teach them a way to "chill out" by relaxing their whole body and that they can use this way of relaxing before a stressful event or after something stressful has happened.
5. Have the children sit in chairs (if they are not already) with plenty of space between them. Read the following relaxation script aloud while the children practice it. Circulate to see that they are doing the exercise correctly.

Progressive Muscle Relaxation Training Script

When you feel tense, upset, or nervous, certain muscles in your body tighten. By having you deliberately tense certain muscles in your body, you will learn to identify the muscles that are tight; then you learn to relax them. Practice tightening and relaxing the following muscle groups.

Forehead

Wrinkle up your forehead. Point to where it feels particularly tense (over the bridge of the nose and above each eyebrow). Slowly relax your forehead and pay special attention to those areas that are particularly tense. Spend a few seconds noticing how it feels to have those muscles loosen, switch off, and relax. Notice the difference in how the muscles feel.

Eyes

Close your eyes very tightly. Point to where it feels tight. Your eyes should feel tense above and below each eyelid and on the inner and outer edges of the eye. Pay particular attention to those areas that are especially tense. Gradually relax your eyes as you open them slowly. Notice the difference in the way the muscles feel.

Nose

Wrinkle your nose. Point to the areas that feel tight (the bridge and nostrils). Pay special attention to those areas that are particularly tense. Gradually relax your nose slowly, letting all the tension out. Notice how it feels to have those muscles loosen, switch off, then fully relax. Notice the difference in the way the muscles feel.

Smile

Put your mouth and face in a forced smile. Point to the areas that feel tense (the upper and lower lips and cheek on each side). Your lips should be hard against your cheeks. Gradually relax your face. Notice how it feels to have those muscles loosen, switch off, and relax.

Tongue

Put your tongue hard against the roof of your mouth. Point to where it feels tense (on the inside of the mouth and tongue, and the muscles just below the jaw). Slowly relax those muscles by letting your tongue gradually fall to the floor of your mouth. Pay special attention to those areas that are particularly tense. Notice how it feels to have those muscles loosen, switch off, and relax. Notice the difference in the way the muscles feel.

Jaw

Clench your teeth. Point to where it feels tense (the muscles on the side of your face and also the temples). Gradually relax your jaw and feel the sensation of letting go. Notice how it feels to have those muscles loosen, switch off, and relax. Notice the difference in the way the muscles feel.

Lips

Pucker your lips. Point to where it feels tense (upper and lower lips and side of lips). Pay special attention to those areas that are particularly tense. Gradually relax your lips. Notice how it feels to have those muscles loosen, switch off, and relax. Notice the difference in the way the muscles feel.

Note. From *Relaxation: A Comprehensive Manual for Adults, Children, and Children With Special Needs* (pp. 22–30) by J. R. Cautela and J. Groden, 1978, Champaign, IL: Research Press. Copyright 1978 by the authors. Adapted by permission.

Neck

Tighten your neck. Point to where it feels tense (Adam's apple and on each side and the back of the neck). Pay special attention to those areas that are particularly tense. Gradually relax your neck. Notice how it feels to have those muscles loosen, switch off, and relax. Notice the difference in the way the muscles feel.

Arms

Put your right arm out straight, make a fist, and tighten your whole arm from your hand to your shoulder. Point to where it feels tense (biceps, forearm, back of arm, elbow, above and below wrist and fingers). Pay special attention to those areas that are particularly tense. Gradually relax and lower your arm, bending it at the elbow; relax so that your arm is resting on your lap in the relaxing position. Notice how it feels to have those muscles loosen, switch off, and relax. Notice the difference in the way the muscles feel. Repeat with the left arm.

Legs

Now lift your left leg, turn your toes in towards you, and tighten your whole leg. Point to where it feels tight (top and bottom sides of thigh, knee, calf, front and back of arch, and toes). Gradually relax and lower your leg until your foot is squarely on the floor, bending your knee as you relax. Make sure your leg goes back to the relaxing position. Notice the difference in the way the muscles feel. Repeat with the right leg.

Back

Move forward in your chair. Bring your elbows up and try to get them to meet in the back. Notice where it feels particularly tense (shoulders and down the middle of your back). Gradually relax by moving back into the chair while you straighten out your arms and put them on your lap in the relaxing position. Notice how it feels to have those muscles loosen, switch off, and relax.

Chest

Tighten your chest. Try to constrict it or pull it in. Point to where it feels tense (middle of the chest and above and below each breast). Gradually relax your chest. Notice how it feels to have those muscles loosen, switch off, and relax. Notice the difference in the way the muscles feel.

Stomach

Tighten your stomach by pulling it in and making it as hard as a board. Point to where it feels tense (navel and circle around navel encompassing about 4 inches in diameter). Gradually relax your stomach to its natural position. Notice how it feels to have those muscles loosen, switch off, and relax. Notice the difference in the way the muscles feel.

Below the Waist

Tighten everything below the waist, including your thighs and your buttocks. You should feel yourself rise from the chair. You may notice that you have to tighten your legs a bit. Notice where it is particularly tense (top, bottom, and sides of thighs; muscles from the rear that make contact with the chair). Gradually relax and move back in your chair. Notice the difference in the way the muscles feel.

6. Discuss the following questions to help children process the experience:

> What did it feel like when you were doing the relaxation exercise?
>
> What does it feel like now that you have finished?
>
> How did this exercise help you?
>
> When do you think you could do this exercise to help you feel more relaxed?

Process Time

1. Discuss the following questions:

> What did you learn about stress today?
>
> Does anyone else in the group have stress signs like yours? If so, tell that person how yours are the same.
>
> What did you learn about being able to handle stressful times?
>
> Who in the group did you connect with when we talked about being able to handle stress? Tell that person how you feel.
>
> What did you learn about eating right to help your body be able to manage stress?
>
> What did you learn about getting enough sleep and exercise to manage stress?
>
> Would you be willing to practice the relaxation exercise before the next session, either before a situation that is going to be stressful (for example, going to visit a new member of the family) or after a stressful time (for example, an argument)?

2. Share snacks, if desired. Before saying good-bye, thank group members for coming and remind them of the meeting time for the last session.

Saying Good-bye

Goals

1. To give children the opportunity to review and process what they have learned during the group experience
2. To encourage children to keep on working on ways to deal with the divorce situation
3. To model a leavetaking experience in which children can say good-bye in a positive manner

Materials

Paper lunch bags

Crayons/markers

Paper strips about 2 × 8–inches long

Whatever snacks or other materials children have chosen to celebrate the last session

Group Session

Review

1. Welcome the children to group and thank them for their efforts in coming to the sessions. Remind them that the confidentiality rule holds even after the group is over.
2. Give group members the chance to bring up any additional thoughts about the last session's topic, on ways to manage stress. Did anyone use the relaxation technique? If so, what happened?

Working Time

1. Review the content of the previous sessions. The following discussion questions may help:

   In what ways has your family changed since the divorce?

   What did you learn about why people get divorced?

   When you learned this, how did you feel?

   What kinds of feelings do kids have when their parents divorce?

   What kinds of feelings do parents have?

   What did you learn about feelings being low, medium, or high level?

   Why is it important to speak up and share our feelings when we are upset or need something changed?

   What did you learn about the "wicked stepmother" myth?

   What ways did you learn to manage your stressful feelings? Have these helped you cope?

2. Pass out the lunch bags, crayons or markers, and strips of paper. Have children write their names and draw a circle face on the front of the lunch bags, then place the bags in front of them.

3. Tell group members that these are their "warm fuzzy bags" and that warm fuzzies are positive, nice things people can say to one another. Explain that because they have shared so much and learned from one another in the group, they will now have the chance to write a few warm fuzzies to the other group members. For example:

> Joey, you helped me be more relaxed.

> Marina, thanks for hugging me when I cried.

> Larna, you are brave and good.

> Zach, thanks for helping me see I need to be more patient.

Help the children spell any words they don't know and put the slips in one another's bags. Be sure to include a bag for yourself, too.

Process Time

1. Discuss the following questions:

> Did someone in the group help you understand how to be more patient? Tell that person so and say thank-you.

> Did someone in the group help you learn how to deal with your stepfamily? Tell that person so and say thank-you.

> Did someone in the group help you to understand what is going on with your feelings? Tell that person so and say thank-you.

> Did someone in the group help you to understand how the other members of your family must be feeling? Tell that person so and say thank-you.

2. Thank children for participating and remind them that there are going to be rough times ahead but that they now have one another as a "support team." If appropriate, let them know that you will be available after the group to help them individually.

3. Share snacks and celebrate. End with a group hug.

Grieving and Growing: Learning From Losses

Children are especially vulnerable when they experience a loss, and some special guidelines for conducting a group on loss and grief apply. This is a time when the counselor must be especially sensitive, as well as possess knowledge about children's specific issues and needs.

Frequently, the first loss experience for a child comes in the form of the death of a beloved pet. Adults are sometimes surprised by the strength of the child's reaction to such a loss. In a study by Greene (1988), 84 children in the fourth through sixth grades described events they considered stressful. Whereas 60% of the children mentioned the death of a relative, 69% listed the death of a pet. The affective response to death of either a relative or pet is usually sadness and anxiety, and the disruptive impact is experienced in school activities, general routine, and sleep disturbances. The child who has experienced loss of a pet is grieving just as deeply as the child grieving the death of a grandparent and needs to be included in the group if other selection guidelines are met.

Stages of Grief and Children's Response

Some researchers and practitioners postulate that children go through approximately the same stages of grief as adults. However, major differences exist in how children behave as they deal with grief and in the needs they have in relation to the stages of grief. Although the "stages of grief" theory is just that—a theory—the conceptualization of the loss experience as a process can be helpful in working through the major issues and emotions involved (Schaefer & Lyons, 1988).

Jewett (1982) identifies three overlapping stages that both adults and children go through in the resolution of grief. The first stage is generally characterized by shock, followed by alarm in the child who loses a parent or significant caretaker. Reactions are physiological, emotional, and behavioral. Physiological reactions include insomnia, increased heart rate and muscle tension, inability to attend or sit still to complete school tasks, withdrawal from social interactions, and/or temporary regression to earlier phases of

development (thumb sucking, bed wetting, tantruming, and so forth). Emotional and behavioral reactions include flat affect, panic outbursts, denial and disbelief, disrespectful or contemptuous statements about the person who died, extreme anger, or depression and withdrawal. The second stage of grief is usually characterized by feelings of anger, guilt, sadness, and shame. These feelings cycle and recycle, usually lasting for several weeks to several months. If the child has lost a parent, it may take as long as 2 years for these intense feelings to subside and for the child to work through the grief process. During this time the child slowly comes to the realization that the loved one will not return. The last phase, resolution, is reached when the intense feelings of the second phase are mastered, finality is understood, and life style is reorganized (Thomas & Grimes, 1987).

The length and intensity of each stage of grief is affected by the child's age and coping skills at the time. Children 4 to 9 years of age frequently regress to earlier learned behaviors, become possessive and clingy, and engage in tantrums and other behaviors more characteristic of 2- and 3-year-olds. If you are selecting first graders for a group, they may be wetting their beds and sucking their thumbs. They need kindness, sensitivity, and encouragement to talk about their feelings in whatever ways they can express them. It is important for adults to let younger children talk and work out through play their feelings about what it is like to die, events surrounding the death, and the funeral. To reinforce security, adults should reassure children that they will be taken care of and will receive continued love and attention (Worden, 1982).

Children this age may also exhibit fears of anything associated with death, such as hospitals, doctors, getting injections—even getting colds or the flu. They are frequently embarrassed by their behavior and play games and joke about death, using these responses to defend against the terrifying anxiety of not really knowing what death is all about. Be aware of this in your group, gently encouraging children to deal with their underlying fears rather than trying to stop them from acting silly. In addition, children from 4 to 9 are more likely to demonstrate anger about dying and the loss of the loved one than are younger children. Such responses can emerge in group as hostility, defensiveness, resistance, silence, sullenness, or outward attacks on other children or group activities. Take the time to answer children's questions honestly and on their level to affirm the idea that it is acceptable to discuss the death. Affirm their memories of the dead person or pet and spend time discussing feelings and behaviors associated with life events such as a recent Christmas or birthday. The children need to be given clear, straightforward answers, to be taken seriously, and to learn to ask to be included in family events and discussions of the loss (Grollman, 1967, 1974).

Other Considerations for Children

Cognitive-Developmental Level

A child's experience in grieving and letting go of pain when a loss occurs is very different from that of an adult. Perceptions of death are directly affected by our age and maturity level, so it is critical that the group counselor be aware of the level of cognitive and emotional development in the children who will participate.

Children from about 4 to 9 years of age are unaware of the finality of death, usually believing that it is like sleep or a journey and that the person who died will wake up or return soon (Papalia & Olds, 1993). This way of thinking is consistent with younger children's general inability to conceptualize long periods of time. Younger children are also prone to making inaccurate connections between the death and other events. For example, if told that Grandma died in her sleep, a child may become afraid to go to bed for fear of dying during sleep. In addition, children at this age frequently have the unrealistic wish or dream that if they behave in a certain way or pray enough the beloved person will return. For example, a child might say, "I'll be good, and then Grandma will come back for Christmas."

Older children—from approximately 10 to 12 years of age—usually understand that death is final, but they may still harbor some doubts about whether the dead person will return. Although they may understand the finality of a particular loss, children this age are only beginning to be aware that death occurs to every living thing. They may not realize that death will occur to themselves or to all of those they love and cherish. Children in middle childhood do not think logically but rather tend to believe that illness, death, and other phenomena they do not understand are produced by magic, human agency, or supernatural actions (Brewster, 1982; Papalia & Olds, 1993). Such explanations may serve to protect and defend the child against feelings of helplessness and anxiety (Kastenbaum, 1967).

Previous Experience With Crises

If a child has been through a previous crisis and has emerged without serious emotional difficulties, the grief group experience will likely be more successful. Most children, however, will not have had a major emotional crisis up to this point, and their level of coping skills will be unknown. It is therefore important in the screening process to query both child and parent/guardian about other major life events so you will have some feeling for the child's emotional stability. If a child is still dealing with another major issue, such as a family divorce, he or she might not have the emotional strength or coping ability to deal with a loss in a group setting. Having several other children sharing their losses may be too overwhelming for the vulnerable child. Individual counseling would be more appropriate in this instance.

Social Hunger

Because the child dealing with a loss is so vulnerable, it is important to look closely at the selection variable of "social hunger," or degree to which the child has the ability or at least the potential ability to work with others in a cooperative way, share sensitive topics and feelings, and practice new behaviors. A child who is a social isolate or who is extremely shy and lacking in communication skills will probably not be a good candidate for this particular group experience. Children who are just learning to experience and understand their feelings or who have extreme difficulty doing so may find that the topic of loss is too much to deal with in a group. Group members need to have at least an average ability to share themselves with others— thus, it is important to select group members who appear to want to deal with their pain in a social way.

The best way to assess this variable is to inquire about or observe the degree to which the child is influenced by others in the social environment. The extremely shy, unassertive, or culturally different child who does not appear to want to play in a group would probably not find this group experience rewarding.

Emotional Stability and Frustration Tolerance

Discussing and sharing personal losses necessarily means that strong emotions associated with the loss will be reexperienced as the tale of the loss unfolds. Children who become highly anxious, lose control, or are emotionally unstable should not be invited to be part of a grief group. Participants must have at least a normal tolerance for frustration to be able to function as group members.

Group Goals

1. To provide children with a place to clarify and work through their feelings of loss over the death of a loved one

2. To provide a safe, supportive environment for children to explore the issues of death and loss and to learn more effective coping skills and behaviors

3. To provide accurate information on issues related to death, dying, and loss in order to eliminate distorted concepts

4. To encourage children to express grief in healthy ways both at home and elsewhere

5. To teach children to ask for and express their emotional and social needs related to the loss

6. To encourage and support children in learning to communicate their grief to one another and to family members

7. To allow children to explore memories as part of the legacy of their loved one

8. To help children understand and come to terms with the concept of the finality of death and its part in the life cycle

Selection and Other Guidelines

In selecting children to participate in this group experience, carefully follow the general guidelines for selection suggested in Part 1. The following specific indicators may suggest that a child is a good candidate for a group counseling intervention on this topic:

1. Currently dealing with the loss of a parent, relative, friend, or pet

2. Able to function academically and socially at school without major emotional

disturbances—that is, neither severely acting out nor extremely withdrawn

3. Having difficulty grieving, as indicated by inability to stop talking about the death or acting as though the loss never occurred (for example, by talking about the person as if he or she were still alive or constantly referring to the dead person)

4. Depression, as evidenced by withdrawal, moodiness, irritability, problems sleeping and/or eating, or difficulty concentrating/ remembering

Even though a child might need counseling services very badly to work through a loss, the group modality might not be appropriate due to the child's maturity level and/or lack of coping skills in general. In particular, the child who exhibits the following behaviors probably would not be an acceptable candidate for a time-limited group but would profit from more intense therapeutic intervention:

1. Engages in bizarre behavior such as self-destructiveness, hurting animals, giving away possessions, playing with knives, and the like

2. Has frequent panic attacks or otherwise appears still to be in a state of shock over the loss

3. Engages in serious socially inappropriate or delinquent behaviors, such as stealing or vandalism

4. Withdraws or refuses to socialize with other children

5. Refuses to do schoolwork or go to school

6. Is assessed as being suicidal

Children dealing with loss and grief are at risk for developing other emotional problems if their issues are not resolved. For this reason, it is important that you or someone else with appropriate training be available to talk to group members between group sessions. You will also need to keep close contact with the parents of children selected for the group, letting them know if you become aware of anything indicating that the child may need other psychological services. Although suicide is rare among young children, it does happen. Refer immediately for individual or family therapy to deal with suicidality or other issues beyond the scope of group counseling.

References and Suggested Resources for Professionals

Brewster, A. B. (1982). Chronically ill hospitalized children's concepts of their illness. *Pediatrics, 69,* 355–362.

Elizur, E., & Kaffman, M. (1983). Factors influencing the severity of childhood bereavement reactions. *American Journal of Orthopsychiatry, 53,* 668–676.

Greene, A. L. (1988). Early adolescents' perception of stress. *Journal of Early Adolescence, 8,* 391–403.

Grollman, E. (Ed.). (1967). *Explaining death to children.* Boston: Beacon.

Grollman, E. (Ed.). (1974). *Concerning death: A practical guide for the living.* Boston: Beacon.

Grollman, E. (1976). *Talking about death: A dialogue between parent and child.* Boston: Beacon.

Hannaford, M. J. (1982). *The joy of sorrow.* Dunwoody, GA: Pettit Publications.

Heath, C. P. (1987). Children and reactions to death. In A. Thomas & J. Grimes (Eds.), *Children's needs: Psychological perspectives.* Silver Springs, MD: National Association of School Psychologists.

Jewett, C. (1982). *Helping children cope with separation and loss.* Harvard, MA: The Harvard Common Press.

Kastenbaum, R. (1967). The child's understanding of death: How does it develop? In E. Grollman (Ed.), *Explaining death to children.* Boston: Beacon.

Kübler-Ross, E. (1969). *On death and dying.* New York: Macmillan.

Papalia, D., & Olds, S. (1993). *A child's world: Infancy through adolescence.* New York: McGraw-Hill.

Rando, T. A. (1984). *Grief, dying, and death: Clinical interventions for caregivers.* Champaign, IL: Research Press.

Schaefer, D., & Lyons, C. (1988). *How do we tell the children? Helping children understand and cope when someone dies.* New York: Newmarket.

Thomas, A., & Grimes, J. (Eds.). (1987). *Children's needs: Psychological perspectives.* Silver Springs, MD: National Association of School Psychologists.

Worden, J. (1982). *Grief counseling and grief therapy: A handbook for the mental health practitioner.* New York: Springer.

Bibliography for Children

Berry, J. (1990). *Good answers to tough questions about death.* (Available from Paperbacks for Educators, 426 West Front Street, Washington, MO 63090) (Grades 3–6)

Boyd, C. (1985). *Forever friends.* New York: Puffin. (Grades 5–9)

Brown, M. (1965). *The dead bird.* Reading, MA: Addison-Wesley. (Kindergarten–Grade 3)

Buscaglia, L. (1982). *The fall of Freddie the leaf.* Thorofare, NY: Slack. (Preschool–Grade 12)

Carrick, C. (1976). *The accident.* New York: Clarion. (Grades 1–3).

DePaola, T. (1973). *Nana upstairs and Nana downstairs.* New York: Penguin. (Kindergarten–Grade 4)

Heegaard, M. (1990). *Coping with death and grief.* Minneapolis: Lerner. (Grades 3–6)

Holden, L. D. (1989). *Gran-gran's best trick: A story for children who have lost someone they love.* New York: Magination. (Kindergarten–Grade 3)

Jukes, M. (1985). *Blackberries in the dark.* New York: Yearling. (Grades 2–5)

O'Toole, D. (1988). *Aarvy Ardvark finds hope: A read aloud story for people of all ages.* Burnville, NC: Rainbow Connection. (Grades 3–6)

Pringle, L. (1977). *Death is natural.* New York: Beech Tree. (Grade 1 and up)

Rogers, F. (1988). *When a pet dies.* New York: Putnam. (Kindergarten–Grade 4)

Simon, N. (1986). *The saddest time.* Niles, IL: Whitman. (Grades 1–4)

Stein, S. (1984). *About dying: An open family book for parents and children together.* New York: Walker Press. (Kindergarten–Grade 4)

Varley, S. (1984). *Badger's parting gifts.* New York: Lothrop, Lee & Shepard. (Grades 1–6)

Viorst, J. (1971). *The tenth good thing about Barney.* New York: Aladdin. (Kindergarten–Grade 2)

Getting Started

NOTE: By the end of this first session each group member should have shared with the other members the person or pet they are grieving and perhaps the circumstances of the loss. Use supportive and reinforcing statements as the children share so they will begin to understand the norm that what they are thinking and feeling is accepted and appreciated in the group.

Goals

1. To introduce children to the group experience and help them begin to get acquainted
2. To establish ground rules and discuss the issue of confidentiality
3. To discuss the purpose of the group and prepare children for the sessions ahead
4. To provide a safe and supportive environment for the discussion and sharing of painful thoughts and feelings
5. To help children become aware that others in the group have similar experiences and feelings about loss (in other words, that their feelings are universal)

Materials

Easel pad and marker

Drawing paper

Crayons/markers

A healthy snack, such as raisins in individual boxes, fruit, crackers, or juice *(optional)*

Group Session

Ice Breaker

1. Welcome the children to group, briefly going over the purpose of the group and some of the topics that will be covered.
2. Ask the members to go around the circle and share their names, their favorite pet or person, and a pet or a person they know who has died. Some children may wish to share about a different loss than the one that brought them to the group—if so, give them a session or two to get comfortable before asking any questions to stimulate discussion of the recent loss. It will help if you share some information about a loss you have experienced yourself.
3. Discuss basic ground rules for the group, giving group members a few examples:

    Everyone gets a chance to talk.

    No hitting or fighting in group.

    Take turns.

    Ask for the children's input to help them develop "ownership." List the ground rules on an easel pad so everyone can see, then post them during every session.

4. Discuss the confidentiality rule and its limits. For example, you might say:

> When we talked about your being in the group, I told you that whatever we say in our group is *confidential*. That means what we say is private. You may talk about your own thoughts, feelings, and actions, but you may not share anything others in the group talk about. There are some special times when I would have to share what you say—if you say something about harming yourself or others, if you share something about child abuse, or if the court (a judge) asks me about what goes on.

Working Time

1. Distribute the drawing paper and crayons or markers and ask the children to draw a picture of the pet or person who has died, letting them sit on the floor if they wish. Tell them they are going to share their pictures with the rest of the group when they are finished. Encourage them to be sure to put anyone else they want to in the picture.

2. Reassemble in the group circle. Ask the children to share what is in their picture and tell about the pet or person whom they have lost. Let children who self-disclose easily go first.

3. As the children share their pictures, point out what is common in their experience, such as having sad feelings, going to the hospital to visit the person who died, going to the funeral home, or going to the church and/or cemetery. For example: "Jenny, both you and Shawn went to the hospital to visit someone who was very sick."

4. Encourage group members to name someone else in the group they felt connected to and have them speak directly to that person. Ask, "Did anyone share something that made you feel connected to that person?" If a group member names someone he or she felt connected to, say, "Tell_____you connected with him/her." In this way you are teaching group members to communicate directly, share thoughts and emotions, and empathize with one another.

Process Time

1. Discuss the following questions:

> What did you learn about in group today?
>
> What feelings do we all seem to share about a person or pet close to us dying?
>
> What was it like for you to tell us about your special person or pet?
>
> Who else in the group feels the way you do? Tell that person how you feel the same.
>
> What did you learn about yourself in group today?

2. Share snacks, if desired. Before saying good-bye, thank group members for coming and remind them of the meeting time for the next session. Tell them that if they need more help dealing with their feelings about the loss they can come to you (or name someone else they can talk to if you will not be available).

Losing Someone Hurts

Goals

1. To establish the norm of reviewing what happened during the previous session and give children an opportunity to discuss anything they still have questions about

2. To help children expand their affective vocabulary for talking about loss and grief

3. To help children begin to distinguish among thoughts, feelings, and behaviors

4. To encourage children to contrast how they felt immediately after the loss with how they feel in the here and now

5. To encourage children to try talking about their feelings with their friends and family members

6. To reinforce the idea that it is healthy to talk about feelings and that the group is a safe place to do so

Materials

Feeling Faces Chart (Handout 1, p. 46)

Thinking-Feeling-Behaving Diagram (Handout 4)

Blank Face Drawing (Handout 5—two copies per group member)

A healthy snack, such as raisins in individual boxes, fruit, crackers, or juice *(optional)*

Group Session

Review

1. Welcome the children to group and thank them for coming. Briefly go over the ground rules and the confidentiality rule.

2. Ask group members if they have anything they want to say about the last session.

Working Time

1. Pass out copies of the Feeling Faces Chart (Handout 1), Thinking-Feeling-Behaving Diagram (Handout 4), and Blank Face Drawing (Handout 5).

2. Refer to the Thinking-Feeling-Behaving Diagram, sharing the idea that we all think (represented by a brain), feel (represented by a heart), and behave (represented by a hand). For example:

   Thinking: Understanding how to do a math problem, remembering something a loved one said or did, imagining what summer vacation will be like

   Feeling: Anger, fear, guilt, hurt, joy

   Behaving: Washing the dishes, doing homework, going to a funeral

   As the children talk during the rest of the session, point out the difference between thinking, feeling, and behaving to reinforce this concept.

3. Have the children look at the Feeling Faces Chart and encourage them to share some of the feelings they have had lately and what they believe might be some reasons for these feelings. Ask those who respond to describe what happened when they had a particular feeling.

4. Have the children select a word from the Feeling Faces Chart (or suggest another word, if they like) that best represents how they felt when they first heard about the death of their special person or pet. Have them write this word in the space provided on one copy of the Blank Face Drawing. Ask them to think of how they are feeling right now about losing their special person and write that word in the space provided on the second copy of the Blank Face Drawing. Then have the children finish drawing and coloring the two faces.

5. Go around the circle and have children share their two drawings and feelings, pointing out the differences in intensity. Help them learn to discriminate between intense feelings and moderate or low-level feelings, telling them that feelings change as time goes on after someone experiences a loss. Continue to differentiate feelings from behaviors or thoughts as children share; help them connect with others who had similar feelings.

Process Time

1. Discuss the following questions:

> What did you learn about today in group?
>
> What did you learn about feelings being stronger or weaker?
>
> What did you learn about the other group members?
>
> Would you be willing to share your sad feelings with someone in your family? What person would that be?
>
> What is good and healthy about sharing your sad feelings?
>
> What happens to strong feelings after time passes?
>
> What can you do to help yourself heal from your hurts?

2. Share snacks, if desired. Before saying good-bye, thank group members for coming and remind them of the meeting time for the next session. Tell them that if they need more help dealing with their feelings about the loss they can come to you (or name someone else they can talk to if you will not be available).

Thinking-Feeling-Behaving Diagram

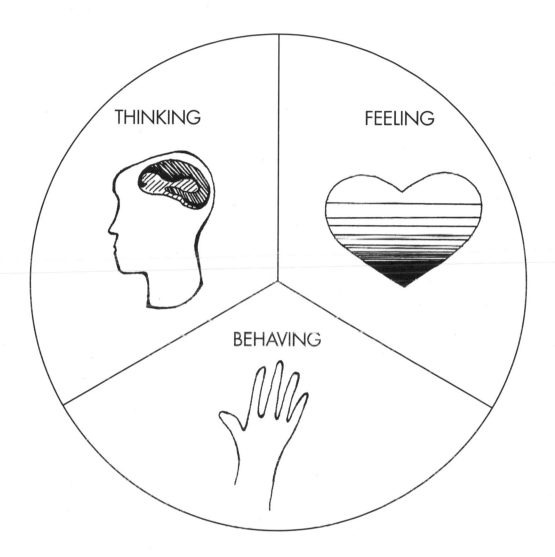

Blank Face Drawing

How I felt

Remembering

NOTE: Before this session, draw a picture to illustrate a positive memory you have about a pet or person who has died. Write a brief description of the memory on the drawing. This will serve as a model for group members' own examples.

Goals

1. To facilitate thinking about memories of the pet or person who has died

2. To encourage the realization that memories are a special legacy

3. To help children understand that it is important to share their memories and feelings of grief with persons they love

Materials

A story about pet loss, such as *The Tenth Good Thing About Barney*, by Judith Viorst (Aladdin, 1971)

Drawing paper

Crayons/markers

A healthy snack, such as raisins in individual boxes, fruit, crackers, or juice *(optional)*

Group Session

Review

1. Welcome the children and thank them for coming to the session. Briefly go over the ground rules and the confidentiality rule.

2. Ask whether anyone has anything they want to say about the last session.

Working Time

1. Read the story selected.

2. Discuss with children the idea that sometimes when people or pets die, they leave us things to remind us of them, like a ring, a picture, or a toy. They also leave things we cannot touch—memories about them. Encourage each child to share some of the good memories the person or pet left for him or her. Begin the discussion by talking about some of your own memories.

3. Pass out the drawing materials. Show the children your picture about a loved one. Read what you have written, explaining the memory you have.

4. Ask the children to make a similar drawing for their loved one and to write one of the memories they shared on it. Help them express their thoughts in writing if necessary.

5. Reassemble the group in a circle and have members share their drawings and special memories.

Process Time

1. Discuss the following questions:

   What did you learn about in group today?

   What feelings (both sad and happy) did you have when we talked about memories of your loved one?

   What ways can you preserve your memories so that you won't forget them as time passes and you grow up? (For example: logs, videos, photographs, diaries)

   Did you connect with anyone in the group today? If so, tell that person how you feel.

   What good memories could you share with someone in your family that might make them smile and remember?

2. Share snacks, if desired. Before saying good-bye, thank group members for coming and remind them of the meeting time for the next session. Tell them if they need more help dealing with their feelings about the loss they can come to you (or name someone else they can talk to if you will not be available).

Why Funerals?

Goals

1. To help children understand their feelings of stress as a result of their loss

2. To help children learn the technique of progressive muscle relaxation as a way to deal with stressful events like going to a funeral home or to the hospital to visit someone who is very ill

3. To show children that funerals are a special time to say good-bye, just as other services are times to say hello (for example, weddings or birthing events)

4. To help children understand that funerals are not to be feared

Materials

A chair for each child

Progressive Muscle Relaxation Training Script (pp. 99–100)

A healthy snack, such as raisins in individual boxes, fruit, crackers, or juice *(optional)*

Group Session

Review

1. Welcome the children to group. Briefly go over the ground rules and the confidentiality rule.

2. Ask whether anyone has anything they would like to say about the last session. Give group members the chance to share additional memories if they wish. (They usually do, so try to keep the discussion short.)

Working Time

1. Discuss the fact that times when we deal with grief and loss are times when we have a lot of stress. Point out that stress can come out in many ways—perhaps a feeling of being anxious, irritable, worn out, and so on. Let group members tell how they experience stress.

2. Have the children share ways they know of to deal with stress—for example, taking a walk, playing outside, or resting. Tell them that using relaxation skills is another good way to deal with stress.

3. Have the children sit in chairs (if they are not already) with plenty of space between them. Begin slowly reading the Progressive Muscle Relaxation Training Script.

4. Discuss the following questions to help children understand the experience:

   What does your body feel like after having done this relaxing exercise?

   How do you think doing this exercise could help you in tense or stressful situations?

   What do you like best about feeling relaxed?

5. Discuss group members' ideas about funerals. The following discussion questions may help:

   What are funerals for?

   What happens at funerals?

   Who goes to the funeral home?

   What happens at the funeral home?

   Why do people send so many flowers and plants?

Why do people go up to the casket and look in or kneel down?

How do you feel when you go to a funeral home?

What happens on the day of the funeral?

What feelings do you have at the cemetery?

Where do the family members go after the funeral?

Why do some people have a dinner or get-together after a funeral?

Process Time

1. Discuss the following questions:

    What did you learn about relaxing today?

    Where can you use this new skill? Will you try it?

    How can you use relaxing to help you cope with your sad feelings?

    What did you learn about your feelings today?

    What did you learn about the other kids in group and their feelings?

    What did you learn about funerals that helps you understand and not be afraid of them?

2. Share snacks, if desired. Before saying good-bye, thank group members for coming and remind them of the meeting time for the next session. Tell them that if they need more help dealing with their feelings about the loss they can come to you (or name someone else they can talk to if you will not be available).

Coping With Stages of Grief

NOTE: The stages of grief described in this session are the ones identified by Elisabeth Kübler-Ross in 1969. Group members in the upper elementary grades will grasp the concepts in this session better than younger ones. Even though younger children may have an incomplete understanding, what they can understand will help them cope with their loss.

Goals

1. To help children understand the stages of grief on their own intellectual level
2. To prepare children for the renewed grief that may occur at certain times, such as holidays and birthdays
3. To encourage children to identify and express their current feelings of grief
4. To instill hope in children that the pain they feel will change and lessen as time goes on

Materials

Easel pad and marker

Stickers (preferably red hearts)

Crayons/markers

A healthy snack, such as raisins in individual boxes, fruit, crackers, or juice (*optional*)

Group Session

Review

1. Welcome the children to group. Briefly discuss the ground rules and remind them of the confidentiality rule.
2. Ask whether anyone has anything they would like to say about the last session, on funerals. Review the relaxation exercise and ask whether anyone tried it out after the last session.

Working Time

1. Tell the children that when we lose a pet or a person we love, we have lots of different feelings and thoughts. Explain that on some days we may feel more one way and that on other days we may feel more another.
2. Go over the five major stages of grief, writing each on the easel pad. Ask group members what thoughts and feelings a person might have at each stage. For example:

    Denial: Pretending it didn't happen, acting happy when you're really sad

    Anger: Being moody, irritable, grouchy, nasty, picky, vulgar, hostile, or bitter

    Bargaining: Thinking if I'm better, smarter, or nicer, my loved one will return

    Depression: Feeling sad, lonely, tired, withdrawn, sullen, or hopeless

    Acceptance: Thinking I can go on, life is OK, I can deal with this, I can remember my loved one and smile, I don't like it but I can accept it

3. Pass out the stickers and ask group members to put their names on them. Ask them to think about which set of thoughts and feelings reflects how they feel right now then take their stickers and put them up on the chart at the stage they are experiencing now.

4. Discuss the placement of the stickers. Most likely, group members will be at different stages. This will give you the opportunity to stress that having different feelings is OK and that people experience losses in uniquely individual ways.

5. Explain that people move forward and backward experiencing these feelings or stages—just when you think you are over feeling one way, you could start feeling that way again. Discuss special times when people might start feeling very sad after they had been happier for a time—birthdays, anniversaries, holidays, and the like. Encourage children to share their own experiences.

Process Time

1. Discuss the following questions:

> What did you learn about in group today?
>
> What is scary about going backward to a stage you think you are over?
>
> What is good about knowing the stages of grief?
>
> What ways can you relax and learn to accept the feelings of grieving?
>
> Whom can you share with at home when you feel like crying?
>
> What can you do this week to help you understand the grief stages?

2. Share snacks, if desired. Before saying good-bye, thank the children for coming and remind them of the meeting time for the next session. Tell them that if they need more help dealing with their feelings about the loss they can come to you (or name someone else they can talk to if you will not be available).

Understanding Causes of Death

> NOTE: If a child is to some extent responsible for the loss, you will need to address this individually. For example, a child might have been charged with the care of a pet that dies because the child did not feed or restrain the pet correctly. Try to help the child let go of the guilt and realize that making mistakes is a way we learn to be more careful in the future.

Goals

1. To help children be able to explain the cause of a loved one's death to themselves and others

2. To promote understanding that children are not responsible for their loved one's death

3. To help children learn that there is nothing they could have done in the past or could do now to change the death

Materials

Easel pad and marker

A book about a particular cause of death, such as *The Accident*, by C. Carrick (Clarion, 1976)

A healthy snack, such as raisins in individual boxes, fruit, crackers, or juice *(optional)*

Group Session

Review

1. Welcome the children to group. Briefly review the ground rules and the confidentiality rule.

2. Ask whether anyone has anything to say about the previous session, on the stages we go through after a loss.

Working Time

1. Read the story selected.

2. Discuss how and why pets and people might die. Let the children brainstorm various causes of death and write these on the easel pad. Some possible causes include old age, suicide, illness, accident, war, and murder.

3. Tell children that sometimes we think we are to blame for a pet's or a person's death, but that is not true. Everything has a time to live and a time to die. The people left behind are the ones who have to learn to live without the pet or person who died, and the more sudden the death is, the harder it is for us to understand it. Blaming ourselves will not bring the loved one back—it only makes us feel worse and doesn't help us grow and learn from the experience.

4. Discuss the following questions:

> Even though we can't control dying or bring the person back, what can we do to feel better?
>
> Even though death is something that makes us feel awful for a time, what can we learn from the experience of losing someone?
>
> What seems harder to accept, someone's dying suddenly or someone's dying after a long illness? Why?

Did anyone else in the group have someone die the same way your loved one did? Tell that person how what happened to you was the same.

When someone asks you about the death of a loved one, how can you explain so the person knows how it happened and how you are feeling about it now?

5. Explain that there are ways to say good-bye even if you couldn't before the person died, such as writing a letter. Encourage children to write a good-bye letter sometime before the next session if they wish.

Process Time

1. Discuss the following questions:

What did you learn in this session about the ways people die?

What causes of death are hardest for us to understand and deal with?

What do we know about feeling responsible for a death?

Since we can't bring the dead person back, what can we do to say good-bye to them in other ways?

2. Share snacks, if desired. Before saying good-bye, thank group members for coming, tell them the group will meet only two more times, and remind them of the meeting time for the next session. Tell them if they need more help dealing with their feelings about the loss they can come to you (or name someone else they can talk to if you will not be available).

Talking to Grieving People

Goals

1. To help children understand that other people feel the same way they do when they experience a loss

2. To show children how they can help these people by telling them they understand (in other words, to learn the skill of empathic responding)

3. To give children the opportunity to practice this skill in the group

4. To encourage children to practice this skill with someone outside the group

Materials

Easel pad and marker

A variety of sympathy cards

Stationery and envelope for each child

Pencils/pens

A healthy snack, such as raisins in individual boxes, fruit, crackers, or juice *(optional)*

Group Session

Review

1. Welcome the children to group and briefly review the ground rules and the confidentiality rule. Remind them that next week will be the last time the group will be meeting. Tell them that later in the session you will ask them to suggest ways they can celebrate and end in a positive and fun way.

2. Ask whether anyone has any unfinished business from the last session, on the causes of death and not taking responsibility for someone's dying. Share good-bye letters, if children have written them

Working Time

1. Discuss the idea that the group members are not the only ones who are experiencing grief—our friends and relatives also have to experience the deaths of loved ones. It is hard for us to talk about our feelings, and we feel good when people let us know they care. We can also help other people by letting them know we care about what they are going through. Understanding other people's feelings and letting them know is called *empathy*.

2. Pass the sympathy cards around. Read some aloud and discuss, explaining that sending such cards is one way for people to show they care.

3. Explain that in this session children will practice saying things to show empathy, or that they care. Brainstorm some things group members could say to someone who has just lost a loved one. For example:

> I'm sorry to hear about the death of your Aunt Mary.
>
> You must be very sad.
>
> My grandma died too, so I know you feel lonely.
>
> It's OK to cry and feel blue.

4. Pass out the stationery and envelopes and tell the children that they can write a letter or draw a card for someone they know who has had a loss. Help them write a simple sentence or two along the line of the statements they have just generated.

5. Let the children share their letters or cards if they choose to.

Process Time

1. Ask the following questions:

   What good does it do to express feelings of empathy for someone who has had a loss?

   How do you feel when someone says one of these things to you?

   How does writing a letter to someone help?

   How do you feel after you write a letter or send a card with a note?

2. Remind the children that the next session will be the last one. Ask them how they would like to use the session to say good-bye to one another and give them the opportunity to plan a good-bye party.

3. Share snacks, if desired. Before saying good-bye, thank group members for coming and remind them of the meeting time for the next session. Tell them if they need more help dealing with their feelings about the loss they can come to you (or name someone else they can talk to if you will not be available).

Saying Good-bye

Goals

1. To give children the opportunity to review and process what they have learned during the group experience
2. To support children's sharing of painful feelings and situations during the group
3. To teach children that saying good-bye is a positive way to end relationships

Materials

Whatever snacks or other materials children have chosen to celebrate the last session

Group Session

Review

1. Ask the children if they would like to talk about anything from last week's session, on empathy for others. The following discussion questions may help:

   Have you made any caring statements to someone else who has experienced a loss?

   Has anyone said any caring things to you about your own loss? If so, how did that make you feel?

Working Time

1. Refer to the session topics, asking children to share what they learned and how it has helped them cope with their grief:

   How did it feel to know that other group members had similar experiences and even some of the same feelings you did?

   How do we feel when we lose someone special?

   What are the differences between thoughts and feelings? Feelings and behaviors?

   What ways do we have to remember a pet or person who has died?

   Why is it important to share your memories and feelings with people you love?

   Why do people have funerals?

   What ways can you relax when you think about funerals or have to do something else difficult for you?

   How do our feelings change over time after we have a loss?

   What are some of the stages of grief?

   What are some of the causes of death?

   Are we responsible if someone we love dies?

   How can we help other people who are hurting because of a loss?

2. Discuss the following general questions as well:

   How do you feel now that you have been to group eight times?

   What was the best thing you learned?

Process Time

1. Let children know you appreciate their coming to group and sharing their feelings. Tell them that you will be available to them after the group is over if they want to talk (or name someone else they can talk to if you will not be available).

2. Share the snacks and celebrate in the way children have chosen. End with a group hug.

I CAN Kids: Control Anger Now!___

Anger—the fiery emotion that drives us to interact socially in both positive and negative ways—is the feeling that seems to cause the most referrals to counseling. It is a complex emotion, expressed at three levels: behavioral, cognitive, and somatic (Bowers, 1987). We express anger behaviorally through our actions. The child who is tantruming, clenching fists, or kicking, fighting, and screaming is expressing anger in this way. Cognitively, we experience anger as beliefs, perceptions, and interpretations of situations. For example, a child sees another child take a book off his desk and thinks, "She's stealing my book—I'll get her back!" This is what the child sees and interprets the action to mean, whether the child taking the book meant to steal it or not. Physiologically, we experience anger as a burst of adrenalin flowing through the bloodstream, causing a variety of responses in different individuals— for example, becoming red in the face, shaking, or perspiring.

Getting angry is normal. Anger is a healthy reaction that can motivate positive, constructive social interactions such as working out individual differences and learning to deal with conflict. It is also a normal part of the grieving process and the process of being ill or injured, as well as an expected result of abuse. The problems anger generates usually fall into one of two categories: excess or deficit. The latter expression appears as anger turned inward in the passive, shy child who is unable to get along socially. It is the former, excess of anger, that usually comes to the attention of mental health professionals and even law enforcement personnel.

Two frequently used and fairly well-researched approaches exist for working with children whose acting-out problems create difficulty in social interactions. The first is stress-inoculation training, a type of cognitive-behavioral approach (Meichenbaum, 1976; Novaco, 1975, 1976, 1977). The second, the behavioral approach, includes several different types of techniques. This approach includes anger management strategies that deal with observable, rather than

cognitive, behavior. Behavioral techniques are tailored to the age, severity of problem, and individual circumstances of the child. Social skills training is often a component of both these approaches; such training emphasizes acquisition of specific behaviors (e.g., Bowers, 1987; Feindler & Fremouw, 1983; McGinnis, Goldstein, Sprafkin, & Gershaw, 1984).

Keep in mind that the purpose, format, and process of group counseling differs substantially from that of classroom educational groups and that group counseling is not geared toward skill mastery. Rather, the intent of group counseling is to provide children with a safe environment in which to explore their ideas, feelings, values, attitudes, and hopes. The emphasis in this agenda is group counseling; however, Sessions 2 through 7 do focus on techniques derived from cognitive-behavioral, behavioral, and social skills training. These sessions center on specific coping skills. If one or more children in the group have trouble with a specific area of anger management, you will need to encourage them to practice the skill outside the group before the next session.

Group Goals

1. To promote awareness that anger is normal

2. To raise children's understanding of why certain behaviors are unacceptable

3. To teach children strategies to choose from when they are angry

4. To teach alternative ways to deal with the stressful situations that arouse anger

5. To provide appropriate role models for expressing anger

6. To encourage honest expression and exploration of anger and its consequences

Selection and Other Guidelines

Follow the general selection guidelines discussed in Part 1 of this book, especially the guideline

---

Note. The CAN acronym for Control Anger Now is the invention of Ann McAfee, elementary school counselor at North Harrison Elementary School, Ramsey, Indiana. I am grateful for her kind permission to use it in the title of this group.

pertaining to heterogeneity. If you are not careful to balance roles, the group could end up being "you against them." In other words, if there are too many children with acting-out behavior problems and not enough with some well-developed anger coping skills, a short-term group will not reach the working stage. It will take all of the sessions to develop the norms of taking turns, listening while others are speaking, being supportive, practicing the skills, and so forth. By the time you get control of the problem behaviors, the group will be over. So select some children who act out their anger, some who "act in" their anger, and some who are able to manage anger in some but perhaps not all situations.

The following are some specific indicators that might be present in children who would be good candidates for this group:

1. Low frustration tolerance

2. Inability to avoid situations that are anger producing

3. Few choices of appropriate behaviors

4. Lack of role models for dealing appropriately with anger

5. Lack of thought before acting

References and Suggested Resources for Professionals

Averill, J. R. (1982). *Anger and aggression: An essay on emotion.* New York: Springer-Verlag.

Bowers, R. C., Jr. (1987). Children and anger. In A. Thomas & J. Grimes (Eds.), *Children's needs: Psychological perspectives.* Silver Springs, MD: National Association of School Psychologists.

Feindler, E. L., & Fremouw, W. J. (1983). Stress inoculation training for adolescent anger problems. In D. Meichenbaum & M. S. Jaremko (Eds.), *Stress reduction and prevention.* New York: Plenum.

Goldstein, A. P. (1983). Behavior modification approaches to aggression prevention and control. In Center for Research on Aggression (Ed.), *Prevention and control of aggression.* New York: Pergamon.

Goldstein, A. P., Sprafkin, R. P., Gershaw, N. J., & Klein, P. (1980). *Skillstreaming the adolescent: A structured learning approach to teaching prosocial skills.* Champaign, IL: Research Press.

McGinnis, E., Goldstein, A. P., Sprafkin, R. P., & Gershaw, N. J. (1984). *Skillstreaming the elementary school child: A guide for teaching prosocial skills.* Champaign, IL: Research Press.

Meichenbaum, D. (1976). A self-instructional approach to stress management: A proposal for stress inoculation training. In C. Spielberger & I. Sarason (Eds.), *Stress and anxiety in modern life.* New York: Winston.

Novaco, R. W. (1975). *Anger control: The development and evaluation of an experiential treatment.* Lexington, MA: Lexington.

Novaco, R. W. (1976). Treatment of chronic anger through cognitive and relaxation controls. *Journal of Consulting and Clinical Psychology, 44,* 681.

Novaco, R. W. (1977). Stress-inoculation: A cognitive therapy for anger and its application to a case of depression. *Journal of Consulting and Clinical Psychology, 45,* 600–608.

Southern, S., & Smith, R. L. (1980). Managing stress and anxiety in the classroom. *Catalyst for Change, 10,* 4–7.

Vernon, A. (1993). *Counseling children and adolescents.* Denver: Love Publishing.

Bibliography for Children

Berry, J. (1988). *Disobeying.* (Available from Paperbacks for Educators, 426 West Front Street, Washington, MO 63090) (Kindergarten–Grade 3)

Berry, J. (1988). *Fighting.* (Available from Paperbacks for Educators, 426 West Front Street, Washington, MO 63090) (Kindergarten–Grade 3)

Berry, J. (1988). *Throwing tantrums.* (Available from Paperbacks for Educators, 426 West Front Street, Washington, MO 63090) (Kindergarten–Grade 3)

Best, A. (1989). *That makes me angry!* Racine, WI: Golden Books. (Preschool–Grade 3)

Boulden, J., & Boulden, J. (1993). *Feelings and faces.* Weaverville, CA: Boulden Publishing. (Kindergarten–Grade 3)

Boyd, L. (1991). *Bailey the big bully*. New York: Puffin. (Preschool–Grade 3)

Duncan, R. (1989). *When Emily woke up angry*. Hauppauge, NY: Barron's. (Preschool–Grade 2)

LeShan, E. (1972). *What makes me feel this way? Growing up with human emotions*. New York: Aladdin. (Grades 3–7)

Mayer, M. (1983). *I was so mad*. Racine, WI: Golden Books. (Preschool–Grade 3)

Merriam, E. (1992). *Fighting words*. New York: Morrow. (Kindergarten–Grade 5)

Mitchell, E. (1969). *The temper tantrum book*. New York: Puffin. (Preschool–Grade 2)

Powell, R. (1990). *How to deal with parents*. Mahwah, NJ: Troll. (Preschool–Grade 2)

Reader, D. (1990). *I want one!* Grand Rapids, MI: Fleming H. Revell Co./Ideals. (Preschool–Grade 3)

Simon, N. (1974). *I was so mad*. Morton Grove, IL: Whitman. (Preschool–Grade 3)

Terrell, R. (1992). *A kid's guide to how to stop the violence*. New York: Avon. (Grades 4–8)

Thaut, P. (1991). *Spike and Ben—Angry feelings: A loving story about angry feelings*. Deerfield Beach, FL: Health Communications. (Kindergarten–Grade 4)

Viorst, J. (1972). *Alexander and the terrible, horrible, no good, very bad day*. New York: Macmillan. (Kindergarten–Grade 4)

Zolotow, C. (1969). *The hating book*. New York: HarperCollins. (Preschool–Grade 3)

Getting Started

Goals

1. To introduce children to the group experience and help them begin to get acquainted
2. To establish ground rules and discuss the issue of confidentiality
3. To discuss the purpose of the group and prepare children for the sessions ahead
4. To begin to develop a positive, accepting atmosphere for children to begin exploring the emotion of anger and its behavioral consequences
5. To suggest that feelings come in different levels of intensity
6. To help children understand that anger itself is not bad, but the reactions we have to it may have positive or negative consequences

Materials

Easel pad and marker

A roll of newsprint

Crayons/markers

Tape

Feeling Faces Chart (Handout 1, p. 46)

A healthy snack, such as raisins in individual boxes, fruit, crackers, or juice *(optional)*

Group Session

Ice Breaker

1. Welcome the children to group. Go over the purpose of the group and discuss some of the session topics and benefits of participating.
2. Discuss basic ground rules for the group, giving group members some examples:

   > Everyone gets a chance to talk.
   >
   > No hitting or fighting in group.
   >
   > Take turns.

   Ask for group member's input to help them develop "ownership." List the ground rules on an easel pad so everyone can see, then post them during each session.
3. Discuss the confidentiality rule and its limits. For example, you might say:

   > When we talked about your being in the group, I told you that whatever we say in our group is *confidential*. That means what we say is private. You may talk about your own thoughts, feelings, and actions, but you may not share anything others in the group talk about. There are some special times when I would have to share what you say—if you say something about harming yourself or others, if you share something about child abuse, or if the court (a judge) asks me about what goes on.

Working Time

1. Cut sheets of newsprint as long as the children are tall. Give each group member a sheet and some crayons or markers.

2. Tell group members that in order to help them get acquainted with one another, you ask that they choose a partner. One person will lie down on the paper and have the partner trace his or her body outline, then the two will reverse roles.

3. Invite group members to write some things about themselves on certain areas of their "me" shapes. For example:

   Waist: Name

   Right arm: Things I can make

   Left arm: People/pets I like to hug

   Head: Things I worry about

   Chest: People I love

   Right leg: Places that are special to me

   Right foot: Sports I like

   Left leg: People I get so angry at I could kick

   Left foot: Things I get so mad at I could stomp

4. Tape the "me" shapes up on the wall for viewing. Have the children introduce themselves and share some things about themselves. Tell them they don't have to share everything on the "me" shape—just whatever they feel comfortable with.

5. Distribute copies of the Feeling Faces Chart (Handout 1). Talk about the emotion of anger, showing group members on the Feeling Faces Chart that it is one of several feelings we might have and explaining that all of these feelings help enrich our lives. Make sure the children understand that the feeling of anger is not bad. Explain that while what we *do* when we are very angry can be hurtful to ourselves and others, feeling angry is OK.

6. Go over the idea that feelings have different levels—low, medium, and high—something like heat on a stove. Some angry feelings are like low heat, when you are just warming something up (annoyed or cross). Some are like medium heat (disgusted or hostile). Some are so hot they are like boiling over (furious or outraged).

7. Help group members identify times they have felt each of these levels of anger. It may help to refer to the anger situations they wrote on their "me" shapes.

Process Time

1. Discuss the following questions:

   What did you learn about the feeling of anger today?

   What does it mean that anger can be low, medium, or high?

   What did you learn about being in a group?

   What did you like about coming here today?

   What was scary about it?

   Did anyone else share something that you connected with? Tell that person how you feel the same.

2. Repeat the idea that anger can be low, medium, or high. If children are feeling mad about something before the group meets again, do they think they could try to "turn down the heat"?

3. Share snacks, if desired. Before saying good-bye, thank group members for coming and remind them of the meeting time for the next session.

Helpful Ways Versus Hurtful Ways

NOTE: Session 3 in the "Good Citizen's Club" agenda presents an alternate technique for controlling anger, appropriate for second grade and up. This session and the next one detail a technique appropriate for children about fourth grade and up.

Goals

1. To establish the norm of reviewing what happened during the previous session and allow children time for "unfinished business"

2. To introduce a three-step process for dealing with events that provoke angry responses (in other words, the stress-inoculation procedure)

3. To help children distinguish responses to anger as being either helpful or hurtful

Materials

Drawing paper

Crayons/markers

A healthy snack, such as raisins in individual boxes, fruit, crackers, or juice *(optional)*

Group Session

Review

1. Welcome the children to group. Remind them of the ground rules and the confidentiality rule.

2. Ask whether anyone has anything more to share about the last session, on how anger is OK and how we can feel different levels of anger. Did any group members notice times since the last session when they had different levels of anger? If so, did they do anything to try to feel less angry?

Working Time

1. Pass out the art materials and ask the children to draw a time they got very, very angry. Encourage them to illustrate the way they showed their anger and the people involved. Ask group members to draw another picture on the other side of the paper to show a time they got a little bit angry—maybe just peeved or irritated.

2. Ask the children to share their drawings and tell what happened in each case. The following discussion questions may help:

> How did you feel when you were a little bit angry?
>
> Where in your body did you feel the anger?
>
> How did you feel different when you were very, very angry?
>
> What did you do to deal with the anger?
>
> Did what you choose to do help or hurt yourself?
>
> Did it help or hurt the other people in the situation?

3. Clarify the idea that some ways to express anger help us get our feelings out and known to the other people involved and other ways just end up hurting everyone.

4. Present the following three steps and explain that they will help group members get control of their anger:

> *Step 1:* Know what is coming. Try to relax.
>
> *Step 2:* Say calming things to yourself. Try to relax.
>
> *Step 3:* Praise yourself! Try to relax.

5. Ask for a volunteer to practice the three steps. Work through the process, applying it to whatever specific situation the child describes:

> *Step 1:* When did you know you were getting very angry? Could you tell you were getting angry when you saw the situation? What were the signs that you were going to get really mad?
>
> *Step 2:* Pretend you are in that situation now. Try to make your muscles relax. Say some calming things, like "I can deal with this," "Stay cool," "Don't blow up," "Relax," and "It's not so bad."
>
> *Step 3:* Imagine you've gotten through the situation without blowing up. Now reward yourself by saying, "I did it!" "I can handle tough things!" "I'm in control of me!"

6. Help children apply these three steps to as many other situations as time allows.

Process Time

1. Discuss the following questions:

> What did you learn about helpful and hurtful ways to deal with anger?
>
> How do you feel about yourself when you use better ways to deal with anger and don't end up getting in trouble or hurting other people?
>
> Does anyone else in the group feel the same way you do? Tell that person how you feel the same.
>
> What did you learn that you could try before the next session?
>
> Who would be willing to try these three steps?

2. Share snacks, if desired. Before saying good-bye, thank group members for coming and remind them of the meeting time for the next session.

Mad, Bad, Sad, Glad

Goals

1. To continue exploring the idea that anger is a normal feeling and that we need to learn to manage and express this emotion better
2. To encourage children to use relaxation as a way of dealing with tension and frustration that can lead to anger
3. To help children express their frustration or feelings of being overwhelmed or unable to cope.
4. To give children additional practice in the three-step stress-inoculation procedure

Materials

Puppets or stuffed animals

A chair for each child

Progressive Muscle Relaxation Training Script (pp. 99–100)

A healthy snack, such as raisins in individual boxes, fruit, crackers, or juice (*optional*)

Group Session

Review

1. Welcome the children to group. Briefly go over the ground rules and the confidentiality rule.
2. Ask whether anyone has anything to share about practicing the three-step plan presented during the last session. Ask children to describe what worked and what didn't work in using the plan. What would they need to do to help them remember to use the plan in the future?

Working Time

1. Tell the children you are going to teach them a way to relax. They can use this way of relaxing before getting in a situation that may cause them to get very angry and upset or after the situation is over to calm down.
2. Have each group member choose a puppet or stuffed toy (if age-appropriate), then sit in a chair so there is plenty of room between them. Let them keep their animals or puppets beside them.
3. Read the Progressive Muscle Relaxation Training Script, going around to make sure each group member is doing the exercise correctly.
4. After the exercise, ask the children to have their puppet or stuffed animal "talk" to share a situation in which they felt afraid that they would get so mad they would be out of control. (Older children may prefer to voice their own ideas instead of using the puppet or stuffed animal.)
5. Use the situations children generate to practice the three steps in the stress-inoculation procedure, giving examples of coping and reinforcing statements:

   Step 1: Know what is coming. Try to relax.

   Step 2: Say calming things to yourself. Try to relax.

   Step 3: Praise yourself! Try to relax.

Process Time

1. Discuss the following questions:

   What is it about anger that is scary?

   (If appropriate) Was it easier to tell about your situation by using a puppet or stuffed animal?

   What did you learn about yourself today in group?

   What did you learn about the other group members?

   Did anyone share something that made you feel connected? Tell that person how you feel.

   What situation might be coming up that you could make better by using your relaxing and coping skills?

2. Share snacks, if desired. Before saying good-bye, thank group members for coming and remind them of the meeting time for the next session.

Worry Warts

> NOTE: This session presents the technique of behavioral contracting. Behavior contracts require that teachers and/or parents be willing to monitor, encourage, and reinforce appropriate behaviors. You will need to arrange to have the contract monitored every day or even every half-day if the children cannot maintain appropriate behavior for an entire day. If a child is unable to manage behavior even for a half-day, he or she will likely need a more concentrated form of individual therapy.

Goals

1. To continue to clarify the idea that anger can be managed before it is out of control
2. To encourage appropriate expression of angry feelings
3. To suggest that worrying doesn't help us control anger—making a plan to change behavior does
4. To introduce the idea of using individual contracts for behavior change and to help children develop such contracts

Materials

A bag of jelly dots

Behavior Contract Form (Handout 6)

Progressive Muscle Relaxation Training Script (pp. 99–100) or some soothing music

Group Session

Review

1. Welcome the children to group. Briefly go over the ground rules and the confidentiality rule.
2. Ask whether anyone has anything to share from the last session, on using relaxation to deal with situations in which the children tend to get angry.
3. Ask whether anyone is noticing being able to deal with anger any better:

   What is working?

   What is not?

   What do you need to do better?

   Who else in the group is having problems like yours? Tell them so and ask them to give you some words of encouragement.

Working Time

1. Bring the bag of jelly dots to the group circle. Ask whether anyone has ever had or seen a wart. (A child may actually have a wart—usually everyone has seen one.) Tell them that a wart on your body is a growth that sometimes becomes very irritating because it rubs against something else. If the wart is on your foot, it might rub against your shoe. If it is on your finger, it might rub against a pencil. Stress the idea that a wart is something irritating but that we can do something about it by getting treatment. Worries about managing anger are the same: They will get better faster if you have the courage to do something about them.

2. Ask group members whether they have ever heard of being a "worry wart." This means someone who worries a lot about things he or she can't control. Ask them whether they ever worry and worry and worry and feel as though they can't do anything about a situation.

3. Let each child take a handful of "worry warts" (jelly dots). Share one of your own worries first. For example: "This purple worry wart reminds me that I have been worrying about the window on my car that I need to get fixed. I'll call today and make an appointment to get it worked on." Then eat the "worry wart" (jelly dot). Go around the circle and encourage children to do the same.

4. Next ask group members whether they know what a *contract* is and show them the Behavior Contract Form (Handout 6). Talk about the kinds of contracts adults make (for example, a contract to buy a car or house or to do a job) and explain that a contract means giving your word that you will do something. Tell group members that they will have the opportunity to make a contract to try to change their behavior before the next session.

5. Contract individually with each child who wishes to do so to meet a specific anger management need. Explain that you may need to consult teachers and/or parents to work out all of the details of the agreement and to provide a good reward for working on behavior.

6. If time permits, read from the Progressive Muscle Relaxation Training Script or have group members relax by listening to some soothing music.

Process Time

1. Discuss the following questions:

> What did you learn about yourself in group today?
>
> How did it feel when you got to eat your "worry wart"?
>
> What did you learn about making contracts to do something?
>
> Did anyone share something that made you feel connected? If so, tell that person how you feel.
>
> What problems do you think you might have with your contract?
>
> How will having a contract help you get control of your anger?

2. Let the children finish eating the jelly dots. Before saying good-bye, thank group members for coming and remind them of the meeting time for the next session.

Behavior Contract Form

Name _____

Dates of contract: From _____ to _____

The angry behavior(s) I will work on is/are: _____

_____

_____

The way(s) I am going to change my behaviors is/are:

_____Count to 10 before saying anything.

_____Decide just how angry I am about the situation (low, medium, high).

_____Think about consequences of my behavior.

_____Walk away from the situation.

_____Tell the person I am angry.

_____ Ask an adult to listen and give me a hug.

_____Other_____

_____Other_____

The person(s) I am going to practice controlling my anger with is/are:_____

_____

_____

The reward I want to receive for controlling my anger is:_____

_____

The bonus I will receive for using _____positive behaviors to deal with anger in one day/week (circle) is:

_____

The penalty for using angry, hurtful behaviors is:_____

_____

Agreed to by_____ and _____

Date signed _____ Date reviewed _____

Shake It Till You Make It

NOTE: This session is designed to help children get in touch with their angry feelings, but participants must remember not to hurt other kids in the group. Therefore, emphasize that there is to be no hurting of other group members.

Goals

1. To encourage children to keep using behavioral contracts and the other techniques they have learned to deal with anger

2. To promote awareness of the role of physical tension in anger

3. To help children learn appropriate loud, physical ways to manage anger as well as soft, soothing ways

4. To give children the opportunity to experience physical relief from some frustrating circumstance and gain a sense of control over the situation/environment

Materials

Any materials you have on hand for aggression release—for example, a large wastebasket and a stack of magazines; a basketball, volleyball, or soccer ball; a clean, new flyswatter; a stack of old newspapers; nerf balls or pillows; bean-bags and target

A healthy snack, such as raisins in individual boxes, fruit, crackers, or juice *(optional)*

Group Session

Review

1. Welcome the children to group. Briefly go over the ground rules and the confidentiality rule.

2. Ask group members to share progress on their contracted behaviors and discuss how their contracts worked or didn't work. Let anyone who wants to continue with the contract do so. (You may need to make contract changes individually outside of group time.)

Working Time

1. Discuss the idea that anger has a physical component—that we feel anger in our bodies. Encourage group members to identify exactly where in their bodies they feel anger (for example, neck muscles tense up, face flushes, palms sweat).

2. Discuss the idea that sometimes you can help yourself deal with anger by relaxing, listening to music, or doing other calming things. Other times you may feel the need to do something physical, to get out the anger and feelings of wanting to destroy something.

3. Show children the various materials you have brought and tell them that there are ways to get angry feelings out without hurting themselves or anyone else. Illustrate how to use the materials— for instance, tearing up magazines and throwing them in the wastebasket or throwing the bean-bags at the target as hard as they can.

4. Tell group members that you are going to ask them to close their eyes and imagine a situation that makes them very angry—for example, going home and finding out that a little brother or sister has been in their room and left things all over the floor. Tell them that when they imagine the scene they should try to make it as real as possible so they begin to feel in their bodies how angry they are. Instruct them to raise one finger when they have the physical feeling of being angry. Tell them not to raise a finger until they can see the scene and feel the angry feelings.

5. As the children raise their fingers to let you know they have visualized the scene, tell each one that he or she may choose one of the items available to reduce anger. Allow about 5 minutes of the aggression reduction activity.

6. Call the children back to the group circle and process the experience.

Process Time

1. Discuss the following questions:

> How are you feeling now about the angry scene you imagined?
>
> Did any other group members feel the same way you did? Tell them how you felt the same.
>
> What was it like for you to allow yourself to work your anger out without hurting anyone?
>
> What did you learn about yourself?
>
> How do you think you can use these ideas after you leave today?

2. Share snacks, if desired. Before saying good-bye, thank group members for coming and remind them of the meeting time for the next session.

I Am Not a Crybaby!

Goals

1. To encourage children to keep using behavioral contracts and the other techniques they have learned to deal with anger

2. To help children learn a way to deal with teasing without becoming aggressive

3. To give children the opportunity to watch someone else model this way of responding, then role-play the behaviors themselves

4. To encourage members to use these skills outside of the group

Materials

A healthy snack, such as raisins in individual boxes, fruit, crackers, or juice *(optional)*

Group Session

Review

1. Welcome the children to group. Briefly go over the ground rules and the confidentiality rule.

2. Ask whether anyone had the opportunity to try using one of the ways learned last session to get rid of angry feelings without hurting anyone else. Encourage children to share and be supportive of one another's attempts.

3. Ask group members to share progress on how their behavior contracts are working. Let anyone who wants to continue with the contracts do so, giving individual help outside group time as needed.

Working Time

1. Ask group members whether they know what a *model* is. (They usually say something about television or magazine models for clothing or beauty products.) Tell them that they can be models for one another to learn from and that today you are going to let them practice new ways to deal with teasing and bullying.

2. Explain that you are going to read two short stories or role-plays about teasing and bullying and that group members will have a chance to act out these stories and be models for one another. Read each of the following role-plays.

   #### Role-Play 1

   Phillip is 10 years old. He lives with his grandma because his mother doesn't have a job and can't afford to keep him with her and his dad is in prison. This situation has Phillip very upset because he is scared he is never going to have a home with his mom and dad. He used to, but now he has to live with his grandma. The bigger kids at school tease and razz him on the school bus—not too loud because the bus driver, Mr. B., makes them hush. But as soon as they get off the bus it gets really bad for Phillip. The kids call him names like "Gramabama baby" and "snot-nose Gramma's boy," and say cruel things like "Your daddy's a jailbird!" Phillip hates this, and it makes him furious. What can he do?

   #### Role-Play 2

   Rosie is 9 years old. She is partially sighted, which means that she has poor vision and has to wear special glasses to be able to see at all. Even with her special glasses she has to be careful because her eyes are not strong and she cannot see clearly. Some kids at school call her names, like "four-eyes," "bug-eyes," and "O' Great Blind One." Rosie gets very hurt and doesn't say anything, but you are Rosie's friend and want to help her deal with her hurt and anger. What can you do?

3. Have the children assign roles and act out Role-Play 1. Tell the person playing the main character to be angry and yell back at the persons doing the teasing and bullying.

4. Encourage group members to brainstorm some positive ways of dealing with the situation. For example:

> Ignore the person and walk away fast.
>
> Walk right up to the person and say, "Mind your own business."
>
> Say, "I feel hurt and angry when you say mean things."

5. Have the children act out Role-Play 1 again, this time having the main character use some of the more positive ideas. Have the group members who observed the role-play give their feedback on how well they think the approach would work. Help observers praise and encourage the actors.

6. Act out and process Role-Play 2 in the same way. Some positive ways of dealing with the situation would be as follows:

> Go up to Rosie and offer to walk with her away from the teasers.
>
> Ask her to share her feelings with you so she has someone who listens and understands.
>
> Offer to practice "I" statements with her (for example, "I feel hurt when you call me names, and I want you to stop")

7. Invite the children to share some of their own experiences in being teased and bullied. Role-play and process as many of these situations as time permits.

Process Time

1. Discuss the following questions:

> What did you learn about yourself today in group?
>
> How can you deal with people who bully or tease you?
>
> What does it feel like when you are not able to defend yourself with the right words?
>
> Do any other group members feel the same way you do? Tell them how you feel the same.
>
> How does it feel when you know what to do and don't let other kids get to you?
>
> What could you practice before the next session?

2. Share snacks, if desired. Before saying good-bye, thank group members for coming, tell them that the group will meet only two more times, and remind them of the meeting time for the next session.

Self as Model

Goals

1. To encourage children to keep using behavioral contracts and the other techniques they have learned to deal with anger

2. To help children practice appropriate assertive responses in difficult situations

3. To promote children's awareness of feelings of increased control associated with skill development

Materials

Easel pad and marker

A tape recorder and a couple of blank audiotapes (or a videotape recorder and videotapes, if available)

A healthy snack, such as raisins in individual boxes, fruit, crackers, or juice *(optional)*

Group Session

Review

1. Welcome the children to group. Briefly go over the ground rules and the confidentiality rule.

2. Ask whether anyone had an opportunity to practice the new way to deal with teasing. Did it help to watch other kids model what to say and do in a situation? Praise the children for their efforts.

3. Ask group members to share progress on how their behavior contracts are working. Let anyone who wants to continue with the contracts do so, giving individual help outside group time as needed.

4. Remind group members that the next session will be their last. Discuss any special celebration they would like to plan to help them say good-bye.

Working Time

1. Ask group members whether they have ever heard themselves on a tape recorder or seen themselves on videotape. Tell them that by using the tape (or videotape) recorder they can practice saying what they want and need in difficult situations.

2. Write the following steps on the easel pad:

   Step 1: Record statement/question.

   Step 2: Listen and get feedback.

   Step 3: Edit and rerecord.

   Step 4: Listen and get feedback.

   Step 5: Practice your statement with another person.

   For example: Jason needs to ask for help from the teacher, but the teacher is upset because Jason hasn't done his work all day and has been bugging her. How can he ask her without both of them getting mad?

   Step 1: Record statement/question. Ms. Lamb, uh, uh, would you please, uh, help me? I, well, I just don't know, let me see, I don't know what, uh, homework to do, or anything.

   Step 2: Listen and get feedback. You need to stop saying "uh" so much. Your voice needs to be stronger. Try not to be so wishy-washy (passive).

Step 3: Edit and rerecord. Ms. Lamb, I need some help to know what pages of math to do for homework. Would you please help me?

Step 4: Listen and get feedback. Much better! You sounded really good this time!

Step 5: Practice your statement with another person. Say the same thing to a group member.

3. Have group members think of situations in which they might be very angry or upset and have to say something to someone, then help each one follow the process just outlined. Do this with as many group members as time allows. Encourage everyone in the group to give helpful feedback.

4. Tell group members they can use this technique in many situations, not just those in which they think they may need help controlling their anger. For example, if they are going to sell candy bars or magazines for the school band and have to go door to door asking people to buy, they can record their sales speech and practice it a couple of times to improve.

Process Time

1. Discuss the following questions:

> What did you learn about yourself in group today?
>
> What was it like for you to practice saying things to manage stressful and anger-provoking situations?
>
> What was scary about it?
>
> What was fun about it?
>
> What helped you?
>
> Is this something you could use or practice at home? How?
>
> How do you feel now that you have learned a number of ways to deal with your anger?

2. Share snacks, if desired. Before saying good-bye, thank group members for coming and remind them of the meeting time for the last session.

Saying Good-bye

Goals

1. To give children the opportunity to review and process what they have learned during the group experience

2. To support and encourage children to continue to work on their anger-related issues

3. To model saying good-bye in a positive way

Materials

Construction paper in various colors

Crayons/markers

Whatever snacks or other materials children decided on for their good-bye party

Group Session

Review

1. Thank the children for coming to group. Briefly review the ground rules; remind them that the confidentiality rule holds even after group is over.

2. Ask whether any group members practiced saying something difficult to someone else. Did rehearsing what they wanted to say help them say it in a positive way?

3. Ask group members to share progress on how their behavior contracts have worked for them so far. Does this seem like a good way to change behavior?

Working Time

1. Review the content of the previous sessions, asking children what they learned and how it has helped them manage their anger:

> How did it feel to know that other group members have some of the same angry feelings you do?
>
> What are three steps you can use to help you deal with your anger?
>
> What was it like to use a behavior contract?
>
> How can you use relaxing before you get in a difficult situation?
>
> What can you do to get rid of your worries?
>
> How did it feel to work out your anger in an active way—for example, by tearing magazines or throwing a bean-bag?
>
> What are some ways to deal with teasing and bullying?
>
> What can you do before you have to say something difficult to someone to help you control your anger?

2. Ask the following kinds of general questions as well:

What did you like best about coming to this group?

What was the most boring part of it?

What was the scariest part of being a group member?

What did you learn that you think will be the most help to you?

Who did you learn something from that you think will help you a lot? Tell that person what you learned and say thank-you. (Encourage everyone to connect with at least one other person in the group.)

3. Pass out the construction paper and crayons or markers. Have the children fold a sheet of construction paper in half, top to bottom, then hold it sideways so it opens like a greeting card. Have them trace around a hand on the front, then write their names and "says good-bye" (for example, "Mindy says good-bye").

4. Encourage children to circulate and write a line on each other group member's card telling that person something positive. For example: "Joey, you sure have a lot of patience! Thanks for helping me calm down." At the end of this activity everyone should have his or her own card back to remember the group.

Process Time

1. Discuss the following questions:

What did you like about the activity today?

What will you remember most about this group?

2. Thank group members for coming and let them know you appreciate all their hard work. If appropriate, tell group members that you will be available to them so they can continue working on their problems with anger.

3. Share the snacks and celebrate!

I'm Responsible _____

Most parents and teachers today have been affected by the two opposing philosophies of child rearing prevalent during the 1950s and 1960s: the authoritarian approach and the permissive approach. These polar extremes in child-rearing practice appear to have produced a great many individuals who are largely inflexible or self-centered (Sheehan, 1987). Since that time we have experienced an upheaval in our ways of thinking about, valuing, and educating children. Movements to secure personal rights, such as women's liberation, gay rights, and civil rights for racial minorities, have affected our views of how we raise and educate children. Increased child abuse and involvement of children with the justice system, the changing legal status of minors in custody decisions, and other societal changes have also prompted child development specialists, researchers, educators, and the therapeutic community to devise ways of teaching personal, moral, and social responsibility (Dinkmeyer & McKay, 1973, 1982; Dreikurs, 1968; Glasser, 1969; Hall, 1979; Simon & Olds, 1976). The current emphasis is on children's rights and responsibilities—on helping children become fully functioning members of a multicultural, pluralistic society.

At first responsibility appears to be a simple, straightforward concept. However, personal responsibility actually occurs in several spheres, including responsibility toward the self, responsibility toward others, moral responsibility, and legal responsibility. How does one go about inculcating these abstract concepts in a child so that he or she will become a responsible adult? The literature seems to agree on one thing: Children will learn to become responsible only if given responsibility and if their efforts are monitored and reinforced by significant adults.

In our society, adults have accepted much responsibility for the child. This tendency is evidenced by the emotions we feel about our children's behavior and misbehavior. We still tend to see our children as reflections of ourselves, through our own overly controlling need to be perfect. It is difficult to produce children who can think for themselves and be responsible for their own behavior if the adults in their lives require submission, unquestioning behavior, and little if any democratic discussion of cooperative ventures (Dreikurs, 1968; Sheehan, 1987).

A child does not automatically arrive at the age of 18 being mature and responsible. Responsible behaviors have to be taught and nurtured from infancy. The preschool and early school years are especially important times for the child to become socially independent and sensitive to how he or she fits into the social sphere. Friendships become more and more important as the child moves through elementary school. During preadolescence, the child is still strongly attached to the family as the primary source of emotional strength and values learning. The teenager is most heavily influenced by peers and age-related social figures such as sports and music stars. A sense of responsibility is important throughout all these phases of development. When a child feels inadequate and lacks the skills to progress socially, future relationships as well as academic ability are often compromised. As Dreikurs (1968) asserts, "The greatest obstacle to growth and development, to learning and to improved functioning . . . is discouragement, doubt in one's own ability" (p. 8).

Group Goals

1. To provide a safe and accepting environment for children to explore the concept of responsibility and relate it to their own behavior

2. To provide the opportunity for children to practice responsibility exercises with others their age and skill level

3. To help children learn what goals are and how to set goals and make plans to reach them

4. To encourage exploration of feelings related to being responsible and fulfilling social expectations

Selection and Other Guidelines

The general selection guidelines described in Part 1 apply to this group agenda. The following more specific signals may also indicate that a child might profit from participating in this group experience.

1. Lack of awareness of other children's feelings

2. Difficulty making decisions or choosing between alternatives

3. Shyness or poor impulse control

4. A shorter than average attention span

5. Difficulty knowing right from wrong with regard to the effect of behavior on others

6. Difficulty predicting how others will react to a particular behavior

7. The apparent need to "win" at all costs

Be sure to choose members so that the group is heterogeneous for coping skills in terms of responsibility. Do not overload the group with children having one particular kind of deficit, or the group will have insufficient role models or motivation for change.

If several children have difficulty staying on task and appear to need more help and support, you might want to meet twice weekly with this group or have group members report to you individually once during the week so you can reinforce their efforts. If a child seems to be too far from the norm of behavior—for example, is very shy or has an extremely short attention span—it is probably best to make a referral for individual counseling. Such children may respond to group work after a period of individual therapy.

References and Suggested Resources for Professionals

Dinkmeyer, D., & McKay, G. (1973). *Raising a responsible child*. New York: Simon & Schuster.

Dinkmeyer, D., & McKay, G. (1982). *The parent's handbook: Systematic Training for Effective Parenting*. Circle Pines, MN: American Guidance Service.

Dreikurs, R. (1968). *Psychology in the classroom* (2nd ed.). New York: Harper & Row.

Dreikurs, R., Grunwald, B., & Pepper, F. (1971). *Maintaining sanity in the classroom: Illustrated teaching techniques*. New York: Harper & Row.

Glasser, W. (1969). *Schools without failure*. New York: Wyden.

Hall, R. (1979). *Moral education: A handbook for teachers*. Minneapolis: Winston.

Sheehan, C. (1987). Children and responsibility. In A. Thomas & J. Grimes (Eds.), *Children's needs: Psychological perspectives*. Silver Springs, MD: National Association for School Psychologists.

Simon, S., & Olds, S. (1976). *Helping your child learn right from wrong*. New York: McGraw-Hill.

Bibliography for Children

Berenstain, S., & Berenstain, J. (1983). *The Berenstain Bears' messy room*. New York: Random House. (Kindergarten–Grade 3)

Berry, J. (1986). *Every kid's guide to making and managing money*. (Available from Paperbacks for Educators, 426 West Front Street, Washington, MO 63090) (Grades 3–7)

Berry, J. (1987). *Every kid's guide to laws that relate to school and work*. (Available from Paperbacks for Educators, 426 West Front Street, Washington, MO 63090) (Grades 3–7)

Berry, J. (1987). *Every kid's guide to nutrition and health care*. (Available from Paperbacks for Educators, 426 West Front Street, Washington, MO 63090) (Grades 3–7)

Berry, J. (1987). *Every kid's guide to using time wisely*. (Available from Paperbacks for Educators, 426 West Front Street, Washington, MO 63090) (Grades 3–7)

Berry, J. (1988). *Being messy*. (Available from Paperbacks for Educators, 426 West Front Street, Washington, MO 63090) (Kindergarten–Grade 3)

Berry, J. (1988). *Being wasteful*. (Available from Paperbacks for Educators, 426 West Front Street, Washington, MO 63090) (Kindergarten–Grade 3)

Berry, J. (1988). *Breaking promises*. (Available from Paperbacks for Educators, 426 West Front Street, Washington, MO 63090) (Kindergarten–Grade 3)

Berry, J. (1988). *Disobeying*. (Available from Paperbacks for Educators, 426 West Front Street, Washington, MO 63090) (Kindergarten–Grade 3)

Berry, J. (1988). *Gossiping*. (Available from Paperbacks for Educators, 426 West Front Street, Washington, MO 63090) (Kindergarten–Grade 3)

Berry, J. (1988). *Overdoing it*. (Available from Paperbacks for Educators, 426 West Front Street, Washington, MO 63090) (Kindergarten–Grade 3)

Brown, K. (1990). *Muledred*. Orlando, FL: Harcourt Brace Jovanovich. (Grades 2–5)

Davis, L. (1990). *Kelly Bear behavior*. Layfayette, AL: Kelly Bear Books. (Preschool–Grade 3)

Davis, L. (1991). *Kelly Bear health*. Layfayette, AL: Kelly Bear Books. (Preschool–Grade 3)

Erickson, D. (1992). *More prime time activities with kids*. Minneapolis: Augsburg.

Gauch, P. (1987). *Christina Katerina and the time she quit the family*. New York: Putnam. (Grades 1–4)

Goffe, T. (1990). *Charm school*. New York: Child's Play. (Grades 2–6)

Hallinan, P. (1990). *Live and let live*. Center City, MN: Hazelden. (Kindergarten–Grade 4)

Hazen, B. (1981). *Even if I did something awful*. New York: Aladdin. (Preschool–Grade 3)

Jams, E., & Barkin, C. (1988). *How to be school smart: Secrets of successful schoolwork*. New York: Morrow. (Grades 4–7)

Kostick, D. (1992). *The biography of me: A journey of self-discovery*. New York: Good Apple. (Grades 5–9)

Lester, H. (1985). *It wasn't my fault*. Boston: Houghton Mifflin. (Preschool–Grade 3)

Riger, R. (1993). *One frog can make a difference: Kermit's guide to life in the 90's*. New York: Pocket Books.

Ross, A. (1992). *Grover's 10 terrific ways to help our wonderful world*. New York: Random House. (Preschool–Grade 3)

Schwartz, L. (1990). *What would you do? A kid's guide to tricky and sticky situations*. Santa Barbara, CA: Learning Works. (Grades 1–6)

Schwartz, L. (1991). *Responsible Rascal: Understanding responsibility*. Santa Barbara, CA: Learning Works. (Kindergarten–Grade 3)

Seuss, Dr. (1987). *I am not going to get up today!* New York: Random House. (Kindergarten–Grade 3)

Steel, D. (1990). *Martha's new puppy*. New York: Delacorte. (Kindergarten–Grade 2)

Wilson, S. (1990). *The day Henry cleaned his room*. New York: Simon & Schuster. (Preschool–Grade 3)

Wirths, C. (1989). *Where's my other sock? How to get organized and drive your parents and teachers crazy*. New York: Crowell. (Grade 5 and up)

Zerafa, J. (1982). *Go for it!* New York: Workman. (Grades 5–10)

Ziefert, H. (1991). *Sometimes I share*. New York: HarperCollins. (Preschool–Grade 1)

Ziegler, S. (1989). *Fairness*. Mankato, MN: Child's World. (Kindergarten–Grade 3)

Getting Started

> NOTE: Before the session, prepare a large sheet of butcher paper or newsprint by writing three headings at the top: *Self*, *Others*, and *School*. Post this chart on the wall.

Goals

1. To introduce children to the group experience and help them begin to get acquainted
2. To establish ground rules and discuss the issue of confidentiality
3. To discuss the purpose of the group and prepare children for the sessions ahead
4. To help children become aware that the group is a safe environment for sharing ideas, feelings, and behaviors
5. To introduce the concept of responsibility and help children begin to understand that responsibility is expressed in the form of behavior

Materials

Easel pad and marker

Large sheet of butcher paper or newsprint

4 × 6–inch index cards

Pencils/pens

A healthy snack, such as raisins in individual boxes, fruit, crackers, or juice *(optional)*

Group Session

Ice Breaker

1. Welcome the children to group. Describe the purpose of the group as learning new things about being a responsible person in order to help them at home and school.
2. Discuss basic ground rules for the group, giving group members some examples:

   > Everyone gets a chance to talk.
   >
   > No hitting or fighting in group.
   >
   > Take turns.

   Ask for group members' input to help them develop "ownership." List the ground rules on an easel pad so everyone can see, then post them during each session.
3. Discuss the confidentiality rule and its limits. For example, you might say:

   > When we talked about your being in the group, I told you that whatever we say in our group is *confidential*. That means what we say is private. You may talk about your own thoughts, feelings, and actions, but you may not share anything others in the group talk about. There are some special times when I would have to share what you say—if you say something about harming yourself or others, if you share something about child abuse, or if the court (a judge) asks me about what goes on.

Working Time

1. Discuss the concept of responsibility, pointing out that there are really three kinds of responsibility. Read the following scenarios aloud to the group to help clarify this idea.

Responsibility to Self

Taylor is 11 years old and just got braces on his teeth. He wanted to get the new rainbow braces that are different colors, but they cost more than the regular "ugly" ones and require him to brush after every meal with a special powder to keep his teeth from staining. Taylor begged his parents to get the rainbow braces. He said he would do the extra brushing and his parents would never have to nag or remind him. He got the braces, and for a few weeks he brushed regularly with the special powder, even though it didn't taste as good as regular toothpaste. Then he got tired of brushing with the special powder at school and of the nasty taste it left in his mouth. He didn't even use regular toothpaste for his noon brushing—just gave the braces a rinse with water instead. Soon the braces started losing their rainbow colors, and it was time for Taylor to go to the orthodontist again.

What would you tell Taylor about responsibility?

What kind of responsibility is this?

Responsibility to Others

Madison is 10 years old and delivers sales catalogs for Mrs. Phillips, who sells beauty products. It is Madison's job to take the catalogs around the neighborhood and put them in people's mailboxes so they can look through them and call Mrs. Phillips if they want to make an order. Now Madison has heard about trying out for the Pep Team. If she gets to be on the Pep Team, she can go to the games and do pep cheers when the junior high cheerleaders are not doing their routines. Lots of her friends are going to try very hard to get on the Pep Team, and she wants to try out, too. If she gets on the Pep Team, she will not have time to deliver the catalogs. But she has promised Mrs. Phillips that she will deliver catalogs until Christmas.

What would you tell Madison about responsibility?

What kind of responsibility is this?

Responsibility at School

Sarah is 9 years old and in third grade. Sarah's mom is an orthopedic doctor and tells Sarah all about the clinic she works in and how she helps people with bone problems. Sarah wants to be a doctor like her mom when she grows up. But there is a little problem: Sarah's report card was not very good this time because she has not been taking her homework home and completing it and taking it back to school the next day. She has trouble remembering which books to take home, and when she takes them home, she forgets what papers to complete. Sometimes she completes the papers but forgets to put them in her backpack to take to school the next day. And sometimes she gets them finished and takes them to school but loses them at school or forgets to turn them in to the teacher on time. All in all, Sarah has a real problem with homework!

What would you tell Sarah about responsibility?

What kind of responsibility is this?

2. Encourage children to brainstorm some responsible behaviors. Have them list these behaviors on the chart under the appropriate headings. (There may be some overlap among the three categories.)

> *Self*
> Raking the yard
> Taking a bath
> Keeping your room clean
> Putting your bike away
> Brushing your teeth
>
> *Others*
> Feeding pets
> Stopping at stop signs
> Walking your sister to the bus
> Saying thank-you
> Putting cans in the recycle bin
>
> *School*
> Doing homework
> Taking care of books and materials
> Talking nicely to teachers
> Walking (not running) in the halls

3. Next ask the following questions:

> What kind of responsibilities do you have?
> Where do responsibilities come from?
> How do you feel when you have finished or met one of your responsibilities?
> How do you feel when you do not behave responsibly?
> Does anyone else think or feel the way you do? If so, how?

4. Ask the children whether they would be willing to name one responsibility that they have a difficult time meeting and make a pledge to the group that they will do it and then report back to the group the next session. Try to get each child to "name and pledge." If desired, as a group decide on a reward that children who "do the responsible thing" can earn. Some possibilities include special pencils, erasers, stickers, and so forth.

5. Pass out the index cards. Have each child write on an index card the responsibility he or she is going to work on. Explain that group members are to have the adult who supervises that responsibility sign the card before the next group session. Remind them to bring the card to group next time—emphasize that completing the task is part of being responsible.

6. Have the children make encouraging statements to one another. For example:

> Chris, you can do it!
> Yusef, give it your best effort!
> Tiffany, do the tough thing!

Process Time

1. Discuss the following questions:

   What did you learn about responsibility today?

   How do you feel about your responsibilities?

   What are you going to do to remind yourself of your pledge?

   What can you do to reward yourself every day for being responsible?

2. Share snacks, if desired. Before saying good-bye, thank group members for coming and remind them of the meeting time for the next session.

Responsible by the Light of the Moon

Goals

1. To establish the norm of reviewing what happened during the previous session
2. To help children understand how being responsible affects everyone
3. To promote the realization that some responsibilities are difficult and some are easy to meet
4. To help children learn that meeting our responsibilities, whether difficult or easy, will help us feel good about ourselves

Materials

Rewards specified in Session 1 *(optional)*

4×6–inch index cards

Pencils/pens

A healthy snack, such as raisins in individual boxes, fruit, crackers, or juice *(optional)*

Group Session

Review

1. Thank the children for coming to group. Briefly go over the ground rules and the confidentiality rule.
2. Ask group members whether they would be willing to share their pledge cards. If desired, give the children who attempted the behavioral homework the reward specified. Praise them for working on being a responsible person and encourage the other children in the group to praise them also.

Working Time

1. Read the following story aloud.

Responsible by the Light of the Moon

In the land of Idego there lived a boy named Frank and his stepsister Ena. Now Frank and Ena used to play together down the street where new houses were being built. There they could climb around the stacks of lumber and peek in as the houses went up.

In the land of Idego everyone was very responsible. Even the dogs and cats were responsible. Frank and Ena came from a very responsible family, where their mom and dad held responsible jobs and taught them to be responsible kids. Sometimes Frank and Ena thought that they would like to have things different, that all of this being responsible was too much work and no fun. Now what you need to know is that all of this responsibility was caused by an extra moon shining on Idego.

One day, the people of Idego saw a great meteor shower, and they knew that some humongous event had taken place in the skies. That night they knew because their special moon did not come out!

The next day, things were different in the land. The feeling of wanting to be responsible had disappeared with their moon. They began to call the missing moon the "Responsibility Moon" because when it went away, so did their desire to be responsible. What happened was this: No one wanted to finish any work. The house builders just sat around all day eating sandwiches and talking. The people in the grocery store didn't stock the shelves, so there were no groceries to buy. The teachers didn't feel like being responsible and doing their jobs, so the kids couldn't learn anything.

At first Frank and Ena thought this was terrific, like summer vacation all year round. But then their parents weren't feeling very responsible either, and they wouldn't take care of the kids. The dogs and cats went around tearing up people's yards, and there were constant fender benders because people wouldn't be responsible and stop their cars at stop signs. What a world! It seemed crazy to Frank and Ena. They couldn't even get a hamburger at their favorite burger place because the kids who worked there didn't show up for their shift.

After a while, Frank and Ena didn't like this irresponsible world. They decided they had to find another place to live because this one was so disorganized. They worried and worried about the future, and they felt bad when their friends behaved irresponsibly toward them. They worried when they thought about their property, their pets, their teachers, and certainly about their parents, who were loafing around on the back porch instead of doing their work.

Frank and Ena decided to turn on the evening news and see whether the rest of the world was also in this sad state of affairs. So they watched, and the news reporter said that there had been another meteor shower that day and big things had happened in the skies! The children went upstairs and looked out the windows of their rooms. Both Frank and Ena saw that their special "Responsibility Moon" was back! Did this mean that the land of Idego was back on track, with people doing their jobs, treating one another with concern, and caring about one another's personal rights?

Well, when Frank and Ena woke up in the morning, their mom and dad were ready for work and had a plate of pancakes ready that the whole family ate hungrily. Ena thought that this was a good sign. Frank ran to the window and saw people driving off to work, and the school bus driver was honking for them.

Off they went to school, where everything was back to normal. There was the principal, Mrs. Howard, smiling at the kids as they got off their bus. How comforting! How secure! How wonderful to know that people were going to do what they said they would do, that people would treat one another with respect and kindness and behave responsibly!

Frank and Ena used to think that responsibility was too much work, but now they thought that a world with responsibility was much better than a world without responsibility.

2. Begin a discussion of how being responsible affects other people as well as ourselves. Help group members share how it feels to be responsible. The following questions may help:

Why didn't Frank and Ena like being so responsible? (Responsibility takes planning, energy, follow up, and work. Sometimes it means doing things we don't like to do.)

Why were they upset when all of a sudden people around them stopped being responsible?

What would happen if people around you stopped being responsible?

What would you miss most?

3. Ask group members whether they would be willing to tackle another responsibility. Encourage children to fill out another responsibility card if they wish.

Process Time

1. Discuss the following questions:

    What is fun about being responsible?

    What is hard about being responsible?

    What feels good about being responsible?

    What kinds of feelings do you have when you are not responsible?

    Since the last session, how much effort did it take for you to be responsible?

2. Share snacks, if desired. Before saying good-bye, thank group members for coming and remind them of the meeting time for the next session.

Chocolate, Strawberry, and Vanilla Responsibilities

Goals

1. To help children take a closer look at their responsibilities in terms of their being personal, social, or school related

2. To encourage understanding that some responsibilities cannot be met in a few minutes but take planning, continued effort, and the help and cooperation of others

3. To help children distinguish between short- and long-term responsibilities

Materials

Rewards specified in Session 1 *(optional)*

Chocolate-Strawberry-Vanilla Responsibilities (Handout 7)

My Responsibilities Chart (Handout 8)

4 x 6–inch index cards

Pencils/pens

Chocolate, strawberry, and vanilla ice cream cups (or at least a couple of different flavors)

Group Session

Review

1. Remind children of the ground rules and the confidentiality rule.

2. Ask whether anyone has another completed responsibility card. Reinforce those who are working on their responsibilities with lots of praise and, if desired, special rewards.

3. Discuss any additional thoughts children might have concerning the story read during the last session, about what it would be like if everyone around suddenly became irresponsible.

Working Time

1. Give each child a Chocolate-Strawberry-Vanilla Responsibilities page (Handout 7). Explain that the drawings show that we have responsibilities to ourselves, to others, and at school—like having three "flavors." Ask children what their favorite flavors are and let them color the ice cream drawings.

2. Next give each group member a copy of the My Responsibilities Chart (Handout 8). Have them work on filling in what their responsibilities are in the three areas and deciding how they feel about each one. Help them fill in the charts and spell any words they don't know. The sample on page 160 shows how a filled-in chart might look.

3. Ask children to share what their biggest responsibilities are in the three areas. Discuss.

4. Brainstorm some things people have to do that take a long time. For example:

> Building a dog house
>
> Doing a book report
>
> Doing a science project
>
> Babysitting a brother or sister every day

5. Talk about how long the children's different responsibilities take to meet. Which ones take a short time? Which ones take longer? Help children understand that longer term responsibilities often take planning, persistence, patience, and the help of other people.

6. Encourage children to fill out another responsibility card if they wish.

Process Time

1. Discuss the following questions:

   What did you learn about different types of responsibilities?

   What is different about tasks that take a long time and ones that take a short time?

   How can you use what you learned today to help you before the next session?

2. Share the ice cream. Before saying good-bye, thank group members for coming and remind them of the meeting time for the next session.

Chocolate-Strawberry-Vanilla Responsibilities

SELF

OTHERS

SCHOOL

My Responsibilities Chart (Sample)

Instructions: Write down what responsibilities you have in each area. Draw a face on the line beside each one to show how you feel about it.

😊 = I like it.

😊 = It's OK.

☹ = I don't like it.

My responsibilities to myself

1. _Clean my room._ _____ 😊

2. _Do my homework._ _____ ☹

3. _Feed my cat, JoJo._ _____ 😊

4. _____ _____

My responsibilities to others

1. _Watch my baby sister._ _____ ☹

2. _Walk home with my brother._ _____ 😊

3. _Listen to my other sister read._ _____ ☹

4. _____ _____

My responsibilities at school

1. _Shut off my computer._ _____ 😊

2. _Keep my desk neat._ _____ ☹

3. _Pay my lunch money._ _____ 😊

4. _Keep my feet off the bus seats._ _____ ☹

My Responsibilities Chart

Instructions: Write down what responsibilities you have in each area. Draw a face on the line beside each one to show how you feel about it.

😊 = I like it.

🙂 = It's OK.

☹️ = I don't like it.

My responsibilities to myself

1. _____   _____

2. _____   _____

3. _____   _____

4. _____   _____

My responsibilities to others

1. _____   _____

2. _____   _____

3. _____   _____

4. _____   _____

My responsibilities at school

1. _____   _____

2. _____   _____

3. _____   _____

4. _____   _____

I'm Responsible for Me

> NOTE: This session involves children in cooperating to make cookies. Before beginning, type the steps in making the cookies on separate index cards. Be sure to supervise the children carefully while they are using the hot plate or stove top!

Goals

1. To teach the idea that being responsible means doing what we say we are going to do and being sensitive to other people's needs and rights

2. To help children understand that being responsible is something we do for ourselves, not because someone is forcing us to be responsible

3. To encourage the realization that we can reach goals and get what we want out of life by being responsible

Materials

Rewards specified in Session 1 *(optional)*

Ingredients specified in the recipe for No-Bake Oatmeal M & M Cookies

Mixing equipment (medium saucepan, mixing spoon, measuring cups and spoons, waxed paper, cookie sheet, teaspoons)

Hot plate or stove top

4 × 6–inch index cards

Pencils/pens

Group Session

Review

1. Welcome the children to group. Briefly remind them of the ground rules and the confidentiality rule.

2. Ask group members to share any responsibility cards they have completed since the last session. Reinforce those who are working on their responsibilities with praise and, if desired, special rewards.

3. Ask group members whether they have anything they would like to share from the last session, when they identified some of their biggest responsibilities and how they felt about them.

Working Time

1. Review the idea that we have different kinds of responsibilities: for ourselves, to others, and at school. Present the idea that being responsible for ourselves means that we do what we say we are going to do because people count on us. For example:

   > If I say I will do my chores, I do them.
   >
   > If I say I will brush my teeth, I do it.
   >
   > If I say I am honest, I am honest.
   >
   > If I say I will be back at 6:00, I am back then.
   >
   > If I say I will keep my room clean, I do it.

   Ask the children to generate additional examples.

2. Talk about how being responsible for our actions affects other people. Ask children to speculate on what would happen if you didn't do what you said you were going to do. What would other people think and feel about you?

3. Tell the children that they are going to make some special cookies together to see how being responsible for ourselves works. Then they can eat the cookies! (The recipe makes about 2 dozen.)

4. Have group members wash their hands, then let each one take an index card and follow the instructions written on it. (If you have more or fewer than eight children in the group, you may need to divide the responsibilities differently than suggested here.)

Recipe for No-Bake Oatmeal M & M Cookies

Card 1

Place all the ingredients and supplies on a clean table:

Margarine

Milk

Sugar

Peanut butter

Vanilla

M & Ms

Oatmeal

Medium saucepan

Mixing spoon

Measuring cups and spoons

Cookie sheet

Waxed paper

Teaspoons

Card 2

Put 1 stick margarine, 1/2 cup milk, and 2 cups sugar in the saucepan.
Turn on the heat.

Card 3

Stir the ingredients together in the pan. Cook at a boil for a minute,
stirring constantly.

Card 4

Take the pan off the heat. Add 1 teaspoon vanilla and 1/2 cup peanut butter
and stir, stir, stir!

Card 5

Add 1/2 cup M & M's to the mixture and stir, stir, stir!

Card 6

Add 3 cups oatmeal to the mixture and stir, stir, stir!

Card 7

Cover the cookie sheet with a piece of waxed paper and give each
group member a teaspoon (be sure to include yourself).

Card 8

Put all the ingredients away. Put all the cooking utensils in one place
to be washed up later.

5. Have everyone in the group help to drop spoonfuls of the mixture onto the cookie sheet. Let the cookies cool for 20 minutes or so (or put them in a refrigerator if one is handy to speed up the cooling).

6. While the cookies are cooling, reassemble the group and ask these questions:

   What did it feel like to have responsibility for one part of the recipe?

   What would have happened if you forgot to do your part or did it wrong?

   What would it feel like if you didn't do your part correctly?

   Do we always do everything right?

   What can you learn from making mistakes?

   Why do you think it is important to be responsible?

7. Ask group members whether they would be willing to tackle another responsibility. Encourage children to fill out another responsibility card if they wish.

Process Time

1. Discuss the following questions:

   What did you learn about being responsible for your own actions today?

   What if you are responsible? How will that make your life different than if you were irresponsible and didn't do what you said you would do?

   What are you willing to work on before the next session that would make you feel good about yourself as a responsible person?

2. Share the cookies. Before saying good-bye, thank group members for coming and remind them of the meeting time for the next session.

I'm Responsible to Others

Goals

1. To give children the opportunity to discuss the idea that we are responsible to other people and for our actions toward other people (in other words, social responsibility)

2. To help children understand that when they behave in ways that interfere with the rights of others, other people may view and react to them negatively

3. To help children understand that other children and adults have the right to expect personal respect, respect for belongings, and respect for rules of behavior (at home and in the classroom)

Materials

Rewards specified in Session 1 *(optional)*

4 × 6–inch index cards

Pencils/pens

A healthy snack, such as raisins in individual boxes, fruit, crackers, or juice *(optional)*

Group Session

Review

1. Welcome the children to group. Briefly go over the ground rules and the confidentiality rule.

2. Ask group members whether they have anything left over from the last session to share and whether they practiced any responsibilities since then. Reinforce those who are working on their responsibilities with praise and, if desired, special rewards.

Working Time

1. Present the idea that every person has the right to be treated with respect, including children. We do not like it when someone treats us badly by being unfair, saying ugly things about us, taking advantage of us, lying to us, and so on. Ask children to express how they feel when someone acts this way toward them, then point out that others feel the same way when we act irresponsibly.

2. Tell group members you are going to read some situations and that you will be asking them to pick out the responsible and irresponsible behaviors in each one.

   #### Situation 1

   Jake asked if he could ride his friend Carlos' new bike up and down the hill at the end of the neighborhood. Carlos had just received the bike for his birthday and didn't want to let anyone else ride it. But Jake begged and begged and promised that he would take special care of the fantastic new bike. So Carlos let Jake take the bike for a spin. Jake rode up and down the hill carefully, then he started riding faster and faster until he got out of control on the way down the hill and ran off into a ditch. He got all scratched up on sticker bushes, and he bent and dented Carlos' new bike.

   What is the responsibility involved in this story?

   How do you think Carlos felt?

   What could Jake learn from this situation?

   What could Carlos learn from this situation?

   How could they both do better in the future?

   How do you think Jake felt when he behaved irresponsibly?

Situation 2

Latonya and Kristin were friends in the fourth grade. They agreed to do a science project together because they both liked dinosaurs and thought it would be fun to learn and build a model together. They decided they were going to build a little lake with three kinds of dinosaurs coming to drink. This would show how big the different kinds of dinosaurs were next to each other and that all creatures need water to survive. Latonya and Kristin thought that they could get an A on their project if they did a good job. They decided who was going to do each part of the project. Latonya would work on the display board above the project, writing out the name of the project, types of dinosaurs, and what the project was about. Kristin was to paint the lake on a board and put trees and bushes in the landscape. They were going to make clay models of the dinosaurs together when they got the first parts of their project finished.

Kristin didn't do her part. She kept putting it off and putting it off. First she said she had to go to dance lessons on Saturday so she couldn't do it then. And she had to go to visit her sick grandma on Sunday, so she couldn't do it then. But really she just didn't want to do it and made excuses for not doing her part. Latonya, on the other hand, got busy and went to the library and read all about dinosaurs. She asked the science teacher lots of questions. She also watched a video on dinosaurs so she knew just what to say on the written part of the project. The Saturday came just before the project was due. The girls were going to meet to finish the clay models and put them in the display, but Kristin had not finished the lake and the bushes.

What do you think happened when Kristen and Latonya got together that day?

What happens to our friendships when we are not responsible?

What happens to our work when we are not responsible for what we are supposed to do?

Which of Latonya's rights did Kristin take away?

How do you think the two girls felt toward each other?

Situation 3

Jeremy, age 8, and Angie, age 10, live with their mom, their stepdad, their 16-year-old stepsister, Lisa, and their baby half-sister, Ashley. Every other weekend their dad comes to pick them up and take them for the weekend. Their dad and stepmom live with her children about 40 miles away. Sometimes their dad does not come to pick them up at the time he says he will, and Angie and Jeremy are left waiting and waiting for him to come. Sometimes he doesn't come at all and then calls later that day or another day and tells them he forgot to pick them up and take them wherever it is he promised to take them. This makes them very angry and disappointed!

This Saturday is the Harvest Homecoming, an annual festival in the city. Jeremy and Angie love to go each year because the rides are neat and the booths have stuff to buy. They always eat and eat great stuff like barbecued chicken, curly-q fries, candy apples, and cider and donuts. So they get up early Saturday morning and watch out the window for their dad as they dress. He said he is going to pick them up at 9:30 A.M. so they can get on a lot of the rides before it gets too crowded.

Well, 9:30 comes and goes—no dad. 10:00 goes by—no dad. 10:30—still no dad. More time goes by, and Jeremy and Angie are feeling awful. They know their friends are at the Harvest Homecoming, and they want to be there, too, with their dad! The day slowly drags by, and they stop watching out the window. Finally, it gets dark, and their mom and stepdad come home from their work and shopping, and there are Angie and Jeremy still sitting on the porch, looking very glum.

What are the responsibilities in this story?

Do adults have responsibilities to children?

Do children have responsibilities to adults?

What happens when either one is not responsible?

How do we feel when other people are not responsible toward us?

If people are angry or upset with us, do they still need to be responsible?

Do we still need to consider our responsibilities if we are angry and upset?

What is it about not being responsible that makes people mad?

3. Encourage children to fill out another responsibility card if they wish.

Process Time

1. Discuss the following questions:

What did you learn about the responsibility of adults to children?

What did you learn about yourself today?

What behaviors of yours do you think you could work on between now and the next session so that you can be more responsible?

2. Share snacks, if desired. Before saying good-bye, thank group members for coming and remind them of the meeting time for the next session.

I'm Responsible at School

NOTE: This session centers on a talk by the school principal about the importance of school rules. Before the session, invite the principal to meet with the group; ask him or her to briefly discuss some major school rules, how they got to be rules, and why they are important to keep things in order. Let the children ask why the rules are the way they are and talk about how they could be changed if needed.

Goals

1. To help children understand why there are rules for behavior at school and give children the opportunity to explore responsibility for their actions at school

2. To help children realize that their behavior is what is seen by other children and adults and that it forms the basis for their reputation

3. To help children become better acquainted with their school principal and the principal's part in developing school rules and maintaining order

Materials

Rewards specified in Session 1 *(optional)*

Copies of the student handbook or rules for your school (one for each group member)

4 × 6–inch index cards

Pencils/pens

A healthy snack, such as raisins in individual boxes, fruit, crackers, or juice *(optional)*

Group Session

Review

1. Briefly go over the ground rules and the confidentiality rule.

2. Ask whether anyone has another completed responsibility card. Reinforce those who are working on their responsibilities with lots of praise and, if desired, special rewards.

3. Ask whether anyone has anything to say about the last session, on being responsible to others.

Working Time

1. Distribute copies of the student handbook or school rules. Introduce the principal as a special guest and explain that he or she will be speaking about how school rules help keep order in the school.

2. After the principal's talk, encourage children to ask any questions to clarify why rules are necessary. Thank the principal for coming to the group and say good-bye.

3. After the principal leaves, be sure group members understand what would happen if everyone did not cooperate and live by the rules. An example like the following may help: "One rule is to walk in the halls—do not run. If everyone ran around in the halls, the smaller children might get hurt by the bigger children. This would take away everyone's right to be safe and to get to class on time so they can learn."

4. Discuss the following questions:

> What rule do you think we should always keep here at the school?
>
> What rule do you think is the hardest for you to keep? Why?
>
> What rule(s) do you think need to be changed? Why?
>
> What responsibilities do you have in your classroom?
>
> What responsibilities do you have to yourself in completing your schoolwork?
>
> Who loses if you don't do your schoolwork?
>
> What happens if you are not responsible about your schoolwork and your friendships? (You might get a reputation for being unreliable.)
>
> How is having a bad reputation a problem?
>
> How can you change a bad reputation?

5. Encourage children to fill out another responsibility card if they wish.

Process Time

1. Discuss the following questions:

> What did you learn about in group today?
>
> What were you feeling when the principal was talking about the school rules?
>
> What makes you angry about rules?
>
> What can you do about rules you think are unfair?
>
> What have you learned about being responsible at school?

2. Share snacks, if desired. Before saying good-bye, thank group members for coming, tell them that the group will meet only two more times, and remind them of the meeting time for the next session.

My Responsibilities to Nature

NOTE: Before this session, you may need to write a note to the principal, teachers, or other school staff to alert them that members of your group will be walking around the building looking for things to reuse and recycle.

Goals

1. To help children realize that we have responsibilities to the earth and its creatures
2. To encourage awareness that by taking care of nature we are being good citizens and that nature takes care of us in many ways

Materials

Rewards specified in Session 1 *(optional)*

Garbage bags

4 × 6–inch index cards

Pencils/pens

A story about the environment and why it is important to recycle and reuse, such as *One Frog Can Make a Difference: Kermit's Guide to Life in the 90's*, by Robert Riger (Pocket Books, 1993) or *More Prime Time Activities With Kids*, by Donna Erickson (Augsburg, 1992)

A healthy snack, such as raisins in individual boxes, fruit, crackers, or juice *(optional)*

Group Session

Review

1. Briefly go over the ground rules and the confidentiality rule.

2. Ask whether anyone has another completed responsibility card. Reinforce those who are working on their responsibilities with lots of praise and, if desired, special rewards.

3. Ask whether the children have anything they want to say about the last session, on school responsibilities.

4. Remind the children that the next session is the last one and that you will be spending the time reviewing and saying good-bye. Give them a chance to plan a special "responsibility party" for this last session.

Working Time

1. Review the idea that we have responsibilities toward ourselves, others, and school. Add that we also have to take care of plants, animals, and the earth. Ask group members to share what kinds of responsibilities they think might fit in this category. For example:

   Feeding the birds

   Helping out at the recycling center

   Being careful not to litter

   Helping other people understand the importance of reusing things (for example, reminding parents to reuse grocery bags and recycle newspapers and cans)

Donating time or money to nature preserves or environmental organizations

Cleaning up after ourselves

Not damaging wildflowers or helpful insects and animals

2. Send group members out in the school in pairs to look for things to recycle or reuse. Give each pair a garbage bag and instruct them to bring these items back to the group room or put them in the recycling area in your school, if you have one. Pairs should return within 15 minutes and should be careful not to disrupt classes, children who are studying, or teachers.

3. When the children return, have them wash their hands. Reassemble in the group circle and discuss the following questions:

How do you feel about being helpful and responsible toward your school environment?

What did other people say to you when you were doing this?

What else could you have done if you had more time?

What would happen if we did not recycle and reuse?

What could happen to the earth if we do not learn better ways of taking care of our oceans and land?

How could we let the other kids in the school know about these kinds of responsibilities?

4. Encourage children to fill out another responsibility card if they wish.

Process Time

1. Discuss what group members feel is the most important thing they learned today.

2. Share snacks, if desired. Before saying good-bye, thank group members for coming and remind them of the meeting time for the last session.

Saying Good-bye

Goals

1. To give children the opportunity to review and process what they have learned during the group experience

2. To help children solidify their learning on being responsible

3. To model saying good-bye in a positive way

Materials

Rewards specified in Session 1 *(optional)*

Whatever snacks or other materials children decided on during the last session for their "responsibility party"

Group Session

Review

1. Thank the children for coming to group. Briefly mention the ground rules and remind them that the confidentiality rule holds even after the group is over.

2. Ask whether anyone has another completed responsibility card. Reinforce those who are working on their responsibilities with praise and, if desired, special rewards.

3. Ask whether anyone has anything to share from the last session, on being responsible for things in nature. Did anyone try to be more responsible for the earth or his or her own space on the earth (for example, own yard or room)?

Working Time

1. Review the content of the previous sessions. The following discussion questions may help:

    What does being responsible mean?

    What are the areas in which you have responsibilities? (Self, others, school)

    If you are not responsible in your behavior, who will know this?

    What would the world be like if no one was responsible?

    What kinds of responsibilities do you have that take a long time and a lot of planning for you to accomplish?

    What are your biggest responsibilities?

    What are our responsibilities to nature and the environment?

2. Ask the following general types of questions as well:

    Who in the group has helped you understand your responsibilities better? Tell that person and say thank-you.

    How do you think being responsible will help you in the future?

Process Time

1. Thank the children for coming to group and for trying hard to learn more about responsibility. If appropriate, let them know that if other things bother them that they can come to see you individually and you will try to help them.

2. Use the rest of the time to enjoy your "responsibility party"!

Good Citizen's Club_____

Many children begin school with the need to master not only school readiness skills but also the social interaction skills that will help them become good citizens of the educational community. The reasons for this deficit are varied, including lack of or inappropriate behavioral role models, poor reinforcement or reinforcement for undesirable behavior, poor impulse control, family disorganization, psychopathology, and unaddressed special needs (Miller & Sperry, 1987). Whatever the reason, the result is the same—children who engage in inappropriate behaviors because they cannot cope with the social and learning environment.

The child who has begun to exhibit antisocial behaviors may not appear to understand his or her impact on peers and adults. Many times the child knows what the correct behavior is but is unable to produce that behavior in a social situation (Camp & Ray, 1984). Thus, the problem may be lack of know-how, or skill deficiency. The child also may have learned that maladaptive behavior has secondary gains—that is, it produces a desired outcome. For example, if the child needs attention and recognition, perhaps he or she is willing to accept the negative attention that will surely result from the act of stealing rather than no attention at all.

This group agenda is designed both to provide children with information for insight and understanding and to teach them the skills and coping methods required for appropriate behavior. The topics covered include those most commonly viewed as detrimental to good citizenship: homework problems, aggression, lying, cheating, stealing, and teasing.

Control of aggressive impulses is central to good citizenship. Three major theoretical orientations toward aggression exist, each with a different view of the causes, maintenance, and control of aggression (Harmon & Evans, 1984; Kendall & Braswell, 1985; Kirkland & Thelen, 1977).

The first approach is the biological/psychological approach. Some research indicates that aggressive behavior responds to pharmacological treatment and neurological electrical impulses and that genetic factors may be involved in producing increasingly aggressive generations (Achenbach, 1982; Delgado, 1969). The second approach, Freudian psychoanalytic drive theory,

espouses the idea that aggressive behavior is controlled by basic instinctual drives and is a response to alleviate tension and frustration (Kauffman, 1981). The third approach to aggression, social learning theory (Bandura, 1973), encompasses some psychobiological components but explains aggression primarily as a learned response to a complex series of events. The sessions here are based on social learning theory—in other words, on the assumption that the development and maintenance of aggressive behavior in children is learned.

Three points are important to keep in mind regarding the learned nature of aggression, as well as of lying, stealing, and teasing.

1. Aggressive behavior is learned by observing others, usually those the child values.

2. Aggressive behavior will increase if allowed to continue and when reinforced by social status, recognition, avoidance of punishment, or other means.

3. Aggressive behavior increases or escalates when children experience some type of stress, such as frustration, threat, or crisis.

4. Children maintain aggressive behavior by believing it is justified (Zlomke & Piersel, 1987).

Group sessions on topics other than aggression also involve behavioral and cognitive-behavioral approaches to work with children. Extensive research has been conducted on these topics; specific references for more in-depth study and evaluation appear in the resource list for professionals at the end of this discussion.

Group Goals

1. To clarify what constitutes good and poor citizenship so children can learn which behaviors are acceptable and which are not

2. To help increase children's understanding of why certain behaviors are not acceptable (in other words, to raise their level of moral reasoning)

3. To help children understand how their behavior affects others as well as themselves

4. To provide role models from whom children can learn appropriate behaviors

5. To help children learn to brainstorm alternative, positive ways to behave to get their needs met

6. To teach coping and other appropriate skills so children can make use of alternative strategies

Selection and Other Guidelines

It is important to follow the general guidelines for selection provided in Part 1. In addition, for this topical group it is critical that children be selected because they share the variable of behavioral adjustment problems (homogeneity) but differ with regard to social skills, values, and attitudes toward behavior (heterogeneity). This group will be a tremendous disappointment if all of the children selected have a moderate to high degree of the same maladaptive behaviors. Be sure to have a role model for each child in the group, someone from whom the child can learn positive behaviors.

Avoid including several children who engage in every one of the maladaptive behaviors listed, or you will find that you will use all of the sessions available in this brief group experience to deal with these behavioral problems and not group content. Include at least one high status girl and one high status boy—that is, peers the other children admire and wish to be like. These children do not have to be "perfect." They may have school adjustment issues in some other area but should have a well-developed sense of moral reasoning for their age.

Some specific indicators that might be present in children who would be good candidates for this group experience include the following:

1. Poor impulse control (yet impulse control should be sufficient to deal with the group experience during the time allotted)

2. Presence of one or more of the target behaviors (homework problems, aggression, lying, cheating, stealing, teasing)

3. Moral reasoning level lower than would be expected for chronological age

References and Suggested Resources for Professionals

Achenbach, T.M. (1982). *Developmental psychopathology.* New York: Harper & Row.

Alberto, P. A., & Troutman, A. C. (1982). *Applied behavior analysis for teachers: Influencing student performance.* New York: Merrill.

Bandura, A. (1973). *Aggression: A social learning analysis.* New York: Prentice Hall.

Camp, B. W., & Ray, R. S. (1984). Aggression. In A. W. Meyers & W. E. Craighead (Eds.), *Cognitive behavior therapy with children.* New York: Plenum.

Carlson, N. S. (1991). School counseling implementation and survival skills. *School Counselor, 39,* 30–34.

Delgado, J. M. (1969). *Physical control of the mind: Toward a psychocivilized society.* New York: Harper & Row.

Fehrenbach, P. A., & Thelen, M. H. (1982). Behavioral approaches to the treatment of behavioral disorders. *Behavior Modification, 6,* 465–497.

Forehand, R. L., & McMahon, R. J. (1981). *Helping the noncompliant child: A clinician's guide to parent training.* New York: Guilford.

Harmon, P., & Evans, K. (1984). When to use cognitive modeling. *Training and Development Journal, 38,* 67–68.

Kauffman, J. M. (1981). *Characteristics of children's behavior disorders* (2nd ed.). New York: Merrill.

Kendall, P. C., & Braswell, L. (1985). *Cognitive-behavioral therapy for impulsive children.* New York: Guilford.

Kerr, M. M., & Nelson, C. M. (1983). *Strategies for managing behavior problems in the classroom.* New York: Merrill.

Kirkland, K. D., & Thelen, M. H. (1977). Use of modeling in child treatment. In B. B. Lahey & A. E. Kazdin (Eds.), *Advances in clinical child psychology* (Vol. 1). New York: Plenum.

Miller, P., & Sperry, L. L. (1987). The early socialization of anger and aggression. *Merrill-Palmer Quarterly, 33,* 1–31.

Millman, H. L., Schaefer, C. E., & Cohen, J. J. (1981). *Therapies for school behavior problems: A handbook of practical interventions.* San Francisco: Jossey-Bass.

Snyder, J. (1991). Discipline as a mediator of the impact of maternal stress and mood on child conduct problems. *Development and Psychopathology, 3*, 263–276.

Thomas, A., & Grimes, J. (Eds.). (1987). *Children's needs: Psychological perspectives.* Silver Springs, MD: National Association of School Psychologists.

Wolfengang, C. H., & Glickman, C. D. (1986). *Solving discipline problems: Strategies for classroom teachers.* New York: Allyn & Bacon.

Zlomke, L., & Piersel, W. (1987). Children and aggressive behavior. In A. Thomas & J. Grimes (Eds.), *Children's needs: Psychological perspectives.* Silver Springs, MD: National Association of School Psychologists.

Bibliography for Children

Alexander, M. (1981). *Move over, twerp.* New York: Dial. (Preschool–Grade 2)

Berenstain, S., & Berenstain, J. (1982). *The Berenstain Bears get in a fight.* New York: Random House. (Preschool–Grade 2)

Berenstain, S., & Berenstain, J. (1982). *The Berenstain Bears in the dark.* New York: Random House. (Preschool–Grade 2)

Berenstain, S., & Berenstain, J. (1988). *The Berenstain Bears and the bad dream.* New York: Random House. (Preschool–Grade 2)

Berry, J. (1988). *Being a bad sport.* (Available from Paperbacks for Educators, 426 West Front Street, Washington, MO 63090) (Kindergarten–Grade 3)

Berry, J. (1988). *Being bossy.* (Available from Paperbacks for Educators, 426 West Front Street, Washington, MO 63090) (Kindergarten–Grade 3)

Berry, J. (1988). *Being greedy.* (Available from Paperbacks for Educators, 426 West Front Street, Washington, MO 63090) (Kindergarten–Grade 3)

Berry, J. (1988). *Being rude.* (Available from Paperbacks for Educators, 426 West Front Street, Washington, MO 63090) (Kindergarten–Grade 3)

Berry, J. (1988). *Cheating.* (Available from Paperbacks for Educators, 426 West Front Street, Washington, MO 63090) (Kindergarten–Grade 3)

Berry, J. (1988). *Complaining.* (Available from Paperbacks for Educators, 426 West Front Street, Washington, MO 63090) (Kindergarten–Grade 3)

Berry, J. (1988). *Lying.* (Available from Paperbacks for Educators, 426 West Front Street, Washington, MO 63090) (Kindergarten–Grade 3)

Berry, J. (1988). *Stealing.* (Available from Paperbacks for Educators, 426 West Front Street, Washington, MO 63090) (Kindergarten–Grade 3)

Berry, J. (1988). *Tattling.* (Available from Paperbacks for Educators, 426 West Front Street, Washington, MO 63090) (Kindergarten–Grade 3)

Berry, J. (1988). *Teasing.* (Available from Paperbacks for Educators, 426 West Front Street, Washington, MO 63090) (Kindergarten–Grade 3)

Carlson, N. (1987). *Arnie and the stolen markers.* New York: Puffin. (Preschool–Grade 3)

Cohen, M. (1985). *Liar, liar, pants on fire!* New York: Dell. (Kindergarten–Grade 6)

Colman, P. (1991). *Dark closets and noises in the night.* Mahwah, NJ: Paulist. (Preschool–Grade 3)

Gantos, J. (1976). *Rotten Ralph.* Boston: Houghton Mifflin. (Kindergarten–Grade 3)

Hazbry, N., & Condy, R. (1983). *How to get rid of bad dreams.* New York: Scholastic. (Preschool–Grade 2)

Henwood, S. (1991). *The troubled village.* New York: Farrar, Straus & Giroux. (Kindergarten–Grade 3)

Jampolsky, G. (1991). *Me first and the gimme gimmes.* Deerfield Beach, FL: Health Communications/Recovery Publications. (Preschool–Grade 12)

Kates, B. (1992). *We're different, we're the same.* Racine, WI: Golden Books. (Preschool–Grade 2)

Lindgren, A. (1960). *Mischievous Meg.* New York: Puffin. (Grades 3–6)

Petty, K., & Firmin, C. (1991). *Playing the game.* Hauppauge, NY: Barron's. (Preschool–Grade 2)

Powell, R. (1990). *How to deal with monsters.* Mahwah, NJ: Troll. (Preschool–Grade 2)

Powell, R. (1990). *How to deal with parents*. Mahwah, NJ: Troll. (Preschool–Grade 2)

Sanford, D. (1990). *Once I was a thief*. Portland, OR: Multnomah. (Kindergarten–Grade 2)

Steig, W. (1973). *The real thief*. New York: Farrar, Straus & Giroux. (Kindergarten–Grade 4)

Thaler, M. (1993). *The principal from the black lagoon*. New York: Scholastic. (Kindergarten–Grade 4)

Wilde, S. (1988). *Extraordinary Chester*. Santa Barbara, CA: Red Hen Press. (Kindergarten–Grade 3)

Wilhelm, H. (1988). *Tyrone the double dirty rotten cheater*. New York: Scholastic. (Preschool–Grade 3)

Zolotow, C. (1969). *The hating book*. New York: HarperCollins. (Preschool–Grade 3)

Getting Started

Goals

1. To introduce children to the group experience and help them begin to get acquainted
2. To establish ground rules and discuss the issue of confidentiality
3. To discuss the purpose of the group and prepare children for the sessions ahead
4. To help children become aware that the group is a safe environment for sharing ideas, feelings, and behaviors
5. To introduce the topic of being a good citizen of the school and classroom and begin to define exactly what being a good citizen means

Materials

Easel pad and marker

Polaroid camera and film

A healthy snack, such as raisins in individual boxes, fruit, crackers, or juice *(optional)*

Group Session

Ice Breaker

1. Introduce yourself and welcome the children to the group. Explain the purpose of the group and the content of some of the sessions.
2. Discuss basic ground rules for the group, giving group members some examples:

   Everyone gets a chance to talk.

   No hitting or fighting in group.

   Take turns.

   Ask for group members' input to help them develop "ownership." List the ground rules on an easel pad so everyone can see, then post them during each session.
3. Discuss the confidentiality rule and its limits. For example, you might say:

   When we talked about your being in the group, I told you that whatever we say in our group is *confidential*. That means what we say is private. You may talk about your own thoughts, feelings, and actions, but you may not share anything others in the group talk about. There are some special times when I would have to share what you say—if you say something about harming yourself or others, if you share something about child abuse, or if the court (a judge) asks me about what goes on.
4. Get out the camera and explain that you want to take a picture of each group member as a "super citizen" of the school. Explain that the children will be working in the group on becoming even better.
5. Take the children's pictures individually and as a group if desired. Have a group member take your picture as well. Save all the pictures until Working Time.
6. Model sharing your name and two things about yourself (for example, you like antiques and have a dog named Jenny). Go around the group circle and have the children share similar information.

Working Time

1. Briefly discuss with group members what it means to be a good citizen of a school and of a classroom, emphasizing taking responsibility for behavior. Ask the children to name the kinds of things that a good citizen does and says. Write these ideas on the easel pad so all can see. For example:

   Completes papers the teacher gives.

   Does homework.

   Raises hand before talking.

   Does not talk when the teacher is talking.

   Tells the truth.

   Says please and thank-you.

   Plays fair.

   Shares things.

   Helps other children and adults.

   Keeps desk neat.

   Stays out of fights.

   Does not tease.

   Does not hit or pull hair.

   Does not blame others.

   Does not cheat on papers and tests.

   Is a good sport.

   Does not take things that belong to others.

   Does not harm other kids' things.

   Does not talk back.

2. Ask group members why they think it is important to be a good citizen. Typical responses include the following:

   So others will like being my friend

   So I can get good grades

   Because it's wrong to (cheat, lie, steal, and so forth)

   So I don't get in trouble

3. Give children the pictures of themselves and ask them whether they would be willing to share their picture with the group and tell some ways they are a good citizen and some things they would like to work on improving in the group.

4. After each group member has had a turn, ask the children to guess how they might be acting at the end of the group if they have practiced being a good citizen and worked on their problem areas.

5. If you have time, select a story from this agenda's bibliography for children to read aloud and discuss.

Process Time

1. Discuss the following questions:

   What did you learn about yourself in group today?

   What was it like for you to tell things about yourself to others?

   Does anyone else in the group feel the same way you do? Tell that person how you feel the same.

   Would you be willing to work on improving a citizenship problem area before the group meets again?

2. Share snacks, if desired. Before saying good-bye, thank group members for coming and remind them of the meeting time for the next session.

Homework Buddies

Goals

1. To establish the norm of reviewing what happened during the previous session
2. To help children understand the purpose of homework and put homework in perspective
3. To help children understand why doing homework is important to school success and to reaching future goals
4. To encourage children to learn and follow some basic homework rules
5. To provide children who are having difficulty completing homework with the structure and support they need to do so

Materials

Easel pad and marker

A healthy snack, such as raisins in individual boxes, fruit, crackers, or juice *(optional)*

Group Session

Review

1. Welcome children to the group. Briefly go over the ground rules and the confidentiality rule.
2. Ask whether anyone has anything left over from the last session, on being a good citizen at home and at school.

Working Time

1. Begin by discussing the following questions:

    Do you know anyone who does his or her homework all of the time?

    We all forget our homework sometimes, but when we do, what happens?

    If you're not paying attention to the teacher and miss the instructions, you soon find out that if you snooze, you lose! What exactly do you lose?

    How will doing your homework help you be a better student and citizen?

    How will being a better student help you get what you want in life?

2. Write the following rules for homework on the easel pad:

    Write it down–Take it home

    Do it–Check it–Pack it

    Explain that these rules mean that you write down your homework, take it home, do it, check it, pack it, and turn it in every single day you have homework. Help group members brainstorm ways they can remember these rules.

3. Next explain that everyone can be a "homework hero," but to do so you need a "homework buddy." Homework buddies check with each other before leaving school each day to be sure they have what they need to finish their homework. Older children can check with each other again by phone before bedtime and give support and help if needed.

4. Ask who would like to have a homework buddy in the group to help them over the next few weeks to become a homework hero, then help children pair up. Pairs should include one child who has more difficulties completing assignments, homework, and other classroom responsibilities and one who has better skills—this way the one with the stronger skills can be a role model.

Process Time

1. Discuss the following questions:

> What is neat about having a homework buddy?
>
> How do you think having one will help you remember to get your homework finished?
>
> Suppose you do your homework and turn it in every day during a week. How do you think you will feel?
>
> Who else feels this way?

2. Share snacks, if desired. Before saying good-bye, thank group members for coming and remind them of the meeting time for the next session.

Controlling Anger

NOTE: Sessions 2 and 3 in the "I CAN Kids: Control Anger Now!" agenda present an alternate technique for controlling anger, appropriate for fourth grade and up. This session details a simpler technique, appropriate for second grade and up.

Goals

1. To encourage awareness that anger can be controlled—that instead of "losing our temper" we actually choose to "give our temper away"

2. To help children learn the steps in the Stop-Think-Act method of dealing with anger

3. To give children the opportunity to practice applying this method in real-life situations

Materials

Special stickers or other small rewards *(optional)*

Easel pad and marker

"Dress-up" clothes (some adult and some children's clothing, such as high heels, purses, briefcases, hats)

A healthy snack, such as raisins in individual boxes, fruit, crackers, or juice *(optional)*

Group Session

Review

1. Welcome the children to group. Briefly go over the ground rules and the confidentiality rule.

2. Ask group members to share how working with a homework buddy is going. The following discussion questions may help:

> What does it feel like to share your skills and help someone else learn good homework skills?
>
> Has having a homework buddy helped you?
>
> What did you like about it?
>
> What didn't you like about it?
>
> How did you feel when you turned in your homework each day?
>
> How did you feel at the end of a week?
>
> What did you think about yourself at the end of a week?
>
> What are you doing better now?

If group members need help, let everyone join in to support them. If desired, give stickers or other small rewards to those who used the buddy system. Praise and encourage the children to continue.

Working Time

1. Read the following situations aloud:

   > You come into your classroom and go to your desk. All of your books are on the floor in the aisle, and the other kids are stepping on them as they walk to their seats. The class bully is laughing at you.

   > You go to the cafeteria, and the kid behind you pushes two younger kids aside and cuts in line.

   > Your dad curses and yells at you for leaving your bike on the sidewalk all night.

2. Discuss the following questions:

   > How do you feel in each of these situations?

   > What do you think of when this kind of thing happens to you?

   > What do you feel like?

   > What do you usually do?

   > Does what you do help or hurt the situation?

3. Explain that you don't have to blow up when something happens that pushes your anger button. Present the idea that you don't "lose your temper"; rather, you "give it away." If you say, "I lost my temper," that means you don't control your temper—it just behaves on its own. We do have control of our temper, and we are responsible for what happens because we are the ones who own our temper. So we say, "I gave away my temper," which means that we chose to behave this way instead of in a different way.

4. Explain that by using the Stop-Think-Act way of dealing with anger, it is possible to get control of angry feelings and act in a responsible way. Write the following steps on the easel pad:

   Stop: Say "Stop!" inside your head before you blow up and yell at or hurt someone.

   Think: Think of what you could do in the situation.

   Act: Do something that will help you respect yourself without taking someone else's right to be respected away.

5. Reread the first situation in the list, then help group members apply the Stop-Think-Act steps:

   Stop: Say "Stop" inside your head.

   Think: Think of what you could do in this situation. (Some possible responses are as follows: Hit someone, yell, start crying, tell the teacher, put your things back in your desk, ignore it, think to yourself the custodian or another student might have knocked the books off accidentally.)

   Act: Do something that will help you respect yourself without taking someone else's right to be respected away.

   Encourage group members to generate as many alternatives as they can, then evaluate the outcomes of each one. For example, punching someone might make you feel good at the moment but won't help in the future because it will just cause you to be in more trouble.

6. Reread the second and third situations in the list and apply the Stop-Think-Act steps in a similar fashion.

7. Help group members apply the Stop-Think-Act steps to real-life situations, letting them dress up in the clothes to represent different characters in the conflict.

8. Encourage group members to continue working as homework buddies, giving them the individual help they need.

Process Time

1. Discuss the following questions:

   > What did you learn about using Stop-Think-Act today?

   > What does it feel like to behave in ways that respect your rights and respect other people's rights, too?

   > What might happen at home or at school that might make you want to "give away your temper"?

   > How could you use the Stop-Think-Act steps if this happens?

   > Who else in the group thinks they could use these steps, too?

2. Share snacks, if desired. Before saying good-bye, thank group members for coming and remind them of the meeting time for the next session.

Liar, Liar, Pants on Fire!

Goals

1. To encourage understanding that dishonesty is hurtful and disrespectful to everyone involved
2. To help children learn alternatives to lying
3. To encourage consequential thinking
4. To help children use the reframing technique to express their wishes and desires instead of lying

Materials

Special stickers or other small rewards *(optional)*

A story about lying, such as *Liar, Liar, Pants on Fire!* by Miriam Cohen (Dell, 1985)

A healthy snack, such as raisins in individual boxes, fruit, crackers, or juice *(optional)*

Group Session

Review

1. Welcome the children to group. Remind them of the ground rules and the confidentiality rule.

2. Ask those who are continuing the homework buddies plan to share how they are doing. If they need help, let everyone join in to support them. If desired, give stickers or other small rewards to those who are participating. Praise and encourage them to continue.

3. Discuss whether any group members applied the Stop-Think-Act steps to a real situation. How did using the steps help them stay in control of their anger?

Working Time

1. Read the story chosen aloud, then discuss.

2. Ask the children what kinds of situations they might have experienced in which they felt like telling a lie. Encourage them to consider the consequences of lying by asking the following questions:

> If you told a lie, how would it help you?
>
> How would it hurt you?
>
> Who else would it help?
>
> Who else would it hurt?
>
> What if you told a lie to keep from getting in trouble?
>
> Who would be hurt if no one found out what you did and you escaped getting in trouble?
>
> What else could you do if you didn't want to get in trouble? (Tell the truth and hope for a "lesser sentence.")
>
> What is the best thing to do for you and for other people?

3. Encourage group members to brainstorm ways other than lying to get the attention they need from parents, friends, or teachers. Some possible responses include the following:

> Say, "I need some help."

> Tell parents you need to spend more time together.

> Talk about how lying makes you feel and what would happen if you told the truth in the same situation.

> Learn to negotiate with adults on consequences if you tell the truth (asking for a lesser punishment for being truthful).

4. Explain that sometimes children say things that they wish were true, but you really aren't true. Use the following situations to illustrate.

Situation 1

You really want your mom and dad to buy you a pony, but they won't. You want a pony so bad! You secretly think that if your mom and dad loved you enough they would buy you a pony. So because you feel a little insecure about being loved, you make up stories about the gorgeous pony they bought you. Then you tell all the kids at school.

What is wrong with this?

Why do you think you would tell this lie in the first place?

What could you say that would be the truth? (I'm worried that my mom and dad don't love me enough. I wish they would show me they love me.)

Situation 2

Suppose your mom and dad have been fighting and arguing a lot, and finally your dad moves out into an apartment. You are just sick about this and want them to get back together really soon so things can get back to normal and you can stop worrying and getting stomachaches and staying awake all night. You go to school and tell your friends that everything is OK now, that your dad moved back in.

What is wrong with this?

Why do you think you would tell this lie in the first place?

What could you say that would be the truth? (I hate it that my dad moved out and I sure want him back, but I'm scared that he won't be coming back.)

5. Discuss the following questions, stressing the idea that saying how you feel is a better way to get what you need than telling a lie:

> Why is the truth so scary sometimes?

> What good does it do to fool yourself and other people by telling lies?

> When you realize that you need help, attention, love, or encouragement, or when you need to be held and hugged, what can you do rather than make up stories to get attention?

6. Encourage group members to continue working as homework buddies, giving them the individual help they need.

Process Time

1. Discuss the following questions:

    What did you learn about lying from the story we read?

    When do you need attention? What kind of attention do you need? Who can give you what you need?

    If you can't get the attention from the person(s) you want it from, who else could you get it from?

    How do you feel about yourself after you have told a lie?

    Do you think you could stop before telling a lie and ask yourself whether you might be hurting yourself or someone else?

    If you tell a lie to keep from getting punished for doing something, do you think you could try telling the truth and asking the person to give you a smaller punishment because you told the truth?

2. Share snacks, if desired. Before saying good-bye, thank group members for coming and remind them of the meeting time for the next session.

Copy Cat

NOTE: Before the session, write the following sentence stems on the easel chart:

When I cheat I feel _____.

When I cheat I hurt _____ and _____.

When other people find out that I cheated they _____.

When my parents find out that I cheated they feel _____.

When my parents find out that I cheated I feel _____.

When my teacher finds out that I cheated he or she _____.

When my best friend finds out that I cheated he or she _____ .

Goals

1. To promote understanding of what types of behavior are considered cheating

2. To help children understand that cheating is not an acceptable behavior (in other words, it violates social convention)

3. To help children understand how cheating hurts both themselves and others and how it is both a moral and social problem

4. To encourage children to brainstorm alternatives to cheating

Materials

Special stickers or other small rewards *(optional)*

A story on the topic of cheating, such as *Tyrone the Double Dirty Rotten Cheater,* by Hans Wilhelm (Scholastic, 1988)

Easel pad and marker

A healthy snack, such as raisins in individual boxes, fruit, crackers, or juice *(optional)*

Group Session

Review

1. Welcome the children to group. Briefly review the ground rules and the confidentiality rule.

2. Ask those who are continuing the homework buddies plan to share how they are doing. If they need help, let everyone join in to support them. If desired, give stickers or other small rewards to those who are participating. Praise and encourage them to continue.

3. Discuss whether any group members had a situation in which they felt like telling a lie. What did they do about these feelings?

Working Time

1. Read one of the stories about cheating, then discuss the content of whatever story you read.

2. Talk about what kinds of things are considered cheating. For example:

> Copying someone else's ideas or creation (for example, homework, artwork, or poem)
>
> Allowing someone else to copy your homework

Using "crib" notes

Getting a copy of a test before it is given

Having someone else write your papers for you

Copying from someone else's test

Giving your word you will do or not do something and then breaking your word (for example, cheating on a boyfriend or girlfriend)

Cheating on time owed at a job

3. Discuss why cheating in all its forms is the wrong thing to do, considering moral as well as social reasons. Some ideas to stress are as follows:

Everyone has the right to be respected by others, and taking/stealing someone's ideas shows disrespect.

Life has many competitions—in school, sports, relationships, and work.

Cheating is dishonest and hurts other people. It also hurts us because it damages our feeling of being a good person (self-esteem).

It takes courage to admit mistakes, but we can be proud of ourselves when we do.

4. Brainstorm what you can do in a situation to keep from cheating. For example:

Start projects early so you have enough time to do your own work.

Study regularly so you go to tests prepared.

Get help from a teacher or friend if you don't understand.

Say no when someone asks to copy your homework.

Play fair in games.

Refuse to give in to peer pressure.

5. Go around the circle and have the children respond to the sentence stems on the easel chart. (This experience can be very powerful because the questions presume that the children have actually cheated at some point.)

6. Encourage group members to continue working as homework buddies, giving them the individual help they need.

Process Time

1. Discuss the following questions:

What did you learn about yourself in group today?

What feelings did you have when we read the story?

Did anyone else in the group feel the same way you did? Tell that person how you feel the same.

What do you think you might do in the future rather than cheat?

How could you help someone else keep from cheating without sounding like you are preaching or being a "goody two-shoes"?

What does the saying "honesty is the best policy" mean?

2. Share snacks, if desired. Before saying good-bye, thank group members for coming and remind them of the meeting time for the next session.

Don't Touch My Stuff!

Goals

1. To help children clarify what behaviors constitute stealing

2. To encourage the realization that stealing is not acceptable behavior

3. To give children the opportunity to get in touch with their feelings about stealing or being stolen from

4. To help children understand that they are responsible for avoiding situations in which they could be accused of stealing

5. To encourage children to brainstorm acceptable ways of getting the things they want or need

Materials

Special stickers or other small rewards *(optional)*

A story about stealing, such as *Once I Was a Thief*, by Doris Sanford (Multnomah, 1990); *The Real Thief*, by William Steig (Farrar, Straus & Giroux, 1973); or *Arnie and the Stolen Markers*, by Nancy Carlson (Puffin, 1987)

A healthy snack, such as raisins in individual boxes, fruit, crackers, or juice *(optional)*

Group Session

Review

1. Welcome the children to group. Briefly go over the ground rules and the confidentiality rule.

2. Ask how group members are coming along with the homework buddies project and what their parents and teachers are saying about their progress. If they need help, let everyone join in to support them. If desired, give stickers or other small rewards to those who are participating, along with lots of praise and encouragement.

3. Discuss any unfinished business from the last session, on the topic of cheating.

Working Time

1. Read a story about stealing. Discuss what happened to the characters and how they reacted to the situation. Personalize the story by discussing the following questions:

   What does it feel like when someone takes something of yours?

   What do you think about that person?

   How long are you upset when someone takes or destroys something of yours?

2. Encourage group members to imagine that they are someplace where some other kids have stolen candy, drinks, or toys. Ask, "What if you don't even touch any of these things, but an adult comes in and catches everyone there. Are you guilty?" Explain that if an adult has stolen property in his or her house or car the law says that person is "guilty by association," even if someone else actually stole the property.

3. Ask children what they think is the best thing to do if they get in a situation where stealing is going to happen or has happened. Help them understand that they should not stay around people with stolen things or hang around with kids who steal in the first place.

4. Next discuss the difference between borrowing and stealing: Ask group members to explain how they could go about borrowing something so they don't get accused of stealing. Stress the idea that you ask the person before you take the item—get permission so that if there is any question, you are cleared. Never borrow first, intending to ask later.

5. Discuss ways children might get something they want very much without stealing it. Some possible responses are as follows:

> Ask parents what you can do to earn it or buy it.
>
> Ask the owner if you can borrow it to play with or use for a certain amount of time.
>
> Ask the store owner if you can work to earn it.
>
> Trade one of your own toys or things for it.

6. Encourage group members to continue working as homework buddies, giving them the individual help they need.

Process Time

1. Discuss the following questions:

> What did you learn about stealing today in group?
>
> What is the worst thing about stealing?
>
> What do the other members of your group think about stealing?
>
> What are you going to do if you get in a situation where other kids are going to steal something?
>
> What kinds of things can you do to get what you need without stealing?

2. Share snacks, if desired. Before saying good-bye, thank group members for coming, tell them that the group will meet only two more times, and remind them of the meeting time for the next session.

You Can't Tease Me Anymore

Goals

1. To introduce the idea that teasing is harmful to everyone involved
2. To promote understanding that you can be teased only if you let someone "push your buttons"
3. To help children learn some specific assertion skills to deal with teasing
4. To help children understand that teasers are usually teased by someone else

Materials

Special stickers or other small rewards *(optional)*

Easel pad and marker

Several hand puppets

A healthy snack, such as raisins in individual boxes, fruit, crackers, or juice *(optional)*

Group Session

Review

1. Welcome the children to group. Briefly go over the ground rules and the confidentiality rule.
2. Ask those who are continuing the homework buddies plan to share how they are doing. If they need help, let everyone join in to support them. If desired, give stickers or other small rewards to those who are participating. Praise and encourage them to continue.
3. Ask whether anyone has anything to say about the last session, on the topic of stealing.

Working Time

1. Discuss teasing, asking group members what this means. Encourage the children to generate a number of other words that mean the same as teasing, listing these on the easel pad. For example:

Annoying	Razzing
Bugging	Ribbing
Criticizing	Shaming
Hurting	Mocking
Jesting	Name-calling
Joking	Poking fun at
Laughing at	Putting down
Playing with	Ridiculing

2. Discuss the following questions:

   How does it feel when someone teases you?

   How do you feel when you tease someone else?

   Why do you think you tease others? Why do they tease you?

   Have you ever noticed that some kids do all the teasing and some kids get teased a lot?

Why do you think some kids become teasers? (Possibly to gain power or control. Usually, they are or were teased themselves at home or in some other situation.)

Why do you think some kids get teased all the time? (They don't have the skills or know-how to stop it or do something else.)

Why does it hurt when you are teased? (Because you believe what the teaser says instead of believing in yourself and your own abilities.)

3. Explain that when someone says things to you that they know are going to hurt you and cause you to feel bad, that person is "pushing your buttons." The teaser seems to know exactly what hurts and will do it again and again. But you can only be teased if you let the teaser push your buttons. You have control of your buttons, not the other person.

4. Help group members understand that if they decide that what teasers say isn't going to push their buttons any more, then the teasing doesn't work. Encourage children to brainstorm a number of assertive things they could say to defend themselves. For example:

I don't appreciate your humor.

I'm not bugged by that anymore.

I feel sorry for you, having to get your kicks by hurting people.

Sorry, I just don't have time for you today.

Tell the children that just walking away is also a good way to stop a teaser.

5. Ask for volunteers to share a time they were teased or a situation in which someone they knew was teased. In turn, have each volunteer take one of the hand puppets and, pretending they are the puppet, try to tease you in that way. Model assertive responses to the teasing. Repeat this process with as many volunteers as time allows.

6. Encourage group members to continue working as homework buddies, giving them the individual help they need.

Process Time

1. Discuss the following questions:

What did you learn about teasing in group today?

What was it like for you to watch the teasing role-play we did? Did anyone feel sorry for the person teased?

Did anyone feel sorry for the teaser? Why?

What can you do if someone tries to tease you?

What can you do if someone tries to tease a friend of yours?

Are you willing to try these ideas out if you have a chance before the next session?

2. Remind the children that the next session will be their last one and give them the opportunity to plan a celebration to reward themselves for all their hard work.

3. Share snacks, if desired. Before saying good-bye, thank group members for coming and remind them of the meeting time for the last session.

Saying Good-bye

Goals

1. To give children the opportunity to review and process what they have learned during the group experience
2. To support, encourage, and reinforce children for their work, sharing, and personal disclosures
3. To model saying good-bye in a healthy manner

Materials

Special stickers or other small rewards *(optional)*

A tape recorder and an audiotape of songs children know

Masks, grease pencils, or costumes (whatever you have that represents clowns)

Whatever snacks or other materials children decided on to celebrate the last session

Group Session

Review

1. Welcome the children to group and briefly go over the ground rules and the confidentiality rule. Remind them that the confidentiality rule still holds after the group is over.
2. Ask those who have continued with the homework buddies plan to share their experiences: Did the plan help? What do their parents and teachers say about their homework and grades now? Encourage the children to continue the plan after the group is over. If desired, give those who have been participating stickers or other small rewards.
3. Ask whether anyone would like to share anything from the last group session, on the topic of teasing.

Working Time

1. Refer to the session topics and ask children to share what they learned.

   Homework Buddies
   What did you like about the homework buddies plan?
   What was the most fun about it?
   What didn't you like about it?

   Controlling Anger
   Why do we say you "give your anger away"?
   What did you learn about stopping, thinking, and then acting when you get mad?
   Has this way of dealing with anger worked for you?
   How do you feel about being able to be in control of what you say and do when you get mad?

   Liar, Liar, Pants on Fire!
   What do you dislike most about lying?
   What did you learn to do instead of telling a lie?
   What did you learn from the story we read?

Copy Cat

Who suffers when someone cheats?

What can you do to keep from feeling as though you need to cheat?

Don't Touch My Stuff!

What should you do if you need to borrow something?

What should you do if other kids steal something and you are around them?

You Can't Tease Me Anymore

What can you do to keep someone else from "pushing your buttons"?

What is one thing you can say to stop the person?

2. Thank each child individually, then ask each one to share with the others in the group what he or she learned from them—for example, "Jamie, I learned that you know how to walk away when kids tease you."

Process Time

1. Get out the clown masks, costumes, greasepaint, and so forth. Explain that the group has been talking about some very serious citizenship behaviors, but sometimes we just have to act like clowns and laugh at ourselves so we don't take ourselves too seriously. Let the children dress up like clowns, listen to music, and dance and/or sing songs for a while.

2. Thank the children for participating and let them know you appreciate their effort. If appropriate, let children know you will be available to them after the group is over if they want to see you individually about citizenship or other problems.

3. Share the snacks and enjoy.

SAMPLE FORMS

Sample Group Counseling Needs Assessment for Faculty

Dear Teacher:

Your school counselor will be conducting time-limited topical group counseling activities for children this year. We would like to have your input so that we can better meet your needs and the needs of the children in our school. Please be a part of helping us provide the best services possible so that our children have the opportunity to meet their full potential. Each of the following represents a major topical issue to be covered by an eight-session group counseling experience, with approximately eight children in a group. Each group will be led by a counselor or counselor team. Please help us determine which topics you think need to be covered by placing a check mark beside the topic. Put two check marks beside each of your top two priorities. Add any other topics you think need to be addressed. Thank you very much!

_____   1. Learning peacemaking skills

_____   2. Feeling better about yourself (self-esteem)

_____   3. Learning how to make and keep friends

_____   4. Dealing with a divorce in your family

_____   5. Dealing with the death of a person or pet

_____   6. Learning better ways of dealing with angry feelings

_____   7. Learning to take responsibility for yourself at home and school

_____   8. Understanding social responsibilities and values as part of a group (good citizenship)

_____   9. Other _____

_____   10. Other _____

Name_____ Date _____

Return to_____

Sample Group Counseling Needs Assessment for Students

Dear Student:

Your school counselor,_____ , will be having some small groups of children get together. Sometimes we all need help to learn how to be better students or how to deal with problems like a divorce in the family, being in control of our anger, or getting along with others. Below is a list of some of these group topics. Please tell us what groups you think we need in our school to help you and your friends. Put a check mark in front of those you think we should have. If you have any other ideas, please add them. If you want your counselor to talk to you about being in one of the groups, put your name at the bottom of the page. Thanks very much!

_____ 1. Learning peacemaking skills

_____ 2. Feeling better about yourself (self-esteem)

_____ 3. Learning how to make and keep friends

_____ 4. Dealing with a divorce in your family

_____ 5. Dealing with the death of a person or pet

_____ 6. Learning better ways of dealing with angry feelings

_____ 7. Learning to take responsibility for yourself at home and school

_____ 8. Understanding social responsibilities and values as part of a group (good citizenship)

_____ 9. Other _____

_____ 10. Other _____

Sign your name only if you want to be in a group.

Name_____ Date _____

Return to_____

Sample Letter to School Faculty

Dear Teacher:

The counseling staff will soon be starting a series of small-group counseling experiences for the youngsters in our school. Group counseling is an effective way to reach certain children and help them learn better ways of dealing with personal problems and social skills deficits. Group leader(s) will work with six to eight children for 30 to 40 minutes once or twice per week.

It is important to distinguish between *group guidance* and *group counseling*. Group guidance is educational in nature and involves sharing information that all of the children need, such as friendship skills, being a good citizen of the school, study skills, and so on. The information can be provided to a whole class or even larger group. Group guidance, something every child needs and deserves on a regular basis, is preventive in nature; helps keep issues from becoming problems in the future. In contrast, group counseling is remedial in nature and involves a counseling relationship between each child in the group and the counselor. It is meant to help solve developmental problems that already exist and to keep these problems from getting out of hand.

Group counseling is not the best choice for every child who has problems. For example, if a child is in a personal or family crisis a group experience would not be appropriate, even though he or she might benefit from a group experience in the future. A child who is so shy that he or she cannot interact in a group setting would also not be suited. And a youngster who is very aggressive or who needs constant attention would not be a good candidate. Some children's problems are already so pervasive that short-term group counseling would not be appropriate. So, although a child might need counseling services of some kind very badly, group counseling might not be the best kind of service. If you know of such students, we will be happy to help them find appropriate help.

Here in the school we will interview and select about eight children who are good candidates for each of the groups to be offered. The group counseling experiences planned for this year are on the following specific topics:

_____   _____

_____

_____

_____

They will meet from_____ _____ to _____.

If you know of children you think could benefit from a group counseling experience, please let us know as soon as possible. We will be happy to meet with you and plan how we can cooperate to make this a special learning experience for them.

Sincerely,

School Counselor(s)

Sample Letter to Parent/Guardian

Dear Parent:

Our school developmental guidance program is going to include the opportunity for students to participate in small-group counseling experiences. About 6 to 8 children are selected to be in a group that will meet once or twice a week for 30 to 40 minutes to work on social and personal skills.

Group counseling is an excellent way for children to learn new skills, develop self-confidence, become more aware of others' views and experiences, practice new behaviors, and better understand how to deal with the problems life presents. Children who share a common concern but have different coping skills are able to learn from one another as well as from the group leader. Some of the topics being considered are as follows:

_____

_____

_____

_____

They will meet from_____ to _____.

If you think your child would benefit from a group counseling experience, you are invited to refer him or her for further screening. Your child may have already expressed an interest in being a part of one of the groups that will be starting soon. Enclosed is a form that asks you to give your consent for your child to participate. Your child has not been selected yet and will not be considered until you give your permission. Only a few students will be able to have this opportunity at a time. If your child is not selected but is an appropriate candidate for future services, he or she will have other opportunities to participate. Participation in the group is voluntary and will not affect your child's grades in any way.

Please read the Parent/Guardian Consent Form thoroughly and return it by_____ . If you have any questions, concerns, or comments, feel free to call us at the number and time listed below. Thank you very much for considering this opportunity for your child.

Sincerely,

School Counselor(s)

Telephone number: _____

Best time to call: _____

Sample Parent/Guardian Consent Form

Your permission is requested for your child, _____ , to participate in group counseling activities.

The group will involve eight sessions and will run from _____ to _____ .

Each session will be about_____ minutes long and will take place during the school day.

The group is entitled: _____
and will include discussion of ideas, feelings, behaviors, attitudes, and opinions. The children will do some activities related to the topic, such as drawing, role-playing, relaxation exercises, and practicing new behaviors both in group and between sessions with family members and friends. For example, your child could be practicing telling you how she or he feels about a related issue. Some of the session topics are:

_____

_____

_____

_____

The children will have the opportunity to learn new skills and behaviors that may help their personal development and adjustment. The group will be led by_____ of the school counseling staff.

Because counseling is based on a trusting relationship between counselor and client, the group leader(s) will keep the information shared by group members confidential, except in certain situations in which there is an ethical responsibility to limit confidentiality. In the following circumstances you will be notified.

1. If the child reveals information about harm to himself/herself or another person

2. If the child reveals information about child abuse

3. If the counselor's records are subpoenaed by the courts

4. Other _____

By signing this form I give my informed consent for my child to participate in group counseling. I understand that:

1. The group will provide an opportunity for members to learn and practice interpersonal skills, discuss feelings, share ideas, practice new behaviors, and make new friends.

2. Anything group members share in group will be kept confidential by the group leader(s) except in the situations already noted.

Parent/Guardian_____ Date _____

Parent/Guardian_____ Date _____

Student _____ Date _____

Return to_____ By_____

TAP-In Student Selection Checklist

Date _____ Interviewer _____

Name of student _____

Age _____ Grade _____ Group topic _____

Tell

_____ 1. The name, purpose, and goals of the group.

_____ 2. Where, when, and how often the group will meet.

_____ 3. Who will be leading the group.

_____ 4. The number of children who will be selected (not everyone who wants to be in the group will be selected).

_____ 5. In order to be in the group, you must give your permission, and your parents (or guardian) must sign that you may be in the group.

_____ 6. You will need to share some personal things about yourself, such as how you feel and your ideas, behaviors, and attitudes. No one will force you to share anything you don't want to share.

_____ 7. It could be very good for you to be in the group because (name benefits specific to topic and child's needs).

_____ 8. It can also be scary to be in a group because (name risks—for example, other kids might pressure you to do or say certain things or you might feel different and uncomfortable when you practice new behaviors).

_____ 9. In the group, we all agree to keep whatever is said by anybody in the group confidential. We call it the "confidentiality rule." That means that no one tells what anyone else says or does in the group. The other children will agree not to tell what you say or do in group, and you must agree not to tell what they say or do in group. Because we don't ever have control over what someone else does or says, we can't promise that someone might not tell what happens in group. At the beginning of each group session I will remind every-one about the confidentiality rule, and this helps us remember.

Is there anything you want to ask about this?

_____ 10. There are some times when I would need to share what you say with other adults, such as your parents.

The times are:

If you say anything about harming yourself or someone else

If you say anything about child abuse happening to you or someone else

If the court (a judge) tells me I need to share the information

Is there anything you want to ask about this?

_____ 11. All of the group members are expected to come on time for each meeting. We will work this out with you, your teacher, and your parents to make sure that you are free at the time of the group meetings. When the group starts, the members share things and the group gets to be very important. So if one member doesn't come, it affects everyone.

_____ 12. For everyone's safety, no one is allowed to hit or fight or hurt other group members.

_____ 13. In group we sometimes practice new ways of doing things. Each group member is expected to do some practicing of new skills in group and sometimes outside of group between meetings.

_____ 14. Each person in the group is expected to work on his or her own behavior and make changes.

Are you willing to do self-improvement homework?

Ask

_____ 1. Do you understand everything I've said about group so far?

_____ 2. What else would you like to know about group? About the leaders?

_____ 3. Are you going to any other counselors or psychologists for counseling in a group or by yourself?

_____ 4. If you are chosen for the group, will you come to each meeting and come on time?

_____ 5. Are you willing to share your ideas and feelings and behaviors with the group?

_____ 6. Are you willing to keep what the other children say in group confidential?

_____ 7. Do you understand that there are some special times I might need to share what you say in group with other adults, such as your parents?

_____ 8. What would you most like to learn about in group?

_____ 9. What behaviors would you like to change?

_____ 10. Would you give your permission to audiotape or videotape the group session if you could ask to have the tape turned off if you felt uncomfortable? (Ask only if applicable.)

_____ 11. On a scale of 1 to 10, with 1 meaning very little and 10 meaning a whole lot, how much do you want to be in the group?

NOTE: This completes the interview portion with the child. Complete the "pick" portion after the interview with the child is finished.

Pick

_____ 1. Does the child seem to understand what the purpose and goals of the group are?

_____ 2. Does the child appear to want to participate in and be a productive member of the group?

_____ 3. Does the child have some positive behaviors/attitudes that would serve as a model for some of the other potential members?

_____ 4. Does the child seem compatible with the other group members tentatively selected?

_____ 5. Does the child appear to be making the decision to join the group independently or under the influence of others?

_____ 6. Does the child appear to be giving assent?

_____ 7. What is the child's motivation factor (on a scale of 1 to 10)?

Selected_____ Not selected_____

Potential for future group? Yes_____ No_____

Comments_____

_____

_____

_____

Harm
(to self or others)

Abuse

Courts

ETHICAL GUIDELINES
FOR GROUP COUNSELORS

Preamble

One characteristic of any professional group is the possession of a body of knowledge, skills, and voluntarily self-professed standards for ethical practice. A Code of Ethics consists of those standards that have been formally and publicly acknowledged by the members of a profession to serve as the guidelines for professional conduct, discharge of duties, and the resolution of moral dilemmas. By this document, the Association for Specialists in Group Work (ASGW) has identified the standards of conduct appropriate for ethical behavior among its members.

The Association for Specialists in Group Work recognizes the basic commitment of its members to the Ethical Standards of its parent organization, the American Association for Counseling and Development (AACD) and nothing in this document shall be construed to supplant that code. These standards are intended to complement the AACD standards in the area of group work by clarifying the nature of ethical responsibility of the counselor in the group setting and by stimulating a greater concern for competent group leadership.

The group counselor is expected to be a professional agent and to take the processes of ethical responsibility seriously. ASGW views "ethical process" as being integral to group work and views group counselors as "ethical agents." Group counselors, by their very nature in being responsible and responsive to their group members, necessarily embrace a certain potential for ethical vulnerability. It is incumbent upon group counselors to give considerable attention to the intent and context of their actions because the attempts of counselors to influence human behavior through group work always have ethical implications.

The following ethical guidelines have been developed to encourage ethical behavior of group counselors. These guidelines are written for students and practitioners, and are meant to stimulate reflection, self-examination, and discussion of issues and practices. They address the group counselor's responsibility for providing information about group work to clients and the group counselor's responsibility for providing group counseling services to clients.

A final section discusses the group counselor's responsibility for safeguarding ethical practice and procedures for reporting unethical behavior. Group counselors are expected to make known these standards to group members.

Ethical Guidelines

1. *Orientation and providing information:* Group counselors adequately prepare prospective or new group members by providing as much information about the existing or proposed group as necessary.

   Minimally, information related to each of the following areas should be provided.

   (a) Entrance procedures, time parameters of the group experience, group participation expectations, methods of payment (where appropriate), and termination procedures are explained by the group counselor as appropriate to the level of maturity of group members and the nature and purpose(s) of the group.

   (b) Group counselors have available for distribution a professional disclosure statement that includes information on the group counselor's qualifications and group services that can be provided, particularly as related to the nature and purpose(s) of the specific group.

   (c) Group counselors communicate the role expectations, rights, and responsibilities of group members and group counselor(s).

   (d) The group goals are stated as concisely as possible by the group counselor, including "whose" goal it is (the group counselor's, the institution's, the parent's, the law's, society's, etc.) and the role of group members in influencing or determining the group's goal(s).

   (e) Group counselors explore with group members the risks of potential life changes that may occur because of the group experience and help members explore their readiness to face these possibilities.

Note. From "Ethical Guidelines for Group Counselors," 1990, *Journal for Specialists in Group Work*, 15(2), 119–126. Copyright 1990 by the *Journal for Specialists in Group Work*. Reprinted by permission.

(f) Group members are informed by the group counselor of unusual or experimental procedures that might be expected in their group experience.

(g) Group counselors explain, as realistically as possible, what services can and cannot be provided within the particular group structure offered.

(h) Group counselors emphasize the need to promote full psychological functioning and presence among group members. They inquire from prospective group members whether they are using any kind of drug or medication that may affect functioning in the group. They do not permit any use of alcohol and/or illegal drugs during group sessions and they discourage the use of alcohol and/or drugs (legal or illegal) prior to group meetings which may affect the physical or emotional presence of the member or other group members.

(i) Group counselors inquire from prospective group members whether they have ever been a client in counseling or psychotherapy. If a prospective group member is already in a counseling relationship with another professional person, the group counselor advises the prospective group member to notify the other professional of his or her participation in the group.

(j) Group counselors clearly inform group members about the policies pertaining to the group counselor's willingness to consult with them between group sessions.

(k) In establishing fees for group counseling services, group counselors consider the financial status and the locality of prospective group members. Group members are not charged fees for group sessions where the group counselor is not present and the policy of charging for sessions missed by a group member is clearly communicated. Fees for participating as a group member are contracted between group counselor and group member for a specified period of time. Group counselors do not increase fees for group counseling services until the existing contracted fee structure has expired. In the event that the established fee structure is inappropriate for a

prospective member, group counselors assist in finding comparable services of acceptable cost.

2. *Screening of members:* The group counselor screens prospective group members (when appropriate to their theoretical orientation). Insofar as possible, the counselor selects group members whose needs and goals are compatible with the goals of the group, who will not impede the group process, and whose well being will not be jeopardized by the group experience. An orientation to the group (i.e., ASGW Ethical Guideline #1) is included during the screening process.

Screening may be accomplished in one or more ways, such as the following:

(a) Individual interview

(b) Group interview of prospective group members

(c) Interview as part of a team staffing

(d) Completion of a written questionnaire by prospective group members

3. *Confidentiality:* Group counselors protect members by defining clearly what confidentiality means, why it is important, and the difficulties involved in enforcement.

(a) Group counselors take steps to protect members by defining confidentiality and the limits of confidentiality (i.e., when a group member's condition indicates that there is clear and imminent danger to the member, others, or physical property, the group counselor takes reasonable personal action and/or informs responsible authorities).

(b) Group counselors stress the importance of confidentiality and set a norm of confidentiality regarding all group participants' disclosures. The importance of maintaining confidentiality is emphasized before the group begins and at various times in the group. The fact that confidentiality cannot be guaranteed is clearly stated.

(c) Members are made aware of the difficulties involved in enforcing and ensuring confidentiality in a group setting. The counselor provides examples of how confidentiality can nonmaliciously be broken to increase members' awareness, and helps to lessen the likelihood that this breach of confidence will occur. Group counselors inform group members about the potential consequences of intentionally breaching confidentiality.

(d) Group counselors can only ensure confidentiality on their part and not on the part of the members.

(e) Group counselors videotape or audiotape a group session only with the prior consent and the members' knowledge of how the tape will be used.

(f) When working with minors, the group counselor specifies the limits of confidentiality.

(g) Participants in a mandatory group are made aware of any reporting procedures required of the group counselor.

(h) Group counselors store or dispose of group member records (written, audio, video, etc.) in ways that maintain confidentiality.

(i) Instructors of group counseling courses maintain the anonymity of group members whenever discussing group counseling cases.

4. *Voluntary/involuntary participation:* Group counselors inform members whether participation is voluntary or involuntary.

(a) Group counselors take steps to ensure informed consent procedures in both voluntary and involuntary groups.

(b) When working with minors in a group, counselors are expected to follow the procedures specified by the institution in which they are practicing.

(c) With involuntary groups, every attempt is made to enlist the cooperation of the members and their continuance in the group on a voluntary basis.

(d) Group counselors do not certify that group treatment has been received by members who merely attend sessions but did not meet the defined group expectations. Group members are informed about the consequences for failing to participate in a group.

5. *Leaving a group:* Provisions are made to assist a group member to terminate in an effective way.

(a) Procedures to be followed for a group member who chooses to exit a group prematurely are discussed by the counselor with all group members either before the group begins, during a prescreening interview, or during the initial group session.

(b) In case of legally mandated group counseling, group counselors inform members of the possible consequences for premature self-termination.

(c) Ideally, both the group counselor and the member can work cooperatively to determine the degree to which a group experience is productive or counterproductive for that individual.

(d) Members ultimately have a right to discontinue membership in the group, at a designated time, if the predetermined trial period proves to be unsatisfactory.

(e) Members have the right to exit a group, but it is important that they be made aware of the importance of informing the counselor and the group members prior to deciding to leave. The counselor discusses the possible risks of leaving the group prematurely with a member who is considering this option.

(f) Before leaving a group, the group counselor encourages members (if appropriate) to discuss their reasons for wanting to discontinue membership in the group. Counselors intervene if other members use undue pressure to force a member to remain in the group.

6. *Coercion and pressure:* Group counselors protect member rights against physical threats, intimidation, coercion, and undue peer pressure insofar as is reasonably possible.

(a) It is essential to differentiate between "therapeutic pressure" that is part of any group and "undue pressure," which is not therapeutic.

(b) The purpose of a group is to help participants find their own answers, not to pressure them into doing what the group thinks is appropriate.

(c) Counselors exert care not to coerce participants to change in directions which they clearly state they do not choose.

(d) Counselors have responsibility to intervene when others use undue pressure or attempt to persuade members against their will.

(e) Counselors intervene when any member attempts to act out aggression in a physical way that might harm another member or themselves.

(f) Counselors intervene when a member is verbally abusive or inappropriately confrontive to another member.

7. *Imposing counselor values:* Group counselors develop an awareness of their own values and needs and the potential impact they have on the interventions likely to be made.

(a) Although group counselors take care to avoid imposing their values on members, it is appropriate that they expose their own beliefs, decisions, needs, and values when concealing them would create problems for the members.

(b) There are values implicit in any group, and these are made clear to potential members before they join the group. (Examples of certain values include: expressing feelings, being direct and honest, sharing personal material with others, learning how to trust, improving interpersonal communication, and deciding for oneself.)

(c) Personal and professional needs of group counselors are not met at the members' expense.

(d) Group counselors avoid using the group for their own therapy.

(e) Group counselors are aware of their own values and assumptions and how these apply in a multicultural context.

(f) Group counselors take steps to increase their awareness of ways that their personal reactions to members might inhibit the group process and they monitor their countertransference. Through an awareness of the impact of stereotyping and discrimination (i.e., biases based on age, disability, ethnicity, gender, race, religion, or sexual preference), group counselors guard the individual rights and personal dignity of all group members.

8. *Equitable treatment:* Group counselors make every reasonable effort to treat each member individually and equally.

(a) Group counselors recognize and respect differences (e.g., cultural, racial, religious, life style, age, disability, gender) among group members.

(b) Group counselors maintain an awareness of their behavior toward individual group members and are alert to the potential detrimental effects of favoritism or partiality toward any particular group member to the exclusion or detriment of any other member(s). It is likely that group counselors will favor some members over others, yet all group members deserve to be treated equally.

(c) Group counselors ensure equitable use of group time for each member by inviting silent members to become involved, acknowledging nonverbal attempts to communicate, and discouraging rambling and monopolizing of time by members.

(d) If a large group is planned, counselors consider enlisting another qualified professional to serve as a co-leader for the group sessions.

9. *Dual relationships:* Group counselors avoid dual relationships with group members that might impair their objectivity and professional judgment, as well as those which are likely to compromise a group member's ability to participate fully in the group.

(a) Group counselors do not misuse their professional role and power as group leader to advance personal or social contacts with members throughout the duration of the group.

(b) Group counselors do not use their professional relationship with group members to further their own interest either during the group or after the termination of the group.

(c) Sexual intimacies between group counselors and members are unethical.

(d) Group counselors do not barter (exchange) professional services with group members for services.

(e) Group counselors do not admit their own family members, relatives, employees, or personal friends as members to their groups.

(f) Group counselors discuss with group members the potential detrimental effects of group members' engaging in intimate intermember relationships outside of the group.

(g) Students who participate in a group as a partial course requirement for a group course are not evaluated for an academic grade based upon their degree of participation as a member in a group. Instructors of group counseling courses take steps to minimize the possible negative impact on students when they participate in a group course by separating course grades from participation in the group and by allowing students to decide what issues to explore and when to stop.

(h) It is inappropriate to solicit members from a class (or institutional affiliation) for one's private counseling or therapeutic groups.

10. *Use of techniques:* Group counselors do not attempt any technique unless trained in its use or under supervision by a counselor familiar with the intervention.

(a) Group counselors are able to articulate a theoretical orientation that guides their practice, and they are able to provide a rationale for their interventions.

(b) Depending upon the type of intervention, group counselors have training commensurate with the potential impact of a technique.

(c) Group counselors are aware of the necessity to modify their techniques to fit the unique needs of various cultural and ethnic groups.

(d) Group counselors assist members in translating in-group learnings to daily life.

11. *Goal development:* Group counselors make every effort to assist members in developing their personal goals.

(a) Group counselors use their skills to assist members in making their goals specific so that others present in the group will understand the nature of the goals.

(b) Throughout the course of a group, group counselors assist members in assessing the degree to which personal goals are being met and assist in revising any goals when it is appropriate.

(c) Group counselors help members clarify the degree to which the goals can be met within the context of a particular group.

12. *Consultation:* Group counselors develop and explain policies about between-session consultation to group members.

(a) Group counselors take care to make certain that members do not use between-session consultations to avoid dealing with issues pertaining to the group that would be dealt with best in the group.

(b) Group counselors urge members to bring the issues discussed during between-session consultations into the group if they pertain to the group.

(c) Group counselors seek out consultation and/or supervision regarding ethical concerns or when encountering difficulties which interfere with their effective functioning as group leaders.

(d) Group counselors seek appropriate professional assistance for their own personal problems or conflicts that are likely to impair their professional judgment and work performance.

(e) Group counselors discuss their group cases only for professional consultation and educational purposes.

(f) Group counselors inform members about policies regarding whether consultations will be held confidential.

13. *Termination from the group:* Depending upon the purpose of participation in the group, counselors promote termination of members from the group in the most efficient period of time.

(a) Group counselors maintain a constant awareness of the progress made by each group member and periodically invite the group members to explore and reevaluate their experiences in the group. It is the responsibility of group counselors to help promote the independence of members from the group in a timely manner.

14. *Evaluation and follow up:* Group counselors make every attempt to engage in ongoing assessment and to design follow-up procedures for their groups.

(a) Group counselors recognize the importance of ongoing assessment of a group, and they assist members in evaluating their own progress.

215

(b) Group counselors conduct evaluation of the total group experience at the final meeting (or before termination), as well as ongoing evaluation.

(c) Group counselors monitor their own behavior and become aware of what they are modeling in the group.

(d) Follow-up procedures might take the form of personal contact, telephone contact, or written contact.

(e) Follow-up meetings might be with individuals, groups, or both to determine the degree to which: (i) members have reached their goals, (ii) the group had a positive or negative effect on the participants, and (iii) members could profit from some type of referral. Information is requested for possible modification of future groups. If there is no follow-up meeting, provisions are made available for individual follow-up meetings to any member who needs or requests such a contact.

15. *Referrals:* If the needs of a particular member cannot be met within the type of group being offered, the group counselor suggests other appropriate professional referrals.

(a) Group counselors are knowledgeable of local community resources for assisting group members regarding professional referrals.

(b) Group counselors help members seek further professional assistance, if needed.

16. *Professional development:* Group counselors recognize that professional growth is a continuous, ongoing, developmental process throughout their career.

(a) Group counselors maintain and upgrade their knowledge and skill competencies through educational activities, clinical experiences, and participation in professional development activities.

(b) Group counselors keep abreast of research findings and new developments as applied to groups.

Safeguarding Ethical Practice and Procedures for Reporting Unethical Behavior

The preceding remarks have been advanced as guidelines which are generally representative of ethical and professional group practice. They have not been proposed as rigidly defined prescriptions. However, practitioners who are thought to be grossly unresponsive to the ethical concerns addressed in this document may be subject to a review of their practices by the AACD Ethics Committee and ASGW peers.

For consultation and/or questions regarding these ASGW Ethical Guidelines or group ethical dilemmas, you may contact the Chairperson of the ASGW Ethics Committee. The name, address, and telephone number of the current ASGW Ethics Committee Chairperson may be acquired by telephoning the AACD office in Alexandria, Virginia at (703) 823–9800.

If a group counselor's behavior is suspected as being unethical, the following procedures are to be followed:

(a) Collect more information and investigate further to confirm the unethical practice as determined by the ASGW Ethical Guidelines.

(b) Confront the individual with the apparent violation of ethical guidelines for the purposes of protecting the safety of any clients and to help the group counselor correct any inappropriate behaviors. If satisfactory resolution is not reached through this contact then:

(c) A complaint should be made in writing, including the specific facts and dates of the alleged violation and all relevant supporting data. The complaint should be included in an envelope marked "CONFIDENTIAL" to ensure confidentiality for both the accuser(s) and the alleged violator(s) and forwarded to all of the following sources:

1. The name and address of the Chairperson of the state Counselor Licensure Board for the respective state, if in existence.

2. The Ethics Committee, c/o The President, American Association for Counseling and Development, 5999 Stevenson Avenue, Alexandria, VA 22304.

3. The name and address of all private credentialing agencies in which the alleged violator maintains credentials or holds professional membership. Some of these include the following:

National Board for Certified Counselors, Inc.
3–D Terrace Way
Greensboro, NC 27403

National Council for Credentialing
   of Career Counselors
c/o NBCC
5999 Stevenson Avenue
Alexandria, VA 22304

National Academy for Certified Clinical
   Mental Health Counselors
5999 Stevenson Avenue
Alexandria, VA 22304

Commission on Rehabilitation Counselor
   Certification
162 North State Street
Suite 317
Chicago, IL 60601

American Association for Marriage
   and Family Therapy
1717 K Street, N. W., Suite 407
Washington, DC 20006

American Psychological Association
1200 Seventeenth Street, N. W.
Washington, DC 20036

American Group Psychotherapy
   Association, Inc.
25 East 21st Street, 6th Floor
New York, New York 10010

PRETESTS/POSTTESTS

Peace Begins With Me: Peacemaking Skills

Name _____ Date _____

Instructions: Read each sentence. Put a circle around the number that shows how you think and feel right now.

1 = Strongly agree
2 = Agree somewhat
3 = Agree
4 = Disagree somewhat
5 = Strongly disagree

1. People should only be friends with someone of their own race, religion, or country.	1	2	3	4	5
2. Having friends from other races and countries enriches our lives.	1	2	3	4	5
3. I know that a lot of the kinds of foods we eat first came from other countries.	1	2	3	4	5
4. There are many kinds of churches and ways to think about our religious beliefs.	1	2	3	4	5
5. It is important to help people find homes and jobs.	1	2	3	4	5
6. Having friends of other races and from other countries is fun and interesting.	1	2	3	4	5
7. Taking care of pets and wild birds and animals is a way to be a caring person.	1	2	3	4	5
8. Helping homeless people in my home town is a way of being a good citizen and kind person.	1	2	3	4	5
9. It is more important to be a good person inside than to have a certain skin color or a lot of money.	1	2	3	4	5
10. Being afraid of people who are different is usually caused by not understanding them.	1	2	3	4	5

I'm Somebody Special: Building Self-Esteem

Name _____ Date _____

Instructions: Read each sentence. Put a circle around the number that shows how you think and feel right now.

      1 = Strongly agree
      2 = Agree somewhat
      3 = Agree
      4 = Disagree somewhat
      5 = Strongly disagree

1. I feel good about who I am.   1   2   3   4   5

2. I know how to talk about my feelings to my friends.   1   2   3   4   5

3. It is scary for me to share my feelings.   1   2   3   4   5

4. I can name many things that I do well and am proud of.   1   2   3   4   5

5. Growing up is scary because I will change.   1   2   3   4   5

6. When I can't change things I get very upset.   1   2   3   4   5

7. I feel good about myself when I try hard, even if I don't do well.   1   2   3   4   5

8. I know what I think is important to me and what my values are.   1   2   3   4   5

9. Having a close friend to talk to is very special and important to me.   1   2   3   4   5

10. It is important to be a good friend to others.   1   2   3   4   5

Friends: Getting Along With Others

Name _____ Date _____

Instructions: Read each sentence. Put a circle around the number that shows how you think and feel right now.

> 1 = Strongly agree
> 2 = Agree somewhat
> 3 = Agree
> 4 = Disagree somewhat
> 5 = Strongly disagree

1. I know how to make new friends.	1	2	3	4	5
2. It is fun to make new friends.	1	2	3	4	5
3. Friends never get angry at each other.	1	2	3	4	5
4. Friends are always your own age.	1	2	3	4	5
5. I know how to be a helpful friend.	1	2	3	4	5
6. I know how to get help when I need it.	1	2	3	4	5
7. It is a good idea to say good-bye when friends move away or don't want to be friends any more.	1	2	3	4	5
8. Funerals help you say good-bye to friends.	1	2	3	4	5
9. Cooperating means working together.	1	2	3	4	5
10. Cooperating helps get the job done right.	1	2	3	4	5

Grieving and Growing: Learning From Losses

Name _____ Date _____

Instructions: Read each sentence. Put a circle around the number that shows how you think and feel right now.

    1 = Strongly agree
    2 = Agree somewhat
    3 = Agree
    4 = Disagree somewhat
    5 = Strongly disagree

1. It is scary to think about dying.	1	2	3	4	5
2. I can remember and talk about the good things about my loved one who died.	1	2	3	4	5
3. I can tell my mom or dad when I feel sad.	1	2	3	4	5
4. I know what funerals are for and what happens in them.	1	2	3	4	5
5. I can share my feelings with my friends.	1	2	3	4	5
6. I have said good-bye to my loved one who has died.	1	2	3	4	5
7. I know that dying happens to everyone.	1	2	3	4	5
8. I can ask for help when I feel very bad about death and dying.	1	2	3	4	5
9. It is OK to feel sad or cry when someone dies.	1	2	3	4	5
10. I know the grief will not be so bad as time passes.	1	2	3	4	5

KIDS: Kids in Divorce Stress

Name _____ Date _____

Instructions: Read each sentence. Put a circle around the number that shows how you think and feel right now.

      1 = Strongly agree
      2 = Agree somewhat
      3 = Agree
      4 = Disagree somewhat
      5 = Strongly disagree

1. I think parents should never get divorced.	1	2	3	4	5
2. I know how I feel about my parents' divorce.	1	2	3	4	5
3. I think divorce can be a good thing.	1	2	3	4	5
4. Divorce always hurts everybody.	1	2	3	4	5
5. I know how to talk to my parents about how I feel when I get sad.	1	2	3	4	5
6. I feel good about myself.	1	2	3	4	5
7. I can get along with my stepparents.	1	2	3	4	5
8. I can get along with my stepbrothers and/or stepsisters.	1	2	3	4	5
9. It is important to be at peace about the divorce.	1	2	3	4	5
10. It is scary to think about growing up and getting a divorce like my mom and dad.	1	2	3	4	5

I CAN Kids: Control Anger Now!

Name _____ Date _____

Instructions: Read each sentence. Put a circle around the number that shows how you think and feel right now.

      1 = Strongly agree
      2 = Agree somewhat
      3 = Agree
      4 = Disagree somewhat
      5 = Strongly disagree

	1	2	3	4	5
1. My anger gets me in trouble.	1	2	3	4	5
2. Sometimes I think I am angry all the time.	1	2	3	4	5
3. There are some ways to be angry that are OK.	1	2	3	4	5
4. I can relax whenever I want.	1	2	3	4	5
5. I never feel just a little angry, I only feel a lot angry.	1	2	3	4	5
6. Sometimes I get so mad I don't know what to do.	1	2	3	4	5
7. I know how to avoid fights.	1	2	3	4	5
8. I can deal with bullies.	1	2	3	4	5
9. I have my temper under control.	1	2	3	4	5
10. I can say things I need to say to someone without getting upset.	1	2	3	4	5

I'm Responsible

Name _____ Date _____

Instructions: Read each sentence. Put a circle around the number that shows how you think and feel right now.

    1 = Strongly agree
    2 = Agree somewhat
    3 = Agree
    4 = Disagree somewhat
    5 = Strongly disagree

1. I am a responsible person.	1	2	3	4	5
2. I know what my responsibilities are.	1	2	3	4	5
3. I don't know if I am responsible.	1	2	3	4	5
4. When I act responsibly, I feel good about myself.	1	2	3	4	5
5. Sometimes I think I can't meet all my responsibilities.	1	2	3	4	5
6. I get upset when other people are not responsible.	1	2	3	4	5
7. Some responsibilities take longer than others.	1	2	3	4	5
8. My first responsibility is to myself.	1	2	3	4	5
9. I know how to set goals for myself.	1	2	3	4	5
10. I feel good about being responsible.	1	2	3	4	5

Good Citizen's Club

Name _____ Date _____

Instructions: Read each sentence. Put a circle around the number that shows how you think and feel right now.

      1 = Strongly agree
      2 = Agree somewhat
      3 = Agree
      4 = Disagree somewhat
      5 = Strongly disagree

1. I know how to get help with homework when I need it.	1	2	3	4	5
2. It is important to keep up with my homework and studies.	1	2	3	4	5
3. Getting angry is something everyone does.	1	2	3	4	5
4. I know how to be angry without hurting myself or anyone else.	1	2	3	4	5
5. It is always best to tell the truth.	1	2	3	4	5
6. Copying homework is stealing someone else's ideas.	1	2	3	4	5
7. I know how to get things I want and need without stealing them.	1	2	3	4	5
8. If someone teases me I can deal with it.	1	2	3	4	5
9. Making up stories to get attention is not a good way to get what I need.	1	2	3	4	5
10. I am the person who can control my temper.	1	2	3	4	5

About the Author

Rosemarie Smead Morganett is Professor and Coordinator of Counselor Education at Indiana University Southeast in New Albany. Dr. Morganett is an accomplished teacher and training consultant, with over 20 years experience working with children and adolescents in school, mental health, inpatient, and family therapy settings. She has presented workshops and training seminars both nationally and internationally to various professional groups, state departments of education, school systems, juvenile treatment facilities, and business and industry.

Dr. Morganett is past president and fellow of the Association for Specialists in Group Work and has received state, ASGW, and university awards for her distinguished teaching and service to the profession in group work. She holds a doctorate in counseling psychology from Auburn University, is a licensed marriage and family therapist, and is a clinical member of the American Association for Marriage and Family Therapy. In addition to her program coordination and teaching responsibilities, she consults with and conducts workshops for school systems, mental health agencies, government agencies, professional organizations, and hospital treatment facilities. Her professional interests are in counselor education and group counseling research with children and adolescents, and she maintains a private practice in marriage and family therapy. *Skills for Living: Group Counseling Activities for Elementary Students* is her second book.